Shakespeare's effect on America's intellectual and artistic life has been much discussed, but what role does he play on the American popular stage? This study changes our understanding of Shakespeare's presence in American life. The book looks at how Shakespeare came to America just before the Revolutionary War. As Americans broke with Britain, they embraced Britain's playwright. Teague re-examines P. T. Barnum's attempt to buy Shakespeare's birthplace, the Astor Place Riot in which twenty-three people died, and the way both Abraham Lincoln and John Wilkes Booth regarded Shakespeare. In the history of Broadway, more musicals have drawn on Shakespeare than on any other author. Shakespearean musicals like *Kiss Me, Kate* and *West Side Story* can tell us much about America's culture, but sometimes failed musicals such as *Swingin' the Dream* can tell us more. With discussion of over twenty Shakespearean musicals, this study demonstrates that Shakespeare has always been present in popular shows.

FRANCES TEAGUE is a Meigs Professor at the University of Georgia, where she teaches in the English Department and is an affiliate member of the Women's Studies Program. Widely published, she has received fellowships from the National Endowment for the Humanities, the American Council of Learned Societies, and the Association of College and Research Libraries. She frequently directs plays in Athens, Georgia, and has a long-time involvement in the Georgia Shakespeare Festival.

SHAKESPEARE AND THE AMERICAN POPULAR STAGE

FRANCES TEAGUE

CAMBRIDGE
UNIVERSITY PRESS

CAMBRIDGE UNIVERSITY PRESS
Cambridge, New York, Melbourne, Madrid, Cape Town, Singapore, São Paulo

Cambridge University Press
The Edinburgh Building, Cambridge CB2 2RU, UK

Published in the United States of America by Cambridge University Press, New York

www.cambridge.org
Information on this title: www.cambridge.org/9780521679923

© Frances Teague 2006

First published 2006

Printed in the United Kingdom at the University Press, Cambridge

A catalogue record for this publication is available from the British Library

ISBN-13 978-0-521-86187-8 hardback
ISBN-10 0-521-86187-x hardback
ISBN-13 978-0-521-67992-3 paperback
ISBN-10 0-521-67992-3 paperback

Contents

Illustrations

Acknowledgments

My first debt is to John Velz, who invited me to edit with him the correspondence of the nineteenth-century Shakespearean Joseph Crosby of Zanesville, Ohio. Work on those letters provided me with a far greater education about my adopted country than I had received in any classroom. I owe a major debt to the Shakespeare Association of America, since it is an organization that features original research and long discussions of that research at its annual conference; its affiliation with the International Shakespeare Congress also encourages American scholars to look behind the screen of their own culture and to set aside parochialism. Several sections of this study began as seminar papers for Shakespeare Association seminars; I am indebted to Alexander Leggatt, Virginia and Alden Vaughan, and Terence Hawkes and John Drakakis for leading such seminars and to the responses I received in those seminars from Helen Whall, Georgianna Ziegler, and Irene Dash. Irene is of particular importance because she so generously shared her own research findings about musical comedy with me and so wisely suggested places where my analyses were weak. A crucial seminar for my thinking on this book was one that Richard Burt and Lynda Boose ran; Richard's encouragement and his interest in what I had to say about musical comedies helped persuade me that I was on the right track in my work. A version of the final chapter went through his hands, and he helped to make it much better. To Susan Cerasano, I owe many thanks for manifold favors and good conversation, and thanks also go to Stephen Buhler and Doug Lanier for their encouragement. The questions and comments I received from Sarah Stanton and the anonymous readers of this book were invaluable. Informal discussions with Douglas Anderson, Susan Baker, Allen Corrigan, Christy Desmet, the late Margaret Dickie, David Gants, Peter Holland, Sujata Iyengar, Allan Kulikoff, Naomi Liebler, Hubert McAlexander, Thomas Moisan, Tim Powell, Tom Riis, David Schiller, Joseph Sigalas, Ben Teague, John Velz, Robin Warren, and Elizabeth Wright have been very important. Naomi's invitation to speak at the Columbia University Shakespeare Seminar, Allan's to participate in the Georgia Workshop in Early American History and Culture, and Thomas Moisan's to lecture at St. Louis University all allowed me to get responses to material at a crucial point. Elizabeth Hardaway gave me some old sheet music that she thought would amuse me: it led me to *Mr. Hamlet of Broadway*, an overlooked production, which may be Broadway's first Shakespearean musical. Grants from the University of Georgia Research Foundation, the Center for the Humanities and the Arts, and the Department of English have made it possible for me to attend professional meetings where I presented sections of this research and profited from exchanging ideas with other Shakespeareans. Recording these debts I am reminded of my good fortune in the work I do.

Finally, I wish to thank the Metropolitan Museum of Art, the Colonial Williamsburg Foundation, the Library of Congress, Scott Tambert of PDImages, Margo Feiden and the Margo Feiden Galleries, the Museum of the City of New York, the Shakespeare Birthplace Trust, and the Shakespeare Centre Library for their assistance in providing illustrations. I am, like all scholars, in awe of research librarians, without whom our work would be impossible. In particular my thanks to the University of Georgia Library and its Hargrett Special Collections, the Folger Library, the British Library, the Yale University Beinecke Rare Book and Manuscript Library, the New York Public Library's Billy Rose Theatre Collection, the Shubert Archive, the UCLA Library, and the Shakespeare Centre Library.

My husband, Ben Teague, has never doubted for a moment that this project was worth doing and for that belief, as well as much more, I dedicate this book to him.

Introduction

As early as 1831 Shakespeare was part of everyday life in America, to judge from Alexis de Tocqueville's remark that

There is hardly a pioneer's hut which does not contain a few odd volumes of Shakespeare. I remember that I read the feudal drama of Henry V. for the first time in a log house.[1]

Nor did it take long for Americans to claim Shakespeare as one of their own: by 1849, in *Representative Men* Emerson could call Shakespeare "the father of the man in America."[2] American writers have felt comfortable using, indeed taking liberties with, Shakespeare. From the Duke and Dauphin in *Huckleberry Finn* to Broadway musicals like *Kiss Me, Kate* or *Play On!* Americans have amused themselves by appropriating, and misappropriating, Shakespearean material. His figure fills American needs. It seemed entirely suitable that in 1976, the year of the American Bicentennial, the International Shakespeare Association held its inaugural World Congress in Washington, D.C., focusing on the topic of "Shakespeare in America."[3] The American experience of Shakespeare was thus institutionalized as worthy of the world's attention (or at least the attention of the academic world).

As critics have increasingly moved away from asking what Shakespeare means to asking what uses we make of Shakespeare, I have become curious about the ways that Americans use Shakespeare idiosyncratically: how he has served American popular entertainment during the founding of the nation, during the nineteenth century, and within America's quintessential theatrical form, the musical comedy.

This book has a long genesis that owes much to the patience and knowledge of others. I might say it began in the 1960s with my family's patience as I played albums of Broadway shows over and over or with my stint as stage manager for the first production of *Hello Hamlet!* in 1967. (A burlesque by George Greanias, today a prominent Houstonian, *Hello Hamlet!* has become a Rice University tradition.) In the 1970s, working with John

Velz to edit the Crosby letters gave me a taste of Shakespeare's importance in nineteenth-century America. But these experiences simply whetted my interest about what happens to Shakespeare in the American book musical.

One evening in the 1980s, I was at a party with a colleague in music, Tom Riis. When I said I thought a book might be written about Shakespeare musicals, Tom was enthusiastic. But as a music historian who was just completing his groundbreaking book on African-American musicals, Tom recognized problems that I hadn't seen. What did "Shakespeare musical" mean? Would I include Verdi and minstrel-show burlesques? When did musicals begin and where did they come from? I had no answers, so went away to read and re-think my project.

The questions Tom had raised took me to nineteenth-century America and some ideas about how Americans had used Shakespeare to explain themselves. For a Shakespeare Association of America seminar, I drafted an essay about the topic, and then ran it by some of my colleagues in American literature. One, Douglas Anderson, who was finishing what would become a major study of reading in early American culture, responded with a long set of marginal comments that made his skepticism clear because he had recognized more problems that I hadn't seen. Why was I assuming that most Americans knew little about Shakespeare? Wouldn't attitudes toward Shakespeare have been as various as Americans were? What of American reading or popular performances? Again, I read further in the material he suggested and re-thought the project.

And so I continued, learning about one area only to discover that I was still poorly read in another. Thanks are due to many, but especially to Richard Burt for a good reading list on popular culture, to historian Allen Kulikoff for guidance through American colonial-history sources, and especially to Irene Dash whose resistance to my interpretations is matched by her generosity of spirit. These conversations have pushed me back in America's cultural history and forced me to reconsider the project. Yet each has also confirmed for me the importance of working across specialist boundaries, despite the discomfort one feels in doing so. This study does not easily fit the fields of performance history, Shakespeare study, or American studies. In fact, those who work in those fields may well wonder why I am bothering with material that seems to them peripheral or digressive. My answer is that I think one can understand what Americans do with Shakespeare only when one works *among* the fields.

To put the matter another way, I do not believe that one can understand what is happening in *Play On!* unless one understands the sources of *The Boys from Syracuse* or *Swingin' the Dream*. Those productions grow out of a performance tradition epitomized by the now-forgotten show, Eddie Foy's *Mr. Hamlet of Broadway*. Foy's work exists in the context of his early experience as a supernumerary for Edwin Booth. To understand Edwin Booth, one must consider the performances both of his predecessor Edwin Forrest, and his brother John Wilkes Booth. Making sense of the way that John Wilkes Booth employs Shakespeare demands close attention both to Shakespeare's text and to the American political tradition that cites Shakespeare as an authority sanctioning violence, a tradition that begins with the years before the Revolution and proceeds through Adams and Jefferson and (tragically) Booth. My original interest in Shakespearean musicals has proven digressive and the musicals themselves transgressive.

Like earlier studies, this one concentrates on various manifestations of Shakespeare – that is, the historical Shakespeare, his works, and the cultural institution that clusters around his name – principally in the United States, all of which elements I will call Shakespeare's American figure. Unlike other scholars, I am relatively uninterested in the role that Shakespeare's figure plays in America's intellectual or aesthetic life, although I do not doubt his importance in these spheres. Nor do I wish to duplicate the examination of American "legitimate" theatre, a project that Charles Shattuck undertook and that other theatre historians have ably continued. Because I am concerned with the origins of twentieth-century Broadway musicals, I will consider only those aspects of both elite and popular culture that lead to shows like *The Boys from Syracuse*, *Kiss Me, Kate*, or *West Side Story*.

Instead, I want to explore the way that Americans have used Shakespeare's figure in idiosyncratic popular ways to screen out certain values and attitudes. But a screen has other functions: it can, for example, cover up an area that one does not wish to acknowledge, without denying its existence; one can also reflect small images on a screen. (That is not to suggest that I shall investigate American film treatments. At one point I had planned to do so, but as I did the preliminary research, I came to believe that Shakespearean films have been international from their outset.) In the first part of my study, I want to use the screen metaphor to show how Americans employ Shakespeare's figure to sift out their values, to conceal what they would prefer to ignore, and to reflect what they consider of most value; in the second part, I shall use a different metaphor.

Although Shakespeare's figure matters to America in the nineteenth and twentieth centuries, America's history begins much earlier. Neither read nor staged in America until the eighteenth century, Shakespeare's plays had little influence on American society during much of the colonial period. The importance that Shakespeare eventually assumed in American life, as well as the speed with which his figure became important after the Revolutionary War, seem to me disproportionate and fascinating, an instance of an idiosyncratically American phenomenon, the ability to make a radical shift in the culture's values with very little fuss or acknowledgment that any change has occurred. (One might think of the sudden change in American foreign policy toward China during the Nixon administration, for instance, or the abrupt popular recognition among whites of the cost of racism when Harper Lee's *To Kill a Mockingbird* was published.) During the decades when colonial America broke away from England, Shakespeare swiftly prospered, and in hindsight the importance of his figure in colonial times serves as a harbinger of that period's end. During the decades when America was most dependent on England, however, Shakespeare was ignored. While earlier studies have both documented and interrogated Shakespeare's importance in American life,[4] none has yet explored why Shakespeare was absent for so long in the early years of America, nor what his figure offered that nineteenth- and twentieth-century Americans found so appealing. Thus, I begin with Shakespeare's absence in colonial America.

I shall try to suggest why Shakespeare was left off stage for so long and why his plays did not appear on an American reader's shelves. After trying to account for the speed with which Shakespeare's plays entered American life, I examine the role that Shakespeare's figure played during the Revolutionary period, as well as in the early years of argument about what sort of culture the new nation would have. I argue that the role Shakespeare takes in this public debate is crucial to his later reputation in America, for from this debate comes the impetus to re-fashion Shakespeare as an American author, or at least as an authority who sanctions American desires.

An important figure who used that re-fashioned Shakespeare is Emerson, as others have suggested; writers like Melville and Whitman also play roles in transforming Shakespeare's figure into a screen that both sifted out American culture from English and concealed other projects behind the shelter of unquestioned or unquestionable value.[5] Such writers are *not* representative men in this discussion, however, because I am less concerned with the role that Shakespeare and his writing played in the development of American culture than in the way that American culture has shaped Shakespeare. The way in which nineteenth-century Americans employed Shakespeare and his work to mark their national, class, or regional identity interests me, especially when such appropriations lead to action that is unethical, even violent or treasonous. Throughout this section, I try to keep an eye on the way that popular entertainment developed in this country, especially in ways that are idiosyncratically American, and to trace Shakespeare's presence in that development.

The final section of this study focuses on the way that American popular theatre has employed Shakespeare as an unacknowledged agent to allow the commercial theatre to make changes that might frighten or upset audiences if they were perceived too plainly. In it I am principally concerned with musicals. When a production was innovative in a threatening way, when it broke the boundaries of taste or social preconceptions, its creators were apt to use the screen of Shakespeare's figure to mask their project. The results have been especially interesting for what they suggest about shifts in American taste and anxiety about that taste.

PART I

Pilgrims, pioneers, and parlors

CHAPTER I

Shakespeare and the spirit of '76

When one turns to a reference book for information, the ideal entry offers a neat array of dates and data and quickly sums up a vast subject in a paragraph. An encyclopedia entry on theatre in the United States of America, for example, divided into discussions of particular periods and regions, might suggest a smooth flow of development, extension, and improvement. While it would begin with the insistence that the subject is complex, the *telos* of the entry is to simplify that complexity into a narrative of progress and promise.

At the root of American theatre, its fundamental source, is the English tradition, and according to *The Oxford Companion to the Theatre* (*OCT*), ". . . it was from a secular, British source that a distinctively American theatre emerged" (s.v. United States of America, 846). The third edition of *OCT* explicitly claimed that Shakespeare is the playwright most influential to American theatre, and Shakespeare's centrality recurs in other reference works. *The Reader's Encyclopedia of World Drama* says that American drama's "first models were the lofty tragedies and extravagant comedies popular in England in the latter half of the eighteenth century" (s.v. United States, 882). *The Oxford Companion to American Theatre* says "Shakespeare came to American stages relatively early" (s.v. Shakespeare, 611); and *The Everyman Companion to the Theatre* remarks that "It was not until quite late in the eighteenth century that serious attempts began to be made to establish for American theatre an identity separate from England's" (57). In all of these works, the principal emphasis is on English and other influences are scanted. Fuller treatments of the subject do acknowledge other traditions than that of the English, although these too move quickly to focus on the Anglo-American stage tradition.[1] Their recitation often sounds mechanically correct, and the various repetitions lend an air of credibility.

Yet one could easily write an encapsulated history of theatre in America that differs widely from these. This received account ignores the variety of cultures that make up America's past, the powerful orature of colonial

9

churches, and the commercial difficulties and rewards of beginning a theatrical tradition.[2] It also ignores one thing that made the earliest English settlements quite different from those of other European nations, an unusual emphasis on education and literacy. Moreover, because the sort of account found in such a reference book must be compact, it smoothes out the interesting complexities of the relationship that people living in America during the sixteenth and seventeenth centuries had with Europe. Nor does it account for the way in which Shakespeare's figure after its introduction to American culture becomes linked to particular political positions or class identities.

Rather than smooth out the narrative of Shakespeare's figure in America, I shall begin with such a variant account, one that initially leaves Shakespeare off the American stage, on the grounds that his absence is more telling of the American character than his presence. European settlements in the Americas took root during the sixteenth and seventeenth centuries. One of Europe's greatest dramatists turned his attention away from his home nation to write a play about the potential richness and present mysteries of America. Yet despite his fascination with its promise, he would never leave Europe. While he never crossed the ocean, his work did. At the end of the sixteenth century, homesick settlers performed his plays; and only twenty years after the first permanent playhouse was built in the city where he wrote, settlers established a playhouse of their own so that they could lose themselves in dreams of their motherland. Indeed, the settlers loved his work so much that his plays were translated into an indigenous language so that the settlers could share the riches of their European background with the native people among whom they lived.

The dramatist in this sentimentalized history was, of course, Lope de Vega, who wrote a heroic drama about Columbus. As the *OCT* notes, "Long before any English plays were presented in the New World, what is now Latin America and the west coast had witnessed performances" (965). Spanish settlers in Mexico first viewed theatrical performances in 1538, less than fifty years after Columbus' first voyage. Seventy years after Columbus landed, Lope de Vega was born in 1562. A playhouse was built in Mexico City by 1597, "only twenty years after the first permanent theatre was established in Madrid itself. Priests used miracle plays to teach converted Indians about Roman Catholicism; and work by Lope de Vega was translated into native languages such as Nahuatl or Quechua.[3] In Peru the earliest touring company arrived in 1599" (*OCT* 895). The theatrical tradition in Hispanic America is a particularly rich one: not only were plays by Golden Age dramatists performed, but native American playwrights soon developed in part because missionaries in Mexico City offered an annual prize for the best *auto sacramentale*.[4]

The dramatic traditions of Spain stand in marked contrast to those of another great nation. It, too, had a great playwright, but his plays went unperformed in the Americas until more than a century later than the Mexican performances, although these Europeans had mounted an American production of an open-air pageant in 1604. Still he was not altogether neglected: a mere ten years after his greatest play was first performed, it received an amateur production across the ocean. Drama was produced as a diversion for the troops guarding the settlements. Unfortunately, some of the settlers objected to plays on moral grounds, blocking their performance, so the theatrical history of the French in America is not so rich as that of Hispanic drama. Nevertheless, the French garrison at Port Royal did stage *Le Théâtre de Neptune* on the beach to amuse and divert the soldiers in 1604.[5] A 1646 production of Corneille's *Le Cid* in Québec is notable. Finally, however, the Bishop of Québec's objection to Molière's *Tartuffe* led him to block the production that Governor Frontenac proposed in 1694, for many of the same reasons that led to protests against the play's anti-clericalism in Paris.[6]

Finally, there is Shakespeare, considered to be England's (indeed, the world's) greatest dramatist. His plays went unperformed in the Americas until more than a century and a half after the first English settlements. Scholars have largely ignored or glossed over this disjunction of timing among the theatrical traditions of European settlers (see table, p. 12). David Hackett Fischer remarks of the English settlers,

Many colonists felt desperately homesick, and regretted what Isaac Johnson called their "voluntary banishment" from the "mother country." Something of this colonial mood persisted for many years.

This aching sense of physical separation from the European homeland became a cultural factor of high importance in colonial settlements. The effect of distance created feelings of nostalgia, anxiety, and loss.[7]

That yearning undoubtedly helps to account for the Spanish and French efforts to produce the plays of their home nations. The English felt it as well, although their sense of nostalgia did not move them to re-create London's drama. The word "nostalgia," which today often denotes a sentimental yearning for an earlier, better time, originally described a disease. As Susan Bennett points out, a Swiss doctor coined "nostalgia" in 1780, meaning home-sickness. When David Hackett Fischer speaks of an "aching sense of physical separation," he does not exaggerate: settlers became physically

Summary of American events before 1750

	Spanish	French	English
First explorers	1492–1540	1524–1635	1497–1630

Although the Spanish were the first, their explorations were concentrated in the early years of contact and fell off as they established settlements. The French did the least significant exploration, although exploitation of the Newfoundland fisheries began in 1507; their activity was concentrated in Canada. After a lengthy period of neglect, following Cabot's initial voyages, the English continued their exploration far longer than either of the other groups.

Early settlements	1521 Mexico City	1608 Québec	1585 Roanoke
	1565 St. Augustine	1642 Montréal	1607 Jamestown

It is worth noting that the Spanish did not settle Mexico City; they sacked and seized it. Initially the English were less successful than either the Spanish or French in establishing major urban centers; New York (1624) was settled by the Dutch, while Boston (1630), Charleston (1670), and Philadelphia (1682) were all settled relatively late. Their first settlement, Roanoke, failed.

First performances	1538 Mexico City	1604 Québec	1703 Charleston

The Spanish and French moved quickly to introduce drama, the Spanish staging plays within 17 years of taking control of the city and the French actually staging a pageant before the establishment of Québec. Charleston's first performance occurred 33 years after the city's founding and 118 years after Roanoke's settlement.

First playhouse	1597 Mexico City	1790 Montréal	1716 Williamsburg

The construction of a building specifically for theatre required a period of peace. Thus the French, plagued by unsuccessful wars with England for control over Canadian territory, built a playhouse quite late.

Major dramatist	1590s Lope de Vega	1646 Corneille	1750 Shakespeare

Lope de Vega was not even born when the Spanish began producing plays in the Americas. Corneille was alive when *Le Cid* was performed in Montréal. Shakespeare had been dead for over a century before one of his plays was performed in the Americas, and that production was of Cibber's revision of his work.

---

ill with desire for England. The point is important because a settler's self-identification as English and the conservatism that nostalgia evoked would produce adherence to the past, to "preserve the cultural dynamics that existed in the hour of their birth" (Fischer 57). This loyalty to a vanished world operated to exclude Shakespeare from the first English settlements. French and Spanish settlements coincided chronologically with the greatest period of their dramatic literature. While the first significant wave of immigrants from England was Puritan, the second major wave was Royalist and Anglican, traditionally groups that valued theatre highly.[8] That second wave lasted three times as long as the first and brought to America over twice as many people. Yet this second wave of immigrants took little note of drama. Although the first professional performance in 1703 did take place outside New England, one might wonder why that Charleston performance was not several decades earlier.

It is tempting to claim that the English performed no plays in their American settlements simply because Puritans thought theatres wicked. Such a generalization is simplistic: Puritans, a remarkably diverse lot, were selectively anti-theatrical. In England, a tradition of Puritan drama is discernible among the plays of Jacobean and Caroline England:

To see all Puritans as automatically hostile in principle to the theatre and the arts generally is . . . to misunderstand the depth and complexity of the intellectual and social movements that led to the upheavals of the 1640s.[9]

John Milton enjoyed plays, after all, and Oliver Cromwell had sanctioned masques and opera performances. Furthermore, sales of play texts flourished during the Commonwealth years. The simplistic explanation obscures the culture's complexity.

Arguably for American theatre history, the more important effect of Puritan opposition to drama is not the forbidding of plays in the America, but rather the closing of playhouses in London from the 1640s until the 1660s. For two decades, the theatrical tradition of England was *non*-performance; thus settlers who might have welcomed theatrical performance in America did not always have a habit of viewing performances formed in their European lives. Their nostalgic attempts, in Hackett Fischer's phrase, to "preserve the cultural dynamics" of England meant that the suppression of the playhouses in the Commonwealth period was reflected in America as an absence of theatrical practice. Yet the powerful language of the English attacks on the theatre survived, as Jeffrey Richards and Jean-Christophe Agnew have shown, in the *theatrum mundi* metaphor that operates so strongly in early Anglo-American religious and civic discourse. In the French or Spanish traditions, plays in the Americas were quickly performed after arrival, although the popular taste seems to lag about one or two decades behind those in Europe. Theatre is part of an institutional presence, whether military or religious, and hence sanctioned. In the English tradition, plays are absent and attitudes are at odds with those of the homeland. The settlers who arrived within one or two decades of a healthy London theatre were opposed to performance; those who were potentially friendly arrived during the decades when no English model for performance existed. From its outset, then, the American Anglophone community regarded plays as unusual, even disreputable.

A factor just as important as Puritanism is the lack of institutional backing for performances. The English army was caught up at home in the problems of the Civil War and its aftermath; Catholic missionaries reserved their efforts for the heretic island of England, not the English settlements. Furthermore, the Spanish and French settlers moved quickly to establish communities that maintained close relations with their home nations. Despite the English settlers' feelings of "nostalgia, anxiety, and loss," most had come to the New World as dissidents. While they might yearn for English homes, they did not, as a rule, yearn for English establishments. Instead, they had come to America in reaction against Stuart kings or Oliver Cromwell, the Established Church or the Puritan meetings. Thus they were less interested than the Spanish or French in replicating the public life of a nation they had left in dissent, however deeply they yearned for the private life they had once known in England.

Although the power elites in French and Spanish settlements were more apt to be drawn from men who had some familiarity with Paris and Madrid, those in the English settlements were not necessarily from London. Indeed, the source of the first wave of English immigrants, that is, the Puritan wave, was from East Anglia and Suffolk, outside of London (Fischer 31–42). Less than 10 percent of the population came from London. The second wave came from the South of England and a much larger percentage of it had lived in London, perhaps as much as one-third. When English theatre began in America, it began in the settlements of this second wave, taking place in Charleston, Williamsburg, and New York. (A performance in 1665 of an entertainment, which may or may not have been a play, named *Ye Bare and Ye Cubbe* at Cowle's Tavern in Virginia was blocked by the arrest of the participants, although the Virginia settlers were no Puritans.)[10] The first two venues were in the midst of areas settled by the second wave of immigrants, while New York had been settled by the Dutch.

In England, it would take the efforts of such eighteenth-century editors as Nicholas Rowe or Edmond Malone and such actors as Colley Cibber or David Garrick to recreate Shakespeare as a figure of importance, a figure that would eventually become the central cultural institution of today.[11] Even though Shakespeare was regarded less highly in the 1600s than he is now, one might still hope to find a copy of his works imported by some settler, but the first definite record that one of Shakespeare's plays reached America occurs in 1699 when a copy of *Macbeth* is listed in an inventory of the books of a Captain Spicer. According to Richard Beale Davis, Spicer was a Virginia lawyer and planter, and the inventory was prepared at his death.[12] Yet Davis also calls the work, "the one known item of Shakespeare in the seventeenth-century colonies, the first quarto of *Macbeth* of 1673." In all likelihood, then, this book was not exactly Shakespeare's text, but rather William Davenant's operatic revision, which includes singing and dancing witches as well as plenty of spectacle: the first version of a Shakespeare play known in America was a musical. Still the advent of a Shakespearean text – however derivative – in America matters, for without a script from which to work, an acting company could not give a production. Before his plays could reach the American stage in 1750, his play texts had to be available in American bookcases.

In America, then, the process of introducing Shakespeare reverses that of recuperating his reputation in eighteenth-century England. There, as Gary Taylor has shown, "Shakespeare had not yet become part of the mental equipment of every educated Englishman" (34), for "In the restoration of Shakespeare's reputation, publishers followed; actors led" (33). In America, by contrast, the books came well before the actors – by at least fifty years. Even when play productions begin in America, the first English play published in America was Lillo's *George Barnwell*, produced at London's Drury Lane in 1731 and already appearing serially in an American weekly magazine in 1732.[13] Addison and Farquhar preceded Shakespeare because they had become fashionable in London in the early eighteenth century, and nostalgic Americans wanted what they had once known in England.

One might argue that Shakespeare was, in fact, part of American culture in the early settlements, but that time has simply erased evidence of his presence. After all, plays in books were regarded less negatively than plays on stage.[14] Early New Englanders like John Harvard did own plays; his library included copies of Plautus and Terence as well as a play that had been produced at his alma mater, Cambridge University. The students at Harvard College read plays by classical authors. Esther Dunn thinks that some seventeenth-century New Englanders might even have read Shakespeare. She points out that John Cotton's son Seaborn included Shakespeare's lyric "Take, O take those lips away," in his commonplace book; he was not the only Puritan to have a passage from Shakespeare in his papers.[15] One even finds a persistent tradition that Cotton Mather owned a Shakespeare First Folio.[16] Thus Dunn concludes

In this relatively "Shakespeareless" century, then, actual evidences of the presence and reading of Shakespeare's plays are scarce. But the evidences are there . . . What the evidence shows, so far as it goes, is a rugged, busy world in which libraries were not common. Yet in those recorded, vaguely or specifically, Shakespeare has a fair chance of being present. The chance is not as good as it was in England, but Puritan restrictions and the austerities of pioneer life have not excluded him. (32–33)

The evidence she cites, however, seems weak: two Shakespeare lyrics, both quoted in student commonplace books, and the traditional story of Cotton Mather's First Folio (first heard of in 1874). Despite her remark that "libraries were not common," Dunn also presents much evidence that Americans owned and valued books, including play texts. Among these, she thinks, one might have found a copy of Shakespeare, a more plausible speculation although it, too, is founded on no concrete evidence.

Indeed, many of the standard studies about colonial reading fail to mention Shakespeare at all in the seventeenth century, although they do note his presence in the eighteenth. See, for example, George E. Littlefield's *Early Boston Booksellers*, Worthington Chauncey Ford's *The Boston Book Market 1679–1700*, or Lawrence C. Wroth's *The Colonial Printer*, none of which mentions Shakespeare. The way the Shakespearean materials spread in the eighteenth century is notable. One cause was the publication of Nicholas Rowe's edition of Shakespeare in 1709 (and of subsequent editions). As Gary Taylor remarks, the "1709 edition of Shakespeare was to previous editions what an operatic Restoration adaptation [like Davenant's] was to the original performances, a spectacular new rendition seasoned to contemporary tastes" (74). After 1709 Shakespeare's plays became more readable thanks to the editions by Rowe and his successors. Any colonist who wanted to import a Shakespeare collection could do so easily and read it with enjoyment. In *A Colonial Southern Bookshelf*, Richard Beale Davis points out that by the eighteenth century some Southern readers owned Shakespeare's plays.[17] In addition to Shakespeare's appearance on bookshelves, his works were cited in periodicals:

Original essays on the quality and nature of his genius appear in the southern gazettes, and in the same newspapers were reprinted British commentary on his plays, such as Steele's *Tatler* No. 53 or Addison's *Spectator* Nos. 40 and 592. (Davis 96)

While Shakespeare does indeed begin to appear, Davis later remarks apropos of the *Spectator* essays that "There are more than three times as many collected editions of the work of Addison and Steele in South Carolina inventories . . . as of Shakespeare, the most popular purely belle lettristic item" (114). Today Shakespeare's figure seems integral to American literary culture, but it was not until the eighteenth century that he made the voyage to America.

What is startling is the way that Shakespeare spread in the years between 1750 and 1776 as the practices of reading and of book production changed: from a figure leaving no significant trace in the culture of colonial America,

Shakespeare moves to become a powerful presence authorizing revolt and empowering colonists to claim cultural superiority over their motherland. Thus, in the first part of the eighteenth century, American colonists began, for the first time, to read Shakespeare. In part, Americans were simply following the tastes of England, where Shakespeare's critical fortunes were on the rise as well. As Richard Beal Davis remarks, "The bard's American popularity coincided with his Georgian revival in Britain" (*Intellectual Life*, 3:1303). One can speculate that another factor was the age's didactic approach to Shakespeare. I do not think that it is a coincidence that Americans began to value Shakespeare's language, whether read or performed, during the Great Awakening (1730s to 1770s), when emotionally charged eloquence swept across the land. For those who had discovered a sudden hunger for emotionalism and rich language, Shakespeare's plays stood ready as secular sermons, and they were less morally suspect than more frivolous, if more fashionable, plays such as Farquhar's *The Beaux' Stratagem*.

But it is no accident that interest in Shakespeare heightened most dramatically in the same years that tensions grew between England and its American colonies. Increasingly Shakespeare appears in a political context, supporting one position over another, used as a voice for authoritative social values. In the twenty-five year period between 1750 and 1775, his plays are suddenly performed, read, and cited, while his image appears in household furnishings and his authority crops up in political discourse. Moreover, when colonial America invokes Shakespeare in the decades just before the Revolution, he serves both sides of the political conflict. Shakespeare functions simultaneously as an index of all that is best about England and as England's sharpest critic, whether on stage, at home, or in the public arena.

To begin with the performances, the popularity of his plays speedily increases after the first Shakespeare production in 1750, *Richard III* by the Murray–Kean Company in New York. (An amateur production of *Romeo and Juliet* was announced in 1730, but no trace of its actual performance exists.)[18] In the latter half of the eighteenth century, as Shakespeare's reputation was rapidly rising in England, his plays were increasingly being produced in America. Rankin considers Shakespeare the most popular colonial playwright, estimating that "In the twenty-four years before the Revolution [i.e., 1750 on], fourteen of his plays were performed at least 180 times, and, in the light of the paucity of information, it would be reasonable to guess the total to be at least 500" (191; Johnson and Burling do not substantially revise Rankin's figures). Those figures are remarkable. From 1600 until 1750, no performances of Shakespeare occurred, but between 1750 and 1776 there were 500, by conservative estimate. Rankin's estimate raises the question of why Shakespeare's plays – so late in coming to the Americas – immediately prospered.

One reason that English plays, including Shakespeare's, were finally performed in the Americas is the same reason that they continued to be performed: a desire for liberty, or rather a desire to be free from restrictive laws. Actors wished to evade English laws against performance and earn a living by acting. In 1737, the Theatre Licensing Act limited the number of theatrical venues in England. A number of actors attempted to get around the law, one of them being a man named William Hallam who ran the New Wells Theatre. In 1747, Hallam abruptly stopped his efforts to put on plays "probably [because] the law was closing in" (Shattuck 1:4); in a recent analysis of the Hallam family, Robert Myers and Joyce Brodowski show that "Throughout their careers, William and the other Hallams were at odds with the patent theatres and the law."[19] A few years later he began investigating the possibility of putting together a company to perform in America. Another London manager, John Moody, was enjoying some success in Jamaica (R. Wright 26–8); Robert Upton, sent to New York at William Hallam's behest to investigate conditions, found them sufficiently promising to set up in business for himself (Shattuck 1:4). Following the lead of Moody and Upton in 1752, Hallam's brother Lewis and nine other actors sailed to Williamsburg and began performances there, soon performing in New York, Philadelphia, and Charleston as well.

These actors' attempts to find theatrical venues in America, since such venues were limited in London, enjoyed success. Whenever the Hallam Company ran into difficulties because of opposition from local authorities, they simply moved on to the next city. When the opposition was particularly intense in 1755–58 and 1764–66, the company went to Jamaica, returning when the climate for performances was friendlier on the mainland. (During the first trip to Jamaica, Lewis Hallam, Sr., died in 1758, and the company was thereafter run first by David Douglass and later by Lewis Hallam, Jr.) Initially known as the London Company, they became the American Company in 1763.[20] In that name change, one may see a new judgment, i.e., that America allowed actors what Europe could not: room to move about and opportunity to evade licensing laws or to duck antitheatrical prejudice. America offered freedom.

That freedom was not political or artistic, but rather freedom from regulation, important to actors on commercial grounds. The prosperity that the Hallam–Douglass Company enjoyed allowed it to recruit new performers from England; over the years some of these actors broke away to form their own companies. By the middle of the eighteenth century, much of the anti-theatrical opposition had died down. The new acting troupes showed no interest in the controversial, and here Shakespeare's plays played an important part because they had become relatively old-fashioned. Thus, in 1759 when the Hallam-Douglass troupe came to Philadelphia, Quakers and Presbyterians pressured the General Assembly to suppress their productions. The General Assembly passed an act forbidding plays in the city, but Governor William Denny delayed its enforcement until January 1760 (Johnson and Burling 189–190). The players quickly built a new playhouse outside the city limits, and their manager, David Douglass,

rearranged his repertoire to feature the plays of Shakespeare and the less offensive efforts of contemporary playwrights. Shakespeare, of course, was presented in the altered or expurgated versions then current on the London stage. (Rankin 83)

Those productions not only used an altered text for Shakespeare's plays, but also included afterpieces and other entertainments, including dancing, fencing, or singing.

In 1761, when Douglass and his company gave the first performances in Rhode Island, they continued to use Shakespeare as a stalking horse to defend against moral objections. Douglass presented Shakespeare in the form of "MORAL DIALOGUES in five parts," beginning with *Othello* and its depiction of "the Evil Effects of Jealousy and other Bad Passions, and Proving that Happiness can only Spring from the Pursuit of Virtue" (Rankin 94). (The Great Awakening may have influenced this ploy.) And when the company returned to Philadelphia in 1770, Douglass toned down the company's performances. "Some concessions were made to the simpler and spiritual tastes of Philadelphia," including a production of Dryden–Davenant's operatic revision of *The Tempest* because, as a newspaper said, Philadelphians could "reflect Honour on our Taste, by patronizing one of the *Chef d'Oeuvres* of the Immortal Genius" Shakespeare (Rankin 137). Having been excluded from sixteenth- and seventeenth-century American life because he did not fit a nostalgia for England, Shakespeare now benefited from a nostalgia for a later England that had designated him as a national representative. Though initially unwelcome, Shakespeare now represented good taste.

By the 1770s, Shakespeare's plays served as a mainstay in the repertory for the touring companies that performed in all the major southern and some of the northern cities, with the most popular being *Richard III* and *Romeo and Juliet* (Johnson and Burling 66–67). In the years before the Revolution, those who would become loyalists and rebels all attended the theatre together. One could relish English plays while dissenting from the policies of the English government. Among the colonists, after all, those of English descent regarded themselves *as* English and laid claim to all that was attractive in that identity, including its theatrical interests. Shakespeare's popularity was somewhat restricted by the coming of rebellion, as the American leaders in the Continental Congress felt that playgoing (like cockfighting and horse racing) had to be discouraged:

We will, in our several stations, encourage frugality, economy, and industry . . . and will discountenance and discourage every species of extravagance and dissipation, especially all horse-racing, and all kinds of gaming, cock-fighting, exhibition of shews, plays, and other expensive diversions and entertainments. (Rankin 187)

The British had no such scruples about going to plays. While the start of the Revolution meant ceding the pleasures of playgoing to British identity, that surrender was not uncontested. Despite the American prohibition on performance, Douglass and his company continued to produce plays in Baltimore, and at least one member of the company, Francis Mentges, became an American officer (Rankin 173). George Washington was an avid playgoer even during the war, evidently ignoring the laws against such activity despite his position as commander-in-chief. Ultimately, both armies would produce Shakespeare's plays.

During the Revolution (1775–83),[21] Shakespearean productions were military entertainments, paralleling the sixteenth-century Spanish productions in Mexico and the seventeenth-century French productions in Canada. Military theatre served to raise morale, providing a pastime for the performers and entertainment both for the troops and the community that housed them. When the community did not want the military, of course, as Boston did not want the English in 1775, the civilians were unhappy. "Proper Bostonians found [General] Burgoyne's theatricals to be offensive from first to last, and Burgoyne seems to have delighted in giving offense" (J. Brown 24). Soon after Burgoyne's play production began, however, the battle of Bunker Hill took place and the British soldiers soon evacuated Boston, moving to New York.

From 1777 until 1782, British officers gave six seasons of drama at the "Theatre Royal" in John Street, New York, for the benefit of "charity" and "the widows and orphans of soldiers." Of Shakespeare they produced *Othello*, *King Richard III*, *King Lear*, *Macbeth*, *King Henry IV, Part I*, and *Catherine And Petruchio*, a list which shows that the officers preferred the martial and heroic. (Gale 43)

Jared Brown has discussed the British military theatre at length. He adds the cities of Philadelphia and Savannah as venues for their performances, and also notes that British prisoners in Virginia gave performances at Staunton and Charlottesville, suggesting that the British soldier–actors were principally interested in supplementing their pay despite the publicized claim of concern for "widows and orphans" of fallen comrades. Whatever their motives, eleemosynary or self-interested, the British military used Shakespearean plays as a mainstay. Indeed, in the first production that Burgoyne staged in Boston in 1775, he wrote a prologue mocking rebellious Americans who objected to his theatrical ambitions and found "Shakespear charm'd no more" (J. Brown 25). In the New York productions, Shakespeare's importance to the military theatre is indicated by an establishment close to the playhouse named the Shakespeare Tavern, where the soldier–actors often celebrated their successes (Silverman 375). During the Revolution, then, Shakespeare was principally performed by the British, not by the American rebels, and presumably his plays embody values of importance to the British forces. Gale thinks those values were the martial and heroic, while Dunn and Brown think they were economic.

It also seems fair to argue that the choice of plays to be performed was, to some extent, affected by the performers' political sympathy for Britain, especially in one instance of a Shakespeare play performed by American troops. Dunn describes the circumstances:

A Shakespearean play, *Coriolanus*, buttressed the low spirits of the American Army in New Hampshire at Portsmouth in 1778. One Jonathan Sewall wrote an epilogue for this occasion, showing the figure of Coriolanus as a man suffering from 'his country's base ingratitude'. This epilogue, later printed, carried a footnote indicating that Shakespeare's Coriolanus spoke for the American soldiers and officers who felt that their efforts for their new country were not appreciated. (120)

Gale and Pollock also record theatrical performances by the American military, both at Valley Forge and in Philadelphia, but it is not clear that these plays were Shakespearean (Gale 46; Pollock 36–9, 131–32). Jared Brown suggests that the Continental Congress's resolution prohibiting performances was a major factor limiting performances by the American army, despite the way that the resolution was frequently ignored. In the case of the New Hampshire *Coriolanus*, those who put the play on were aggrieved with their American commanders. Clearly there is self-identification with a hero who is thrust out from his own nation and unable to come to terms with another nation. The choice of a Shakespearean play may underscore the soldiers' dissatisfaction with the American command, given that Shakespeare on stage was largely associated with British practice during these years.

During wartime, then, Shakespeare's plays served to raise British morale by reinforcing the cultural values that their audiences held. British officers wanted plays that were linked to the motherland, and they enjoyed watching plays like *Richard III*, *Macbeth*, *1 Henry IV*, and *Lear*, in which those who attempt to displace a rightful king are defeated. American officers seem to have preferred non-Shakespearean farces or plays like *Cato* (all by British authors, of course), yet turned to Shakespeare when they sought a way of critiquing their command. But what is one to make of the sudden introduction of Shakespeare in 1750 or the surge in popularity that his plays had in the years leading up to the Revolution? Drama is intensely political in early America, as David Shields has demonstrated,[22] and the sudden performance of Shakespeare's plays coincides nicely with the rising concern that Americans felt about the colonial relationship with Britain.

The experience of the Maryland Company precludes the idea that Shakespeare's theatrical popularity is simply political. Despite the Congressional resolution forbidding plays (as well as cockfights and horse racing), the Maryland Company produced a season in 1782–83, which included seven of Shakespeare's plays (J. Brown 147, 155). American rebels, including some officers and soldiers, attended the plays, suggesting that the law against theatre was enforced intermittently. The company's use of Shakespeare may owe something to one of the players, billed as a Mr. Shakespeare, "who later continued his professional career with another company" (J. Brown 150). But the principal reason that the company (indeed any eighteenth-century company) produced Shakespeare's plays was commercial: they wanted to make money. Presumably the company enjoyed enough success that in the following year they raised their sights higher. Having succeeded in Baltimore, Maryland, they wished to try a larger city with a more sophisticated playgoing public, namely, New York. New York was, of course, under British control. The chameleon pragmatism of theatre become apparent:

When his company performed in Baltimore, Ryan produced plays and prologues that had appealed to American patriotic sentiment. Now that he was in British-occupied New York, however, Ryan abruptly became a Tory. (J. Brown 164)

Shakespeare could, in short, be used by either side theatrically, but the American rules against playgoing limited performance of his plays in the Revolutionary years.

It was not only on the stage that Shakespeare suddenly became popular, but in the home as well.[23] Busts of Shakespeare and other memorabilia become part of colonial domestic furnishings in the period between 1750

1 The Wedgwood chess set depicting the Siddons and Kemble *Macbeth* created by John Flaxman. Such a luxurious import in the colonial American period might signal enthusiasm for the performance, seen while the owner was in London, but more likely it indicated either a political loyalty toward England or a sense of wealth and social standing.

and 1776. Carson notes that the earliest such item was "A beautiful Statuary Marble carved Chimney-Piece and Picture; two fine China Chandeliers, fitted with Flowers and Branches; with three Plaister Figures of Shakespear, Milton, and Pope," which was offered for sale in 1754. In subsequent years, figures of Shakespeare adorned Americans' mantelpieces or mahogany bookcases, and he was the subject of a number of small plaster busts and medallions. In 1769, for example, Samuel Chase, who would sign the Declaration of Independence, began construction of a house that featured a mantelpiece with a marble bas-relief of Shakespeare being visited by the Muse. While there is uncertainty about whether Chase ordered the mantelpiece or Edward Lloyd, who took over the house soon after work on it began, in both cases we have American colonists who valued British art and culture, but who sided with the Revolution against the monarch. A Wedgwood chess set sold in the colonies is notable: the chessmen represented characters from the Charles Kemble and Sarah Siddons *Macbeth* (see figure 1).

Thus Americans began to use images of Shakespeare and his plays in their home to indicate their education and taste. Owners of such objects implicitly claim a privileged status in society. In at least one case, the owner of Shakespearean items was an American who was unsympathetic to the Revolutionary ideas. Elizabeth Graeme Fergusson complained that "twelve small medal Plaister of Paris heads of the Poets" among her domestic goods were seized by the "rebels," a reminder if one were needed that not all American colonists wanted their independence from Britain, and that Shakespeare-ana might be used to indicate allegiance to Britain as well as social status. In the colonial period, then, domestic furnishings offered Americans a way to emulate British taste. As Shakespeare moved into position as "England's poet" for Londoners in the early eighteenth century, adoption of his figure into domestic furnishings allowed Americans to demonstrate that they were current with the fashions of their motherland. Unlike the stage productions before the war, which could appeal to those on both sides of the growing political divide, domestic use of Shakespeare's image seems more often to show sympathy to British interests.

More complex are the rising number of references to Shakespeare.[24] Privately in letters and commonplace books, American colonial writers began to invoke Shakespeare as an authority who lent prestige and weight to their complaints about the political situation, while publicly newspapers appropriated his texts to criticize England. Initially, citation of Shakespeare served aesthetic ends. Hennig Cohen gives one such example:

Another indication of how well Shakespeare was known is the extent to which local writers used quotations from his plays as epigraphs to their own poems and essays. For example, "Humourist," a regular contributor to the [Charleston] *Gazette* in 1753–54, sprinkled his essays with Shakespearian quotations and used several examples of Shakespeare's nature descriptions (along with others by Dryden, Spenser, and Otway) to demonstrate the superiority of the "Moderns" over the "Antients." (Cohen 328)

Such citation soon shifted to politics. Esther Dunn records a number of such references in Massachusetts and New York newspapers between 1770 and 1776, showing that in the popular press, Shakespeare becomes a standard referent for complaints about England's colonial policy. One of the best examples is a parody of *Hamlet* that asks

> Be taxt or not be taxt – that is the question.
> Whether 'tis nobler in our minds to suffer
> The sleights and cunning of deceitful statesmen
> Or to petition'gainst illegal taxes
> And by opposing, end them?   (Dunn 108)

Other journalists produced similar parodies, and in one case the parodist was a loyalist, an American Whig who referenced Shakespeare as he expressed his reluctance to sign an article of "association" favoring the rebels: "To sign, or not to sign?" he asks a few years later (1774–76):

> . . . that is the question.
> Whether 'tis better for an honest man
> To sign – and so be safe; or to resolve,
> Betide what will, against "associations,"
> And, by retreating, shun them.
>
> (Dunn 111–12; Rawlings 29–31)

Another broadside from 1778 refers to "Old Shakespeare, a poet who should not be spit on, / Although he was born in an island called Britain" (Dunn 112). Does this doggerel suggest that rebels showed particular contempt for Shakespeare? Probably not, since rebels as well as loyalists invoked him, but it does suggest how closely Shakespeare was linked in the popular imagination of the day to Britishness. Sturgess traces the way that later Americans, hostile to Britain, increasingly separated Shakespeare from Britain so that they could regard the dramatist as American. For the rebellious colonists, references to Shakespeare's works provided a way for them to reproach what they regarded as a falling away from the traditional British love of liberty, while colonists loyal to the crown could invoke him as a symbol of British greatness. What strikes me as interesting is the way that both sides cite Shakespeare to lend power to their position: Shakespeare makes it possible for them to declare themselves.

Abigail and John Adams, for example, use Shakespeare in their private discussions of George III's government. Thus Abigail Adams writes a letter comparing George III to Richard III, or John Adams compares his revulsion at a political choice to the revulsion that Mistress Ford feels at Falstaff's attempted seduction (Dunn 86, 92). These casual references suggest the couple's familiarity and comfort with Shakespeare's works, to be sure, but they may also suggest that he was particularly congenial in discussions of politics. Michael Bristol suggests that John Adams' later appropriation of Ulysses' speech on degree in *Troilus and Cressida* is especially significant:

Adams invokes Shakespeare to authorize his own refusal of myth as the basis for his constitutional project, the arduous task of making social institutions as opposed to simply affirming either what has been received or what has been newly instituted. Shakespeare clearly functions as part of praxis, that is, political action informed by theoretical as well as by strategic deliberation. (58)

(I would underscore Bristol's point that the way Americans like Adams use Shakespeare is pragmatic rather than aesthetic.) Such references work in a way somewhat different from performances of Shakespeare's plays then: while the American rebels stopped performing Shakespeare's plays for the most part during the war, appropriations of his language were commonplace. And those appropriations were intended to mark American ideas as truer readings of Shakespeare's meaning than conventional British attitudes could be. But it is not Americans only who made such a claim. In 1777 Maurice Morgann, a British official who had actually worked in North America on government service, wrote that when Voltaire and his criticism (that Shakespeare was a barbarian) should be no more, "the *Apalachian* mountains, the banks of the *Ohio*, and the plains of *Sciota* shall resound with the accents of this Barbarian [Shakespeare]" (170). In Morgann's view, it is not England that shall outlast the French Voltaire, but the Americas that shall be Shakespeare's future home. Shakespeare, in this way, becomes more American than British, a suggestion that would continue in American culture.

Political pragmatism also occurs with Thomas Jefferson, who kept a commonplace book that uses Shakespearean passages frequently. These citations are generally passages "of defiance and rebellion" that are "characterized by emphatic outbursts" and entered in an "energetic and flamboyant hand, the most exuberant in the manuscript," "that is called the 'Shakespeare' hand" (D. Wilson 18–19). In his private reading, Jefferson found Shakespeare's works intensely political, concentrating on those plays in which characters struggle with issues of authority: *1 Henry IV*, *2 Henry VI*, *Henry V*, *Julius Caesar*, and *Coriolanus*. In one case, Jefferson makes use of a revision of *Julius Caesar* by John Sheffield, Duke of Buckingham, and Douglas Wilson comments that Jefferson "seems to have been attracted by the same things in Buckingham as in Shakespeare – the strident note of defiance and the insistence that death is preferable to infringements of one's honor or liberty" (158). Wilson also notes the way that Jefferson often linked Shakespeare to Milton, who attracted him because of "strong expressions of rebellion and defiance of authority" (174). Like Adams, Jefferson seems to have found Shakespeare both useful (as a way of authoritatively supporting his own positions) and attractive (perhaps because appropriating Shakespeare to American values diminishes British culture). What seems most striking, however, is that the Shakespearean works Jefferson was most drawn to were those that authorize political violence.

Not everyone in eighteenth-century America found Shakespeare interesting or apropos, of course. Benjamin Franklin, for example, never cites Shakespeare (although his print shop owned a copy of Shakespeare's *Works*), nor are there any Shakespearean allusions in *The Federalist Papers*. I have looked through the indexed papers of such "founding fathers" as John Jay, Henry Laurens, Richard Henry Lee, William Livingston, Alexander Hamilton, James Madison in vain: they never mention Shakespeare. Others such as George Mason, George Washington, and Fisher Ames may quote a tag in passing, but say nothing of substance. Nor is it only notable American political figures who appropriate Shakespeare as an index of America's cultural superiority to England.

In 1770, a production of *Cymbeline* is an especially interesting one, for it results in an object that illustrates several of the points I want to make. (See figure 2.)

The Hallam-Douglass American Company had included *Cymbeline* in its repertoire since 1767, with a Miss Margaret Cheer as Imogen, cross-dressed as Fidele. In 1769, however, Miss Cheer stepped aside and the production featured Nancy Hallam as Imogen/Fidele (Shattuck 1:14–15). Nancy Hallam, niece to Mrs. Hallam Douglass and cousin to Lewis Hallam, Jr., came to America in 1765 in search of her fortune. In 1770, when the company appeared at the New Theatre in Annapolis, they put on *Cymbeline* with *The King and the Miller of Mansfield* as the afterpiece, and Nancy's Hallam's performance was hugely successful. The *Maryland Gazette* reviewer, one Y. Z., praised her with enthusiasm:

She exceeded my utmost Idea. Such delicacy of Manner! Such classical Strictures of Expression! The Musick of her Tongue! The *vox liquida*, how melting! . . . Her whole Form and Dimensions how happily convertible, and universally adapted to the Variety of her Part. (*Maryland Gazette* 6 September 1770)

At the end of the review came "To Miss HALLAM," a poem of adulation, by Jonathan Boucher:[25]

> HAIL wond'rous maid! I, grateful, hail
>   Thy *strange* dramatic Pow'r:
> To thee I owe, that *Shakespeare's* Tale
>   Has charm'd my Ears once more.
>   · · ·
> She speaks! – *What Elocution flows!*
>   Ah! Softer far her Strains
> Than Fleeces of descending Snows,
>   On gentlest vernal Rains.
>
> Do solemn Measures slowly move?
>   Her Looks inform the Strings:
> Do Lydian Airs invite to Love?
>   We feel it as she sings.

2 Charles Willson Peale's 1771 portrait of Nancy Hallam as Fidele in *Cymbeline*. In the portrait one finds a material representation of a Shakespearean performance; the portrait was celebrated in several newspaper items. In the years between 1750 and 1776, Shakespeareana became part of American domestic furnishings, Shakespeare's plays were suddenly and frequently produced, and his works were the topic of American writing.

The poem continues, with a total of twelve quatrains, and concludes with an appeal that the finest painter in Annapolis, Charles Willson Peale, should do a portrait of Miss Hallam.

Peale was a remarkable figure, who had turned to painting after developing an interest in politics. Joining the Sons of Liberty during the Stamp Act troubles of 1764, Peale campaigned for Samuel Chase, the man with the Shakespearean mantelpiece, who was running for the provincial assembly. As a consequence, Peale's creditors, opposed to his politics and more loyal to Britain, had driven him out of the saddlery trade and into painting, a field in which he prospered. Indeed, his sons and daughters also became painters and were well-known through the new American nation, while Peale developed a notable reputation as a portraitist, painting his friend George Washington repeatedly. (Peale would also become famous for his museum in Philadelphia.) In 1771, he placed a lovely full-length painting of Nancy Hallam in his rooms when the American Company returned to play at the West Street Theatre, Annapolis.

Once again the *Maryland Gazette* produced verse tributes, both to Nancy Hallam in *Cymbeline* and to Charles Willson Peale. While the first round of newspaper attention had concentrated on Nancy Hallam's performance, praising her acting, singing, and dancing, the second set of newspaper poetry and comment in 1771 concerns the painting, with much praise of Peale's work. There is one poem by "Paladour," however, that remains focused on Hallam's charm. It suggests that the theatrical production is particularly American, and that its excellence outshines those of England.

> Fair, fair FIDELE! How thy charms
>   The Huntsmans Pity mov'd
> Artless as theirs, such soft Alarms
>   My melting bosom prov'd.
>   . . .
> Methinks I see his [Shakespeare's] smiling Shade,
>   And hear him thus Proclaim,
> "In Western Worlds, to this fair Maid
>   "I trust my spreading fame.
>
> "Long have my Scenes each British Heart
>   "With warmest Transports fill'd;
> "Now equal Praise, by HALLAM's Art,
>   "AMERICA shall yield."
>   *Maryland Gazette* 10 October 1771

This incident shows Shakespeare on stage, in journalism, and in decorative arts in colonial America. Perhaps the first point to make is that

Shakespearean performance in this period was not at all what we are accus-
tomed to today. The playtext was very much an acting edition, shortened
to make room for songs and dancing, as the poems to Miss Hallam suggest
when they praise her singing voice. The Shakespearean play was presented
with an afterpiece, usually farcical, to provide a very full evening's entertainment, well worth the audience's money. The company often struggled with
debt, yet they made enough to continue their performances for decades.
That is not to say that they had earned enough money to commission such a
portrait. A handbill from 1790, reproduced in Sellars' study of Peale (228),
shows that he was then charging forty guineas for a full-length portrait.
Although one art historian suggests Peale was occasionally working as a
scene painter for the Annapolis theatre (Miller, *New Perspectives*, 154), he
would not have done such an elaborate painting for good will. He may
instead have sold (or hoped to sell) to one of the actress's admirers this portrait of Nancy Hallam, who, cross-dressed "as the boy Fidele, prettily clad
in pink trousers and an overdress, stands wonderingly, her sword drawn,
about to enter the cave" (Shattuck 1:15).[26]

Just as commercial and sensual factors are at work in the painting, so,
too, do political interests affect the eighteenth-century audience's understanding of Shakespeare. Such men as Samuel Chase, Edward Lloyd, and
Charles Willson Peale shared a common political position: many colonial Americans valued English taste and art, but disliked English rule.
Shakespeare becomes a figure who is both valuable as England's national
poet, and available for American appropriation, as the Paladour poem suggests. For the acting company, Shakespeare's attraction may lie elsewhere:
his plays are not controversial, but familiar and unlikely to disturb the civic
authories. In itself that observation is quite remarkable given the almost
complete absence of Shakespeare in America before 1700.

How is one to account for the surge in Shakespeare's popularity between
1750 and 1776? A widespread art form in eighteenth-century America was
the silhouette. The subject sat between a light source, such as a candle or
lamp, and a screen. The artist would hold a sheet of paper up to the screen
and trace the sitter's shadow, or silhouette. The screen served as a place onto
which one projected light. Yet when the screen was a piece of glass, as often
happened, rather than opaque material, it was also a medium through which
one could see the object. In a sense, Shakespeare served Americans, whether
they were pre-Revolutionary colonists or post-Revolutionary citizens, as a
silhouette artist's screen, both displaying England and projecting American
emotions about England, sometimes transparent and sometimes opaque.

In the eighteenth century Shakespeare was increasingly identified as "England's poet," and that identification had a powerful and complex effect on the way that England's colonial subjects in America regarded Shakespeare. As symbol of British values, Shakespeare becomes embraced by colonists who want to be *au fait* with what is happening in the motherland, especially in the fashionable world of London. References to Shakespeare occur in expensive domestic wares, such as chess sets or mantelpieces, as well as newspaper columns and private letters. In popular taste, Shakespeare is a commodity offering a way to mark one's class status.

Yet his figure is a political marker as well. Shakespeare also becomes a means of voicing discontent with the British for perceived hypocrisy and a turning away from liberty. He becomes a figure to be ignored (e.g., Franklin), as well as one to be appropriated (e.g., John and Abigail Adams). Those rebels who employ Shakespeare find in such plays as *Julius Caesar* and *Coriolanus* an authorization of political violence (e.g., Jefferson). The British forces, as the war breaks out, employ Shakespeare as a national representative to entertain the troops. This version of Shakespeare is cited by Americans who are sympathetic to Britain and opposed to rebellion. The crucial point, however, is that Shakespeare's figure *has* power. As the American colonists began to examine critically their relationship with Britain, he suddenly appears in American culture. His presence becomes more and more common, and after the American Revolution, Americans would claim him as their own. Colonial and Federalist Americans seem to have recognized that Shakespeare was as available to them as to anyone in England: Shakespeare could be claimed as an American figure just as well as a London one. Appropriating his works, whether in parody or in defense of liberty, was an especially gratifying act of rebellion, precisely because he was so closely associated with England.

Information about Shakespeare provides an index to American attitudes toward Britain: hence the timing of the sudden introduction of Shakespeare in 1750 or the surge in popularity that his plays had in the years leading up to the Revolution. Drama is intensely political in early America, and the sudden performance of Shakespeare's plays coincides nicely with the rising concern that Americans felt about the colonial relationship with Britain. With the performance of Shakespeare's plays comes the addition of other popular performance forms like farcical afterpieces, Harlequinades, singing, and dancing. Today one is apt to associate the performance of Shakespeare's plays with elite culture: if one takes a longer view, Shakespeare's plays become central to America's popular culture as the nation begins to form. Moreover, because Shakespeare is part of popular entertainment at this moment in history, the plays are linked to song, dance, and farce from the outset, for such elements are integral to the conventions of popular performance when Americans finally begin to stage the plays.

Finally, the history of Shakespeare in eighteenth-century America matters because of what would come from it. The impulse that led to Shakespeare's sudden presence is, as I have tried to show, pragmatic, not aesthetic, whether one thinks of actors trying to evade licensing laws, colonists trying to signal their social status, or men like Adams and Jefferson trying to find a solid precedent for violently breaking with a monarch. The outcome of such pragmatic projects is that Shakespeare's figure has power and his power is linked to such concepts as the British, social rank, or political violence. In the next century, his power will grow, as will the violence. In 1847, P. T. Barnum unsuccessfully attempts to purchase Shakespeare's birthplace and bring it to America. In 1849, more than thirty New Yorkers are killed in the Astor Place riots about a production of *Macbeth*. And in 1865, John Wilkes Booth claims a horrifying self-identification with Brutus in *Julius Caesar* as he kills Lincoln. Shakespeare's presence shapes American culture in ways hitherto unexplored.

CHAPTER 2

In the pioneer's hut

If Americans showed little interest in Shakespeare before 1750, when the events leading up to the American Revolution raised their concern with all that symbolized England, then the end of the Revolution and their victory should have marked a decline in that topical interest. To some extent, that is what happened. Charles Shattuck, for example, notes that "With the signing of the peace treaty in 1783, the British military withdrew from New York . . . It should have been time for a Shakespearean revival," yet while Americans performed some of the best-known of Shakespeare's plays, they introduced few new titles and "To a noticeable extent Shakespeare was crowded out by the new drama" of such playwrights as Sheridan and von Kotzebue (Shattuck 1:16). Such interest in the recent and fashionable helps explain why Garrick's *Shakespeare Jubilee* (1769) was produced in New York in 1788 and in Charleston in 1793 (Markels 39). The performance of music, recitation of poetry, and stirring oration that composed the *Shakespeare Jubilee* omitted any passages from Shakespeare's plays: it was not love and enjoyment of Shakespeare but love of fashion and enjoyment of music and spectacle that prompted such productions.[1] Furthermore, after seven years of war, Americans were more concerned about their own national identity than England's, turning away from drama that was older or that recalled their defeated enemy. In an unsigned letter to the *Columbian Centinel* (24 November 1792), for example, one writer complained peevishly that the American theatre was insufficiently nationalistic:

. . . they delineate the virtues, vices, and follies of kings, lords, nobility, and a great variety of other characters, quite as unknown, as uninteresting to the people of this country . . . If we must endure the expense of a Theatre, – for the sake of fashion, let us have one, in which our own vices are depicted; not those of foreigners, which with us, must defeat its principle design. If the authors and the actors of plays are to be supported, let them be of our own production.[2]

For this American, not only actors but playwrights ought to be American, not English. Relations between the two countries continued to be difficult, leading to more war with England from 1812 to 1815. The surprise is not that there was a relatively small revival of Shakespearean drama, but that there was any revival of interest in his plays at all.

While American attitudes toward Shakespeare cannot simply be equated with American attitudes toward England, there is a clear congruence during the first few decades after the Revolution, and there is clear hostility. Paul Langford, for instance, argues that

During the three-quarters of a century that followed the Declaration of Independence, certain stereotypes of British and American life emerged on either side of the Atlantic. Many concerned the make-up of society, its codes of behaviour and its interactions. These may be crudely summarized. In American eyes British society was incorrigibly aristocratic, bound by rigid upper-class rules, preserved by cringing lower-class servility and served by institutional conservatism. In British eyes American society was dangerously egalitarian, conducted according to barbaric ideas, governed by unprincipled democrats and bereft of decorum and order. Put simply, America was too democratic to be genteel, and Britain was too genteel to be democratic . . . [T]he basic pattern of perceptions in each direction is remarkably consistent and coherent. (76)

Sturgess would agree, noting that in the early American republic "this strong anti-English sentiment became institutionalized and an expression of American nationalism while simultaneously Shakespeare gradually became subsumed into national consciousness" (24). An anecdote from 1786 illustrates the prickly attitudes that Langford and Sturgess both describe, as well as indicating the contested place of Shakespeare in Anglo-American relations.

The new nation had sent ministers overseas: John Adams to London and Thomas Jefferson to Paris.[3] In the spring of 1786, Jefferson visited Adams to help with delicate diplomatic negotiations. These meetings went badly, as the Ambassador for the Barbary States set a far higher price on peace with Tripoli (over 30,000 guineas) than the Americans were prepared to pay. Jefferson's presentation at the court of George III went badly as well. The monarch was "ungracious," and after a party at the French embassy Jefferson said of the English: "These people cannot look me in the face: there is a conscious guilt and shame in their countenances when they look at me. They feel they have behaved ill, and I am sensible of it" (McCullough 355, 356). Jefferson and Adams, who often found themselves at odds during their careers, on this occasion were in complete accord. The peace negotiations accomplished nothing, the English were rude, and the English nation oblivious to what was of greatest value in their heritage. Soon the two of them decided they needed a holiday from duty.

From 4–9 April 1786, they amused themselves together with a "little journey into the country." Visiting about twenty gentlemen's seats and stately homes, the two greatly enjoyed examining gardens, discussing landscape architecture, and generally sightseeing. But Adams recorded two journeys that fell short of delight. The first was their visit to Edgehill and Worcester, both scenes of great victories for the Parliamentary forces in the English Civil War over a century before. The American revolutionaries were appalled by English indifference to the Parliamentary revolutionaries, and Adams writes:

Edgehill and Worcester were interesting to us as Scaenes where Freemen had fought for their Rights. The People in the Neighbourhood, appeared so ignorant and careless at Worcester that I was provoked and asked, "And do Englishmen so soon forget the Ground where Liberty was fought for? Tell your Neighbours and your Children that this is holy Ground, much holier than that on which your Churches stand. All England should come in Pilgrimage to this Hill, once a year." This animated them, and they seemed much pleased with it. Perhaps their Aukwardness before might arise from their Uncertainty of our Sentiments concerning the Civil Wars. (*Diary* 185)

Adams found the English awkward socially, just as Jefferson had found them unable to look him in the face. Both Americans think social difficulty is the result of English self-consciousness about Americans, not the consequence of anything that they themselves have done. To the Americans the English behavior might be characterized as chilly, ignorant, ill at ease. It does not occur to Adams, certainly, that he might seem brash or arrogant in his own conduct. He regards the battlefield as part of a history that English and Americans share, and as a shareholder in its significance, he speaks out against its neglect. But one could also regard his impromptu lecture as an instance of a patronizing foreigner telling citizens of another nation about their country's shortcomings. The national stereotypes that Langford mentions surely originated in incidents like this one.

The two Americans' visit to Stratford-upon-Avon likewise suggests the depth of national differences that originate in a shared heritage. Both Jefferson and Adams loved Shakespeare's works, read his plays and wrote about them, and were eager to see his home. Jefferson says little of the visit, noting only how much he paid for admission to various locations, "for seeing house where Shakespeare was born, 1s.; seeing his tomb, 1s.; entertainment, 4s. 2d.; servants 2s," but "years afterward Adams would claim that Jefferson on arriving at Stratford-upon-Avon, had actually gotten down on his knees and kissed the ground" (Dumbauld 81; McCullough 359). Adams was just as irked at the neglect he found in Stratford as he was in Worcester. The birthplace, he complained was

as small and mean, as you can conceive . . . There is nothing preserved of this great Genius which is worth knowing – nothing which might inform Us what Education, what Company, what Accident turned his Mind to Letters and the Drama. His name is not even on his Grave Stone. An ill sculptured Head is sett up by his Wife, by the Side of his Grave in the Church. But paintings and Sculpture would be thrown away upon his Fame. His Wit, and Fancy, his Taste and Judgment, His Knowledge of Nature, of Life and Character, are immortal. (*Diary* 185)

Adams notes, too, that they cut a chip from Shakespeare's old chair in the chimney corner of the birthplace, "according to the Custom." While Adams gave no lecture in the birthplace, he would not be the only American to be struck by how poorly it was maintained. Clearly he regards Shakespeare's plays as part of his own cultural inheritance, and his criticisms arise from the way that one of his heroes has seemingly been neglected. Yet the conclusion of his notes points out his comfort: what he values most about Shakespeare, "His Wit, and Fancy, his Taste and Judgment, His Knowledge of Nature, of Life and Character," has no dependence on the treatment of his old home but is immortally preserved in his works. Adams might well have added that it did not much matter whether the English valued Shakespeare properly since he would be valued by others, like Jefferson and himself, in an appropriate (and appropriating) way.

After all, Americans were not averse to claiming Shakespeare as their own whenever they could. One example from before the revolution came in a review of the American Company's 1770 *Cymbeline*, which I discussed earlier. The reviewer Y.Z. ended by declaring belligerently that, "The Merit of Mr. Douglass's Company is, notoriously in the opinion of every Man of Sense in America, whose Opportunities give him a Title to Judge – take them for all in all – superior to that of any Company in England, except those of the Metropolis" (*Maryland Gazette* 6 September 1770). After the war, such claims continued. Thus in 1811, the *American Review* says, "The sterling poets of England, such as Milton, Shakespeare, Pope and Cowper, are read and admired here by that class of society, which, in Europe, scarcely aspires to the rudiments of letters" (Dunn 130). The writer boasts that democracy enables Americans of all classes to read and admire Shakespeare, even those classes that were largely illiterate in Europe. The idea that Americans might have a superior understanding of Shakespeare would recur powerfully in the nineteenth century, as does the invocation of his figure as a justification for violence. But in some ways, such jingoistic pronouncements about American superiority over the English or Europeans were of less moment in the Federalist period because interest shifted to the development of American playwrights in the early part of the nineteenth century.[4]

American culture was becoming just that: American. From 1750 onwards, Shakespeare's figure proves useful as a means of expressing or displaying one's national identity in America, either as British (and as one sympathetic toward Britain) or as American. For nearly a century, as Sturgess shows, Shakespeare's figure served an important function in establishing American's national identity. As Americans become more sure of that identity in the first half of the nineteenth century, however, and as the anxiety of declaring one's identity as an American grew less pressing, Shakespeare's figure took on a new function. Instead of providing an index to one's national identity as an American, Shakespeare's figure became an index to one's social position among Americans, by marking one's relative education, culture, and class status.

Even during the years of greatest hostility to the British, Americans did not scorn Shakespeare by any means. As Louis Wright has said, "The most popular authors, as one might surmise, were the standard writers in the English tradition. Shakespeare was the best known."[5] One result was a commercial interest: American publishers would produce an edition of Shakespeare in the eighteenth century.[6] There was also civic interest: in 1803, Athens County in Ohio sent a wagon-load of coonskins to Boston to acquire $73.50 worth of books, a library full. The purchase, of course, included Shakespeare (L. Wright, *Culture* 117–18). Again and again one comes across references to ordinary Americans reading Shakespeare's plays for pleasure. Thus in 1820, trappers on the Yellowstone River write of reading Shakespeare, Byron, and Scott (L. Wright, *Culture* 75, 117–19). In 1840 a party of young men surveyed the shores of Lake Superior, seeking copper and iron deposits. One of them, Charles W. Penny, kept a journal and wrote: "We read the Bible I dare say much more than we would have done had we been in Detroit. Shakespeare was duly honored, as he is every day when we travel. When on the water, some one of the party usually reads his plays to the others."[7] Ron Dwelle notes that throughout the journal, Penny "frequently alludes to Shakespeare, often quoting or paraphrasing. For example: 'Night before last we caught three whitefish and one trout; last night two large whitefish. One can never get tired of them in this latitude. The meat is so fine, hard, and white, and so sweet, that all other fish seem "flat, stale and unprofitable" when compared to them.'" And in 1831, Alexis de Tocqueville, touring America to detail its idiosyncratic culture for a

European audience, would comment on how present Shakespeare was in America: "There is hardly a pioneer's hut which does not contain a few odd volumes of Shakespeare. I remember that I read the feudal drama of Henry V. for the first time in a log house" (174). For many Americans, then, reading Shakespeare was a pleasant diversion. Later in the century, American performances of Shakespeare would also be popular, with tours extending to its frontiers.

Mining camps particularly welcomed actors.[8] Indeed, Helene Koon entitled a book about such performances, *How Shakespeare Won the West*, while Jennifer Carrell has the variant title "How the Bard Won the West." In 1879 a New Mexico town was named Shakespeare to honor a mining company that was in turn named for the dramatist. Carrell points out that there were other traces of Shakespeare fanaticism among the miners:

The name is scattered all over the West: "Shakespeare" names a town and a canyon in New Mexico, a mountaintop in Nevada, a reservoir in Texas and a glacier in Alaska. But it was the miners who most often staked Shakespeare to the earth. Nineteenth-century claims called Shakespeare dotted the landscape of Colorado and spilled over into Utah. The mines that still scar Western mountains now seem a curious honorific for a great poet.

Yet, Shakespeare takes his place among heroes and sweethearts. In their quest for distinctive names, the miners delved into the Bard's stories. Colorado sports mines called Ophelia, Cordelia and Desdemona. There is even a "Timon of Athens," revealing that some prospectors dug into remote corners of Shakespeare as well as remote corners of North America, because Timon is one of Shakespeare's least-known plays. It is a fitting name for a mine, though, because the play's hero – a mad, bankrupt misanthrope – accidentally discovers "yellow, glittering, precious gold" while digging in the forest for roots.

As such anecdotal evidence suggests, Shakespeare's figure brought nineteenth-century Americans pleasure that was linked to promise of profit.

But promises of commercial success, civic improvement, and personal enjoyment are not all that account for the increasing interest in Shakespeare throughout the nineteenth century. Like the miners who used a screen to separate gold ore from dross, Americans used the figure of Shakespeare to provide a way of negotiating class and identity. Some Americans felt that with Shakespeare as part of one's social repertoire, one might claim membership in an elite social group, while others felt that Shakespeare and his works were claimed unjustly as a perquisite for that elite. The latter group protested at the very idea of restricting Americans from access to Shakespeare in any way as a fundamental betrayal of the American nation. I am not suggesting that there were two positions only, but rather that those two positions act as the far ends of a range of opinions. And on occasion, individuals from either end of the range came into conflict with explosive results.

I have been considering Americans in general terms as I have discussed the way that Shakespeare's figure functioned to help them form a national identity. In this next section of the book, as I discuss how Shakespeare's figure helped individuals form a personal identity, especially with regard to class, I shall consider individual cases rather than the general society. In each of these cases, an individual's desires, his dream of what he could become, led him to Shakespeare and led him to misconduct. Obviously there were other Americans, many others, who did not misbehave or commit crimes because Shakespeare led them astray, but who rather benefited in emotional, practical, and ethical ways from their affection for all things Shakespearean. Though duller than the Americans I shall discuss, their histories also illustrate that Shakespeare's figure, especially during the nineteenth century, has held real power in American culture and that Americans routinely tried to employ his figure to achieve their dreams. Some of their dreams were far from respectable. Others were nightmares.

Yet each of the cases that I consider offers important information about how popular entertainments developed in America and how Shakespeare's figure fitted into such entertainment. My goal, obviously, is to locate the factors in the history of America's popular entertainment that led to the development of the Shakespearean musical comedy, the form in which England's quintessential theatrical figure became linked to America's quintessential theatrical form. Let me preface the three cases I shall discuss with a summary of where popular theatre stood after the Revolution and where it was headed.

Throughout the colonial and Federalist period, particularly in the years before the Revolution, Americans had had an experience of the stage that was markedly different from other European groups. On the one hand, they did not have institutional sanction for performance of plays and various factors led many Americans to be suspicious of the stage. Another culturally suspect topic in the years after the Revolution was England. One figure who helped assuage concerns about propriety and England was Shakespeare, who also embodied much that Americans regarded with distaste. The tendency to ignore Shakespeare's national origin and to regard him as a naturalized American begins early and continues to the present. After the Revolution, such concerns began to fade, but they have never completely left American culture, as I shall try to show in my discussion of P. T. Barnum.

What does help ensure the eventual coming of theatrical performances is American pragmatism and commercial interest. In many areas actors were less regulated in America than in England, and they could easily move about. Moreover, in America actors could present what they pleased. Initially modeled on the programs of English theatres, the programs in American theatre gradually took on a nationally distinct flavor. While the program would include a play as the main piece with a farce offered as an afterpiece, an evening at the theatre often included other items as well: singing or dancing, fireworks, Harlequinades, lectures – any or all of these performances might be included, according to Rankin. In some sense, then, American stages have hosted musical productions of Shakespeare and others from the outset. Such popular mixed programs at the opening of the nineteenth century changed over the decades to the sort of program one finds today, and once again Shakespeare's figure is a key to that change. As American popular stage divided itself into the legitimate and variety, the legit theatre came to be associated with Shakespearean drama, while variety performances drew (ostensibly) away from Shakespeare. This division, as Lawrence Levine has argued, is how American popular culture became a reflection of one's class identity, and certainly as Americans think of Shakespeare during the nineteenth century, they are apt to consider him an index to one's class status. Yet both the working classes and the upper classes claimed Shakespeare as their own. Even after the legitimate theatre had worked to exclude rowdy or lower-class customers late in the century, Shakespeare had a presence in the variety-stage burlesques, whether in minstrel shows or vaudeville. I shall take a close look at the Astor Place Riot, a key moment in the splitting of high-brow from low-brow, to suggest that Shakespeare was present on both sides of the class divide.

Finally, an American strain that has been lost, one that disappears in the nineteenth century, is the link between Shakespeare and political discord. Indeed, one can go further, an idiosyncratically American element is the sense that Shakespeare's plays sanction political violence. Jefferson's "defiant" handwriting is called his Shakespeare hand, as I noted, and Shakespeare's presence in America coincides with the coming of a war to establish the nation. In the case of the Booth assassination, that sanctioning of violence brings national tragedy.

CHAPTER 3

Shakespeare makes scoundrels

When the painter Charles Willson Peale and his sons opened a museum of "natural curiosities," which would eventually become the Philadelphia Museum, he was participating in an American entertainment practice characteristic of the late eighteenth and early nineteenth centuries: a strong desire to combine education with amusement. Thus his museum offered a wonderful variety of exhibits. There were, of course, paintings, by Peale and others; the displays included, for example, copies of two of Benjamin West's painting for the Boydell Gallery – "King Lear in the Storm" and "Ophelia before the King and Queen" – as well as a copy of his son Rafaelle West's "Orlando Rescuing His Brother from the Lioness" (now lost). But the museum also included natural history specimens such as minerals and fossils, live animals (an eagle and monkeys), dead animals (a mammoth's skeleton as well as a stuffed bison, grizzly bear, kangaroo, and orangoutan), an organ loft for musical performances, magic mirrors, a wax figure of Meriwether Lewis, Oliver Cromwell's salt cellar, and the trigger finger of a murderer (Sellers 333–49). Such museums were popular, but it took a showman like P. T. Barnum to raise such a collection from amusement and edification to an American original like Barnum's Museum.

According to *American National Biography*, P. T. Barnum's entry into the museum business depended on the foundering of the Peales' venture:

In 1841 Barnum learned that Scudder's New York Museum, for years a losing concern, was on the market. "Lacking gold," he wrote, he "intended to buy it with brass." Armed with endorsements he persuaded the building's owner to buy it for him. When Peale's Museum outbid them with a public stock issue underwritten by bankers, Barnum wrote a "variety of squibs" ridiculing "the idea of a board of broken down bank directors engaging in the exhibition of stuffed monkeys and gander skins." The issue foundered, and by 27 December Barnum was in possession; he took over Peale's collections in New York in 1842 and in Philadelphia in 1850.[1]

P. T. Barnum built up his American Museum with exhibits of curiosities like the Fiji mermaid, lectures on subjects like temperance, solo presentations by such figures as Tom Thumb, and performances of such wholesome entertainment as *The Drunkard*. He founded other such "museums" and is also remembered for his role in starting the Barnum and Bailey Circus. Throughout Barnum's memoir, *Struggles and Triumphs* (1871), he lays stress on precisely the three factors I mentioned above: commerce, improvement, and pleasure. These are the elements that underlay the success of his museum, namely the exhibits, stage shows, and personal appearances that offered entertainment, promised improvement, and led to Barnum's commercial success. Robert Lewis notes that "The origins of variety entertainment lay in the traveling shows of the early nineteenth century . . . Show men were less welcome [than peddlers], unless they exhibited mechanical marvels or beasts with unusual qualities that were deemed edifying and educational."[2] Lewis goes on to comment on anti-theatrical legislation in several states, which showmen like Barnum circumvented by claiming their shows offering improvement, a maneuver closely related to that of David Douglass of the American Company who claimed in Philadelphia that his plays were "moral lectures." It is perhaps not surprising, given these circumstances at the outset of his career, that Barnum consistently resisted the equation between what he offered in his establishments and stage performances: he participated in the business of entertainment while insisting his offerings were superior to those of most actors. One can measure America's interest in Shakespeare by P. T. Barnum's attempt to buy Shakespeare's birthplace (see figure 3).

Had he succeeded, then Shakespeare's home might have become another popular novelty, like Jumbo the elephant, that Barnum imported from England. This anti-theatrical element in his career, like the widespread American distrust of the English, has important implications for understanding his failed bid to buy Shakespeare's birthplace.

It seems appropriate that the acquisitive Barnum, always on the lookout for new curiosities to display, should have tried to buy Shakespeare's birthplace, since Barnum is sometimes called the "Shakespeare of advertising."[3] Among the various accounts of what occurred when Barnum went after the birthplace, the differences repay analysis. When Barnum was first in England, living there from 1844 to 1847, he visited Stratford-upon-Avon, which did not greatly impress him. Like John Adams before him, he found the neglect of Shakespeare shocking. He does note his pleasure in finding that the guidebook offered to visitors was that of the American writer, "our illustrious countryman, Washington Irving" (*S&T* 232).[4] Next he went

3 Photograph of Shakespeare's birthplace taken *c.* 1890–1900. After the birthplace
was purchased by "a group of English gentlemen," it was lovingly
restored to this condition.

to Warwick Castle, where he saw "a lot of trumpery . . . and told the
old porter that he was entitled to great credit for having concentrated
more lies than I had ever before heard in so small a compass" (*S&T*
233–34). The tone throughout is dismissive of what Barnum regards as
English pretension. Later in *Struggles and Triumphs* Barnum discusses the
birthplace:

During my first visit to England I obtained verbally, through a friend, the refusal of
the house in which Shakespeare was born, deigning to remove it in sections to my
Museum in New York; but the project leaked out, British pride was touched, and
several English gentlemen interfered and purchased the premises for a Shakespeare
Association. Had they slept a few days longer, I should have made a rare speculation,
for I was subsequently assured that the British people, rather than suffer that house
to be removed to America, would have bought me off with twenty thousand
pounds. (365)

A complementary account used to be given on the website of the
Shakespeare Birthplace Trust:

In 1846, American showman Phinias T Barnum [sic] expressed an interest in buying the birthplace houses, which were being used as a butchers and an inn. He then intended to transport the Birthplace across the Atlantic and back to America brick by brick. The sudden realisation that the Birthplace could be lost forever awakened public concern and the Shakespeare Birthday Committee was hurriedly formed. The Committee grew in strength soon acquiring the patronage of Queen Victoria and Prince Albert. Due to public contributions and fundraising efforts by such esteemed figures as Charles Dickens and Jenny Lind the Birthplace was purchsed [sic] in 1847 for 3,000. The 1850s saw an ambitious and largely faithful restoration of the building, resisting the urge to over-improve.[5]

These accounts seem compatible: Barnum's interest grew out of his delight in commercial speculation, but it was defeated by what he calls "British pride" and what the Birthplace Trust calls "public concern." He comments on the profit he might have made with a bit more time; the Birthplace Trust remarks that he would have taken the birthplace "back to America," a curious bit of phrasing.

Yet when I wrote to the Birthplace Trust to inquire about the archival materials related to Barnum's option, I was sent a very different account. In 1992, Mairi R. Macdonald had investigated the matter and determined that the claim was unlikely:

If he [i.e., Barnum] ever contemplated a purchase of the Birthplace it is unlikely that matters ever reached the stage he wrote about subsequently. Thomas Court, by his will dated 2 June 1814 (proved 7 September 1818), left the Birthplace to his wife Ann for her life, and then to his trustee, to sell for the benefit of his children or their issue. However, Ann Court did not die until October 1846. Had Barnum offered for the house in 1844 it would therefore have been very difficult for the family to sell as Ann still had a life interest.

Barnum, however may well have made an approach of some sort, either in 1844 or later, for when the house did eventually come on to the market in 1847 after the death of Ann Court, several newspapers made reference to vague rumours to this effect

"... we think it will require no very extravagant outlay to rescue it at all events from the desecrating grasp of those speculators who are said to be desirous of taking it from its foundations and trundling it about on wheels like a caravan of wild beasts ... through the United States of America ..." (*The Times*, 21 July 1847)

The only other definite reference is by Sarah Flower, wife of Charles Edward, in her reminiscences, compiled in the 1880s. She records that in 1848 she and a friend contributed to a subscription being raised "for the purchase of Shakespeare's House in order to ... prevent it being bought by Barnum the American showman and being taken away to America ..." It is impossible to say how much her subsequent identification of Barnum is influenced by the autobiography, but it is clear that there was a very real concern at the time that some such fate might befall the house.

The house was put up for auction as the trustee was legally obliged to obtain the best possible·price for the house for the benefit of the legatees, many private approaches being turned down on legal advice. Barnum could not therefore have been treating to buy the house quite as seriously as he later made out and his statement that the purchase by a group of "English gentlemen" was a direct result of his actions is not substantiated by other evidence.[6]

This evidence that Barnum has embellished his account is, of course, perfectly in keeping with his practice; indeed, he prided himself on his control of humbuggery, going so far as to write *Humbugs of the World*, his fascinating and still lively account of various deceptions practiced on the public. The end result of all this is to establish that we shall never know with certainty whether Barnum did try to purchase the birthplace of Shakespeare.[7] More interesting, for my purposes, is the narrative's instability. Clearly it serves Barnum's ends to exaggerate his claims; the Birthplace Trust had two accounts, undoubtedly written by different people without consultation: one that was skeptical for scholars and one that was lively for the general public.

In contrast to these accounts, one has Mark Twain's double version. First Twain gives an account in a letter to the *New York Times* 26 April 1875, and he offers an altered account late in *Following the Equator* (1897).[8] The letter reports that Twain has agreed to help raise funds for the Shakespeare Memorial Theatre among Americans. Twain remarks, "We are not likely to be backward when called upon to do honor to Shakespeare." After giving some account of how Americans have supported previous attempts, Twain goes on to comment:

About three-fourths of the visitors to Shakespeare's tomb are Americans. If you will show me an American who has been to England and has not seen that tomb, Barnum shall be on his track next week. It was an American who roused into its present vigorous life England's dead interest in her Shakespearean remains. Think of that! Imagine the house that Shakespeare was born in being brought bodily over here and being set up on American soil! That came within an ace of being done once. A reputable gentleman of Stratford told me so. The old building was going to wreck and ruin. Nobody felt quite reverence enough for the dead dramatist to repair and take care of his house; so an American came along ever so quietly and bought it. The deeds were actually drawn and ready for the signatures. Then the thing got wind and there was a fine stir in England! The sale was stopped. Public-spirited Englishmen headed a revival of reverence for the poet, and from that day to this every relic of Shakespeare in Stratford has been sacred, and zealously cared for accordingly. Can you name the American who once owned Shakespeare's birth-place for twenty-four hours? There is but one who could ever have conceived of such a unique and ingenious enterprise, and he is the man I refer to – P. T. Barnum.

This letter goes a bit further than Barnum's account. Twain claims that Barnum actually succeeded in buying the house, and he also reports that he knows about the transaction not from Barnum's account, but from "a reputable gentleman of Stratford." Yet as the memorandum prepared by Macdonald shows, Barnum could not have bought the house before the death in 1847 of Ann Court; by the time the house was available for sale, Barnum seems to have returned to America.

Twain enjoyed the story too much to abandon it, and in all likelihood he believed some sort of transaction had occurred, as Barnum had claimed in his autobiography. In *Following the Equator*, Twain begins the passage about Barnum and the birthplace by reporting that on board ship, a Second-Class Passenger and he had fallen into the habit of smoking a pipe in the evening. The S.C.P. (Twain's abbreviation) told of how Barnum and Charles Jamrach, a notable English animal dealer, were talking about the eighteen elephants that Barnum had just bought. Jamrach said to Barnum that it was useless to try to buy Jumbo, that "one might as well think of buying the Nelson monument."[9] Barnum immediately agreed to try to buy it. Jamrach thought he was joking, but Barnum explained that though the effort was doomed to failure, the publicity would be priceless. Then seeing a newspaper story about the birthplace, he decided to act to buy that instead, saying,

There's my chance. Let Jumbo and the Monument alone for the present – they'll keep. I'll buy Shakespeare's house. I'll set it up in my museum in New York and put a glass case around it and make a sacred thing of it; and you'll see all America flock there to worship; yes, and pilgrims from the whole earth; and I'll make them take their hats off, too. In America we know how to value anything that Shakespeare's truth has made holy. You'll see. (641)

Once the news of Barnum's ambition was out, according to the S.C.P.'s account, "England rose!" The purchase was regarded as intolerable, a "sixpenny desecration." Barnum agreed to give up his purchase: "[h]owever, he stood out for compromise; he claimed a concession – England must let him have Jumbo. And England consented, but not cheerfully." In this version, which Twain immediately denies, the emphasis is on the sacred nature of all things Shakespeare. The S.C.P. is a conventional Englishman whose phrases include "sacred thing," "pilgrims from the whole earth," "anything Shakespeare's truth has made holy," and "sixpenny desecration." The character, who is said to be a former employee of Jamrach (and who is not said to be a reputable gentleman of Stratford), clearly finds amusing the American ways of Barnum, who is presented as a kind of confidence trickster, but the S.C.P. is wholly mindful of Shakespeare's importance to the nation, respecting "the master-genius of all the ages and all the climes." While the way that he sees Barnum mirrors the way Barnum presented himself to the public with his claims of being a master humbug, his attitude toward Shakespeare is the sort of worship that annoyed Twain deeply. Twain treats the character of the S.C.P. in a way that is tinged with slight contempt.

Twain's own account follows and begins by dismissing the S.C.P.'s as untrue, for "Mr. Barnum told me [Twain] the story, himself, years ago." With this assertion of his personal authority, Twain separates the purchase of Jumbo and the purchase of the birthplace, although he says the story about Nelson's Monument is true:

[Barnum] said that if he had failed to get Jumbo he would have caused his notion of buying the Nelson Monument to be treacherously smuggled into print by some trusty friend, and after he had gotten a few hundred pages of gratuitous advertising out of it, he would have come out with a blundering, obtuse, but warm-hearted letter of apology, and in a postscript to it would have naively proposed to let the Monument go, and take Stonehenge in place of it.

It was his opinion that such a letter, written with well-simulated asinine innocence and gush, would have gotten his ignorance and stupidity an amount of newspaper abuse worth six fortunes to him, and not purchasable for twice the money. (642)

As for the birthplace purchase, Twain continues, Barnum found the place in poor condition. He paid $50,000, and the papers were drawn up for the sale. In Twain's version, Barnum plans to move the birthplace house initially to his museum in New York, but to bequeath it to the Smithsonian. Twain then reports the uproar from the public, including offers to double Barnum's purchase price. Barnum, however, cancels his purchase, "but took only the sum which it had cost him – but on the condition that an endowment sufficient for the future safeguarding and maintenance of the sacred relic should be raised" (643). Twain's version of Barnum initially makes him an even greater humbug than does the S.C.P.'s, as the showman exploits English assumptions that an American is apt to be "blundering, obtuse, but warm-hearted," naive, and full of "asinine innocence and gush" to manipulate the public press. By the end of his account, Twain abruptly turns Barnum into a model gentleman. He is unwilling to take a profit, although he could do so; reluctant to raid another nation's heritage, except to save it from English irresponsibility; respectful of the past, yet mindful of the future. Twain concludes that Barnum "claimed with pride and satisfaction that not England, but America – represented by him – saved the birthplace of

Shakespeare from destruction." Against this splendid character, it seems a pity to set Barnum's own straightforward complaint that he did not act quite quickly enough and so could not make money on the deal. Yet once one does, it becomes clear that Twain's version is a fictional narrative as well.

What these accounts of Barnum's Shakespearean adventure demonstrate, I would argue, is the way that national tensions between England and America worked themselves into the most ordinary, and extraordinary, dealings. One way we can see that is in the way Barnum and Twain both use American stereotypes about the English. In their work the word "proud" is never far removed from the word "English," and both represent the English as being rather dim, easy pickings for a sharp-witted American. They are also both quite aware of the English stereotypes about Americans, as one can see in Twain's description of the sort of letter Barnum might write to the papers. If such a letter were to appear unironically in a work like *Martin Chuzzlewit*, no reader would be surprised: Charles Dickens repeatedly mocks Americans who show parochialism and ignorance (especially ignorance about England) in writing for the newspapers. Or one can return to Paul Langford's summation: "America was too democratic to be genteel, and Britain was too genteel to be democratic" and find support in these competing versions of Barnum's enterprise. But how, one might ask, does Shakespeare fit into this troubled national relationship?

Both nations regard Shakespeare as desirable, clearly, and the property of the English people. The early attitude that Adams and Jefferson shared, that Shakespeare was part of their own heritage, had passed out of the American culture. Indeed, given that Adams and Jefferson were born and raised as English, their affinity for Shakespeare and their affection for his work cannot be too surprising. But for Americans in the early nineteenth century, who had never known themselves as English and who had never known the English save as rivals and former enemies, Shakespeare was a more difficult figure, belonging to the English but desired by Americans. By the mid-nineteenth century, Shakespeare was reaching his height as *the* English poet. As Gary Taylor notes of Victorian England:

Shakespeare's artistic supremacy had ceased to be debated; it was simply assumed. Consequently, the main movement of Shakesperotics now became lateral: his influence broadened, geographically and socially. What had been the river of his reputation was now "the ocean of Shakespeare," an ocean that surrounded and defined Great Britain. (168)

Yet Americans (and others) also claimed some part of Shakespeare, and the English could do nothing to stop them. Shakespeare is like an attractive member of an English family who keeps running off to live with chance-met colonials. The following was written for a Boston newspaper in 1850, and the tone of casual familiarity *vis à vis* Shakespeare is worth noting:

Judging by external indications, an observer would pronounce that literature was in an advanced stage throughout the United States; that intellectual culture was in full bloom; that Shakespeare was the god of American idolatry. We have the plays of Shakespeare every night in scores of theatres in city and country, packet ships, halls, hotels, steamboats, sailing, steaming, constantly opening and taking their drinks and dinners in the name of Shakespeare; and not long ago we had at a public dinner a veteran actor delivering an unmeasured eulogy on the great dramatic poet, which was received with boundless enthusiasm by a company of one or two hundred members of the press and other representatives of public opinion . . . There cannot be a greater mistake. Shakespeare is not popular in America . . . in fact he is but imperfectly understood, and is rather a tradition than a reality . . .[10]

And that position, that Shakespeare's works are an American tradition, but not particularly popular, seems to obtain in the case of Barnum. To be sure, he was quick to brag about his attempted purchase, but the trans-action probably never occurred. He uses his account to establish himself as someone who recognizes that Shakespeare is valuable but who prefers money, hoping to be "bought off by twenty thousand pounds." He includes the account among others in which he, the crafty albeit crass American, outwits the proud but foolish English.

Certainly he treats Shakespeare throughout his career as yet another com-modity to be used in his public dealings, when he seeks to entertain under the guise of amusing Americans in order to charge customers money. For example, when Barnum gives his famous lecture on "The Art of Money Getting," he illustrates his point that perseverance is important for a busi-nessman by quoting the lines, "There is a tide in the affairs of men / Which taken at the flood leads on to fortune" (*Julius Caesar*); the quotation has almost nothing to do with his argument that one should persevere and is preceded by a tag from Davy Crockett and immediately followed by a few lines from the Bible. Moreover, when plays were performed at the Ameri-can Museum in his theatre, which he insisted be called a lecture room, lest the word "theatre" taint his offerings with suggestions of immorality, Bar-num insisted that the performers could present Shakespeare's plays only if they had been carefully expurgated. He seems to have preferred such works as *The Drunkard, Uncle Tom's Cabin, Moses in Egypt,* and *Joseph and His Brethren,* as exemplifying the "Moral Drama" (Kunhardt 134). Newspaper advertisements for the theatre show that the plays offered there were varied save for their high tone of respectability, including "the touching and moral drama of THE DREAM AT SEA; or, VISIONS OF THE DEAD," "the thrilling Moral Drama of ROSINA MEADOWS," "GENERAL TOM THUMB in the magnificent fairy spectacle HOP OF MY THUMB," "THE GREAT AMERICAN PRIZE DRAMA. – 'New-York Patriots or the Battle of Saratoga,'" "the NEW AND BRILLIANT SPECTACULAR DRAMA, APHROSE; OR THE SPIRIT OF BEAUTY" (*New York Times* advertisements, 6 October 1851, 11 September 1852, 17 January 1854, 16 June 1856, 13 March 1864). Barnum uses Shakespeare to provide a veneer of gentility for his enterprise, but seems otherwise largely indifferent to the "holy truth" of Shakespeare.

The Twain accounts operate similarly: they again make the narrative one of national interest in which Barnum represents Americans and is opposed to the English. But Twain who created the Duke and Dauphin with their monstrous version of Shakespeare's plays in *Huckleberry Finn,* Twain who loathed and mocked humbug, Twain who was decidedly skeptical about the claims that William Shakespeare wrote the plays credited to him, nevertheless participates in the sacralization of Shakespeare and the humbugging of his readers by distorting the crass and crafty Yankee into a genteel and rather prim fellow, a gentleman who excels the English in proper behavior. Twain did know Barnum rather well: both men lectured for James Redpath's Lyceum Bureau, and they visited socially. Evidently it seemed more important to Twain that Barnum be a favorable representative of Americans in his dealings with the English than that Barnum be represented accurately, and that nationalistic desire overrode his own inclination to mock those who worshiped Shakespeare.

While Twain was willing to praise Barnum, others were less so. Barnum's role in American entertainment is monumental, of course. His Museum offered wonders and performances, mixed together in a precursor to the variety or vaudeville shows that would so delight later Americans. But Barnum was decidedly ambivalent about the theatre, complaining that most theatres made use of "profanity and vulgarity"; he prided himself "upon the fact that parents and children could attend the dramatic performances in the so-called Lecture Room, and not be shocked or offended by anything they might see or hear" (Kunhardt 134). In a letter to the *Nation* (10 August 1867), Barnum wrote: ". . . it is a great error to state that I ever permitted 'vulgar sensation drama.' No vulgar word or gesture, and not a profane expression, was ever allowed on my stage! Even in Shakespeare's plays, I unflinchingly and invariably cut out vulgarity and profanity" (Lewis 60) Barnum's fear of Shakespeare's potentially vulgar and profane passages that must be screened out seems to fit oddly with his claimed interest in buying the birthplace. Certainly his contemporaries had great fun scoffing at his claims, especially because they thought they recognized his hypocrisy.

Dr. W. K. Northall in his theatrical memoir, *Before and Behind the Curtain*, comments that

During the past year a very large addition has been made to the Museum, and instead of the old cramped up lecture-room, a really beautiful theatre, (Mr. Barnum will excuse us for calling things by their right names,) has been erected . . . We wish all success to Mr. Barnum and his company of actors, although we do most heartily despise the kind of trickery Mr. Barnum has, we think, unnecessarily stooped to with the public, in relation to his establishment. Is there anything which belongs to the drama, of which Mr. Barnum, who has passed his whole life in the exhibition of shows, ought to feel ashamed? He unblushingly exhibits the skeleton of a whale manufactured in wood, and yet feels no blush mantle his cheek in disavowing the ownership of a stage for the acting of plays . . . The miserable trick is adopted of calling each play and farce presented, a moral affair, as though every well written piece did not teach a moral lesson.[11]

In this light, Barnum's attitude toward Shakespeare would seem to depend on whether he considered Shakespeare as a cultural figure or a theatrical one. The former attracted him, but the latter did not. Whether Barnum tried to buy Shakespeare's birthplace in 1847 or not, that same year saw that same W. K. Northall publish *Chinese Junk* for William Mitchell's company, a play that "burlesques the gargantuan peculiarities of Barnum and his fakeries" (Meserve, *Heralds* 156). In a sense this burlesque does Barnum's work for him, simultaneously celebrating him (as an individual of sufficient importance to deserve a burlesque) and deprecating him (as a notable humbug). That ambiguity is important, and the questions about buying the birthplace fit well with it. Barnum's bid for the birthplace, true or not, was charged with nationalism for both English and Americans; furthermore, his making such a proposal established his identity for others as a boor or a gentleman. It was also a performance of national and social identity, as well as a metaperformance in which Barnum calls attention to himself as the master showman who eschews the immorality of performance, simultaneously the trickster and the honest exhibitor, who delights his audience by parting them from their money.

CHAPTER 4

Treason, stratagems, and spoils

In October 1847, the month before W. K. Northall burlesqued Barnum with *Chinese Junk*, he burlesqued the social pretentiousness of the Astor Place theatre in *Upper Row House in Disaster Place*, mocking the management's failure to attract the wealthy and socially elite by operatic offerings. Opera, it developed, did not pay so well as the usual theatre offering of an evening of Shakespeare with a farce after. Richard Moody quotes the *New York Herald*, which claims that the second season of opera (1848–49) ended with "a dead loss of $20,000 and $900 due to some of the chorus singers" (104).[1] Two theatrical old-timers, William Niblo and James Hackett, took over the opera house's management and returned to the theatrical mainstays of Shakespeare with a farce to follow. Yet they charged more for admission than other theatres, hoping to draw a more distinguished audience than most playhouses did. They also engaged the finest talent, including London's leading Shakespearean of the day, William Macready. Thus the Astor Place Opera House set itself apart from such New York theatres as the Bowery, the Broadway, or the National, or such alternate entertainments as minstrel shows, Barnum's museum, or public lectures. Their decision to seek an elite audience contributed to a disastrous result.

Edwin Forrest, handsome, clever, and rich, with a comfortable career and happy marriage, seemed to unite some of the best blessings of existence; and had lived nearly forty-three years in the world with very little to distress or vex him. The real evils indeed of Edwin's situation were the power of having too much his own way, and a disposition to think a little too well of himself; these were the dispositions which threatened alloy to his many enjoyments. In paraphrasing Austen's *Emma*, I do not mean to suggest that Forrest (1806–72), like Emma, was naive or girlish, but he was someone with great gifts whose willfulness and self-importance make him seem decidedly minor today. In Jacksonian America he was recognized as an American performer in the legitimate theatre whose work was genuinely and generally good. As Charles Shattuck wryly says, "Unquestionably America's first important native-born tragedian, he dominated the American stage for thirty years and lasted fifteen years longer" (1:63). Forrest began performing in 1820 and soon became a star; beginning in 1828, he sponsored literary competitions to encourage American dramatists by assuring them a production of their scripts in addition to a $500 prize. In 1848 his marriage to Catherine Sinclair had prompted him to plan and build "Fonthill Castle" on the Hudson River, which he declared would be

a desirable, spacious and comfortable abode for myself and my wife, to serve us during our natural lives, and at our death [I plan] to endow the building with sufficient income, so that a certain number of decayed or superannuated actors and actresses (*all foreigners* to be strictly excluded) may inhabit the mansion and enjoy the grounds thereunto belonging, so long as they live. (Moody 84)

The irony that Catherine Sinclair Forrest was an Englishwoman, one of those foreigners who were to be so strictly excluded, seems to have escaped him. He was set for a successful season in 1849 at the Broadway Theatre where he would play leading roles in Shakespeare's plays, such standards as Edward Bulwer-Lytton's *Richelieu*, and plays written expressly for him like *Metamora*. Yet the year brought a remarkable combination of misfortune and misjudgment. (See figures 4 and 5).

Forrest was intent on having his excellence acknowledged not only on the American stage, but also on the London stage. On a visit to London in 1836, he had initially enjoyed some success. He and London's leading actor, William Charles Macready (1793–1873), had enjoyed a friendly relationship. On his second visit, however, Forrest enjoyed less success than he thought he should have done, particularly in a series of negative reviews by John Forster, who was a close friend of Macready. Consequently, Forrest blamed Macready himself for what the American actor regarded as failure. Charles Shattuck has shown that Macready actually tried to intervene with Forster on Forrest's behalf, to no avail, but reading Forster's criticism does suggest that some part of his distaste for Forrest's style is rooted in his preference for Macready. In some sense, then, Forrest was correct to think Macready contributed to Forster's negative articles, although Forrest was less skilled than his self-estimate supposed. Forrest was wrong, however, in thinking that Macready initially felt personal animus toward him. Nevertheless, Forrest quickly moved to create such animus: he attended an Edinburgh production in which Macready starred, and hissed his English rival. Forrest claimed that hissing was a perfectly acceptable piece of conduct, but it is worth noting that he seems to have been the only one doing it at that performance since he was easily identified. The ins and outs, the rights and wrongs

4 (left) Portrait of Edwin Forrest (1806–72) as Macbeth in 4.1. Most portraits of Forrest do him a disservice by emphasizing his muscular physique. This portrait suggests the chief strength in his performances, the vigorous energy with which he acted.
5 (right) William Macready (1793–1873) as Macbeth in 1.3. The engraving was done by Thomas Sherratt between 1860 and 1880, from a painting by H. Tracey. The portrait suggests Macready's more thoughtful approach to Shakespeare.

of this case are endless, with both men ultimately publishing accounts, each claiming the other had behaved in an unacceptable fashion. (Most scholars today think that Forrest was wrong, but they agree that Macready could be difficult, and that he might show hostility to competing performers.)

In any case, when Macready decided to tour the United States in 1848–49, with an eye to perhaps settling there after his eventual retirement, Forrest proceeded to stir up trouble, as he believed Macready had stirred up trouble for him. Initially Macready was well received on his American tour, but soon the popular press began to publish attacks on him based on Forrest's claims that Macready had sabotaged Forrest's European tour. Macready denied the claims, but Forrest's partisans were soon joined by members of the American public who simply disliked the English. In October 1848, a satire, *Mr. McGreedy*, was produced in New York at Chanfrau's National Theatre, a venue popular with the Bowery "b'hoys."[2] Moreover, Forrest himself began to stalk Macready, following him about on his tour and performing the same plays: thus in Philadelphia, "at the Arch Street Theatre between November 20 and December 2 Macready played eleven roles; at the Walnut Street, Forrest opposed him on the same night in six of them" (Shattuck 1:80). As the weeks of the tour went by, some of the opposition died down, but when Macready returned to New York for his final appearances before returning to England, the actor met with disaster.

On Monday, 7 May 1849, Macready played Macbeth at the Astor Place Opera House, and part of the audience rioted, closing the play in its third act. An understanding of the physical setting and social context help explain what happened. The Astor Place Opera House was a relatively new theatrical venue that had been completed in 1847 and was operating under the management of Niblo and Hackett. As Moody comments, "its construction [had] been financed by subscriptions obtained from a group of 'wealthy aspirers to fashion,' and [it] was named after John Jacob Astor, who had developed the neighborhood and who, until his death in 1848, maintained his residence nearby at 37 Lafayette Place" (103); he had also acquired much of the surrounding real estate and rented it out. Astor's youngest daughter, Mrs. Walter Langdon, still lived in a house across the street from the theatre (while Herman Melville lived two blocks away). Thus the theatre was associated with the upper classes in several ways: by its placement in the heart of Astor territory, by its name, and finally by its ticket prices, which were substantially higher than those elsewhere in the city, for most seats at the Astor Place Opera House cost $1.00, while comparable seats at the Broadway Theatre where Forrest was performing cost 75 cents.

The theatre had several different levels of tickets, which corresponded to the level of the seats, and those levels provided an index to the audience member's social status. The main floor of the theatre (divided into the dress circle and the parquet) and the boxes had the best seats, and the more prosperous and socially elite audience members sat there. The theatre had balcony or gallery seating: in nineteenth-century theatres, the lower of the two was called the family circle, and the higher was the upper tier. Here one might find middle-class audience members, especially in the family circle, and lower- and working-class audience members in the upper tier. Moody reports that there was another gallery level in the Astor, which was called the amphitheatre (Moody 93, 103–104). This third gallery is almost never discussed, but Claudia Johnson has established that such third-level galleries usually held prostitutes and their clients, along with a separate bar to serve them drinks. On the occasion of Macready's performance, the theatre management had announced "No lady admitted unaccompanied by a gentleman," but such restrictions were unlikely to apply to the topmost level. Despite this announcement's tone of seeming caution, the management had sold far more tickets than they had seats. Indeed, the only contemporary pamphlet, published by H. M. Ranney, says that when Macready's engagement began, "A large portion of the audience consisted of ladies."[3]

During the initial performance on Monday, 7 May, the disruption began in the galleries and parquet, where the audience groaned, hissed, and threw things at Macready. Missiles included vegetables, coins, old shoes, and chairs. One of the leaders flung a banner out over the edge of the gallery; it read, "No apologies, it is too late." Meanwhile, those seated in the dress circle and boxes protested the galleries' behavior with great volubility. Moody quotes a particularly lively account:

several gentlemen in the boxes undertook to remonstrate with the party of rioters who were in the parquette. Among them we noticed John Neal, the poet-barrister of Portland, Me. who happened to be in one of the first seats, near the stage. Rising and taking off his hat, he proceeded to address the "gentlemen" in the parquette, in good set terms (we suppose: for it was all as much as "dumb show" to us, as was Macready's *Macbeth*) and with much impassioned gesticulation. He had not proceeded long before he was interrupted by someone exclaiming, amidst roars of laughter, "When you've done your sermon, we'll go to prayer, old boy!" Another shouted, "Let's have a song first!" and at this the whole lot went at it at the top of their lungs. They sang a methodistical hymn, with a roaring chorus, meanwhile stamping and dancing – (many of them) upon the red plush chairs of the parquette. (109)

The facetious tone of this description suggests the light-heartedness with which most observers received reports of the riot. It seems so silly: a bunch of adults behaving like children, one set mocking the other, all stirred up by newspaper tittle-tattle.

This theatrical riot was not the first in America, to be sure, nor were such riots unheard of in London either. In London in 1809 the Old Price riots continued for six straight nights. In 1821, Edmund Kean had upset Bostonians who thought he sneered at Americans (Shattuck 1:42). When he returned to New York a few years later, a party of Bostonians booed him. Planning to play Boston, Kean wrote an open letter to her citizens on 21 December 1825: "Acting from the impulse of irritation, I certainly was disrespectful to the Boston public; calm deliberation convinces me I was wrong. The first step towards the throne of mercy is confession – the hope we are taught, forgiveness. Man must not expect more than those attributes which we offer to God" (Moody 26, Shattuck 1:42). The memory of the Boston audience was so long, however, that when Kean returned the riots that broke out at his 1825 performance drove him weeping from the stage. Yet Kean continued to tour elsewhere in the United States and to be well received; he did not give up, nor did those who supported him.

In this instance, Macready was obviously unable to apologize to the public because the complaint against him, unfounded though it seems to have been, had nothing to do with his treatment of the general public, but rather of Edwin Forrest. Thus Macready decided to do nothing, simply to withdraw from his final performances, departing a few days earlier from New York. Had he stuck to this resolution, all would have been well. Unfortunately, well-meaning interference persuaded him to return.

The newspapers and New York's citizens had recognized an opportunity. Each newspaper reported on the celebrity feud, repeated the various responses from New Yorkers, and editorialized in sympathy with one or the other of the performers. Socially prominent citizens, anxious to establish that New York was a city not unlike London and that it valued culture and artists, hastened to ally themselves to the English Macready, while citizens who were lower-class and publicly more nationalistic supported Forrest eagerly. These partisan activities took various forms.

Had Forrest made a public declaration that he wanted no rioting, the would-be rioters would probably have respected his wishes. Instead, he simply had Theodore Sedgwick send letters to the newspapers that denied his involvement, without deploring the disturbance. Perhaps Forrest would have been more willing to smooth over things with Macready had he not been beset by other woes that undermined his trust in others and made him suspicious and tetchy. His marriage had fallen apart, chiefly because neither he nor his wife practiced sexual fidelity. There is, for example, this account that Forrest gave during his divorce trial about what had occurred in May 1848 while he and his wife visited Cincinnati with a friend, George W. Jamieson. Returning unexpectedly to his hotel room, he said:

When I entered my private parlor in the City Hotel, I preceded S. S. Smith, who was with me, some yards, and found Mrs. Forrest standing between the knees of Mr. Jamieson, who was sitting on the sofa, with his hands upon her person. I was amazed and confounded, and asked what it meant. Mrs. Forrest replied, with considerable perturbation, that Mr. Jamieson had been pointing out her phrenological developments. Being of an unsuspicious nature, and anxious to believe that it was nothing more than an act of imprudence on her part, I was for a time quieted by this explanation.

But by May 1849 the couple had separated, her phrenological explanations no longer sufficing. They had parted in April and at roughly the same time, Forrest had begun sending letters to the New York press about Macready's dastardly efforts to stir up opposition to the American. While some read these letters with sympathy, others responded by openly mocking Forrest and his dislike of Macready. Moreover, some of the *Herald*'s notices of Forrest's performances were decidedly cool, suggesting that as a performer he was less powerful than his rival. After the Monday night riot at the Astor Place theatre, Macready began circulating a set of documents all of which suggested that Forrest was simply wrong about his claims that Macready had acted against him; these, Macready wrote, would be "the means of vindicating his character," and in doing so, of course, he made Forrest look shabby and foolish.

Perhaps the most troubling circumstance for Forrest was one that he could not address. As a fervent American, Forrest had enjoyed the favor of a number of distinguished men because he had sponsored a play-writing contest. Evert Duyckinck and others affiliated with the Young American movement had supported him and praised him as a man of culture. Now those very friends came out in support of Macready, begging the English actor to perform again in New York. The *New York Herald* reported the story (7 May) and quoted the letter:

To W. C. Macready, Esq.,

Dear Sir: – The undersigned, having heard that the outrage at the Astor Place Opera House, on Monday Evening, is likely to have the effect of preventing you from continuing your performances, and from concluding your intended farewell engagement on the American Stage, take this public method of requesting you to reconsider your decision, and of assuring you that the good sense and respect for order, prevailing in this community, will sustain you on the subsequent nights of your performances.

Among the signatories were Washington Irving, Cornelius Mathews, Duyckinck, and Herman Melville. Forrest, who had valued his friendship with Duyckinck particularly, was ignored as his literary friends hastened to comfort Macready. (Like Forrest, Melville may have his feelings hurt: the same issue of the newspaper had a notice praising a Washington Irving volume and a very negative review of Melville's *Mardi*.) Forrest remained aloof from the public controversy after the initial riot, although he had been quick to stir it up.

And so three days later on Thursday, 10 May, Macready appeared again. And once again Forrest, who could have backed away, announced that he would perform the same role as Macready did. The Astor Place Theatre filled, especially since some of the anti-Macready forces had spent the intervening days working up their rage, recruiting "b'hoys" to protest Macready, and circulating a poster that falsely claimed English sailors were planning to fight on Macready's behalf. "The result was disastrous. Ten to fifteen thousand working-class New Yorkers gathered outside the Opera House and pelted it with bricks and stones. The mob dispersed only when the National Guard fired into the crowd, killing twenty-two and injuring thirty-eight."[4] Other accounts put the death toll higher: the Museum of the City of New York says twenty-three died, Shattuck says thirty-one were killed (1:85), while the Ranney pamphlet claims the riot led to the "Sudden Death or Mutilation of more than Fifty Citizens" (title page). But that simple summary does not begin to describe all that went wrong on the night of 10 May 1849. The city authorities had neglected to clear up a construction site so that the rioters had a plentiful supply of bricks and stones to lob at the police, some of whom were badly hurt. Many of the people who were in the streets had simply come to watch the fun, not to protest for or against either actor. The police, unable to control the crowd, called in the militia. They in turn read the mob the Riot Act but the noise was so great that most could not hear. The result was that the militia fired into the crowd several times, and over twenty people were killed while many others were injured (see figure 6).

It is tempting to see the whole contretemps as nativism run wild: certainly that is how this riot is often represented in accounts of it. The leaders of the rioters went on to achieve some notoriety. One, Captain Isaac Rynders, made a speech in which he proclaimed:

Fellow citizens, for what – for whom was this murder committed? . . . To please the aristocracy of the city at the expense of the lives of inoffending citizens – to please an aristocratic Englishman, backed by a few sympathetic Americans. It was more important to these aristocrats that Mr. Macready, an Irish-Englishman, should play before them, and that they should be amused by him for a short hour, than that they should prevent a riot . . . (Moody 190)

6 Nathaniel Currier's 1849 lithographic engraving of the Astor Place Riot.

Since Rynders was himself a ringleader among the rioters, one needs to view his remarks with some skepticism. Yet he does raise the issue of nationalism, albeit in a singularly muddled fashion. Another ringleader, Ned Buntline, was also nativist in his sympathies and would go on to help found the Know-Nothing party so noted for its dislike of anything foreign (or Masonic). There are complications, however, to such a view. If the anti-Macready forces are resolutely pro-American and anti-foreigner, what is one to make of the list of dead, principally rioters, who include eight people born in Ireland, Scotland, and Canada? Or the way in which the anti-Macready rioters are repeatedly identified in contemporary accounts as being the b'hoys, a reference to their Irish origins? Nor is it clear how these b'hoys, the pro-Forrest forces, felt about the "Irish-Englishman" Macready, as Rynder claimed. Macready had been born in London and lived in Birmingham: Rynder's claim is based on Macready's family's origin. Some of these dead may have been innocent bystanders, to be sure, but at least some were clearly rioters as well. Since the Know-Nothings would later protest against immigrants, how does one reconcile the birth of that movement in the riot leaders who sought out and encouraged a mob that included many immigrants? It is clear that nationalism played a role, but it is decidedly unclear what that role was. Some rioters disliked Macready because he was identified as English and they identified themselves as Irish, some because he was English and they were American, some because he was an Irish-Englishman and they were American, some because he was aristocratic and they were democratic; of course some were indifferent to these issues and simply went along to the theatre that night to see the fun. As Peter Holland remarks of the riot, it resulted from "a clash of culture, class, and nationalism," and sorting these elements out is difficult.[5]

Given the large numbers of the dead and the dramatic nature of the event, one might also ask whether Shakespeare is a relevant factor. When Thomas Jefferson cites Shakespeare in the eighteenth century, he seems to associate the Roman plays with political violence. Did *Macbeth* function in a similar way for the nineteenth-century citizens of New York? Again, the answer is unclear.

Forrest and Macready were Shakespearean actors and that identity was the source of their celebrity. As Holland notes, "Shakespeare and a disagreement about who might be seen as the greatest Shakespearean actor of the period led to a clash that defined not only Anglo-American relations, but also the place of the theatre in the structure of American society, given that Macready had been encouraged to stay by many prominent members of that New York 'society'" (202). Lawrence Levine also identifies the Astor Place Riot as a critical moment in American theatre history, one that helps mark the split of public entertainment into forms we can label as high brow and low brow:

The Astor Place Riot, which in essence was a struggle for power and cultural authority within theatrical space, was simultaneously an indication of and a catalyst for the cultural changes that came to characterize the United States at the end of the century. Theatre no longer functioned as an expressive form that embodied all classes within a shared public space, nor did Shakespeare much longer remain the common property of all Americans.[6]

Cartelli would modify Levine's claims, expressing skepticism about the notion that "Shakespeare was ever 'the common property of all Americans,'" yet he does think that "Shakespeare became, in the quarrel between Forrest and Macready, a charged site around which the theoretically incompatible elements of democratic militancy and demagogic nativism could be reconciled and expressed" (44). But I think it is possible to regard Shakespeare as less central. If one examines the earlier weeks of the Macready tour, however, it becomes clear that Forrest challenged Macready by performing identical roles in plays that were not necessarily by Shakespeare. But for an accident of timing, then, the Astor Place Riot might well have been sparked by Bulwer-Lytton's play *Richelieu*.

Was Shakespeare a factor? Forrest would have been happier performing American roles in the plays he had commissioned. As Bruce McConachie points out, "Forrest's preference for plays expressing Democratic sentiments and embodying the public image of General Jackson is not surprising."[7] (4). McConachie also notes that Macbeth was not a role that the actor liked, for ". . . Forrest avoided Shakespearean roles that required him to portray guilt or weakness . . . Realizing, perhaps, his aversion to portraying vulnerability on the stage, Forrest rarely performed *Hamlet* or *Macbeth*" (12). One should not assume that Forrest's preference for certain non-Shakespearean roles suggests that he was as indifferent to Shakespeare as Barnum was: he read the plays carefully and critically, collected various editions, and died reading *Hamlet* for pleasure. The American Shakespeare scholar Joseph Crosby commented,

Forrest, as a man, or even as an Actor, was never an excrutiatingly great favorite of mine. I have seen & heard him in most of his best characters; & I generally thought him too *boisterous*, as well as "Forresty," i.e., *self*-conceited. But he was a good Shakespearian, & loved our Poet, & had a fine Sh. library, &c., and so one must respect him, and his memory.[8]

Clearly, Forrest recognized, even welcomed, the authority of Shakespeare and he knew he had to succeed in Shakespearean tragic roles if he were to achieve recognition as a major performer. That necessity undoubtedly lies behind his decision to perform such roles during his English tour, although he was not well received in them. Shakespeare did constrain his career, and in Forrest's concern about American excellence, Shakespeare must have been a continuing problem. Whether the power that Shakespeare had in American culture – and, in particular, the association between Shakespeare and violence – was a factor in the Astor Place Riot remains an open question. I would say that while there is no direct link between Shakespeare and violence, his figure occurs at moments in American culture when individuals feel strong desire for a shift in identity, whether personal or national. His figure becomes a screen upon which Americans project their fantasies about identity. The strength of those desires may lead to violence. That powerful association can be seen more clearly two decades later.

What also seems important is the concern that the Astor Place Riot raised – not only in New Yorkers, but also elsewhere as newspaper accounts spread the story. Clearly the gallery's bad behavior and rowdiness had gone too far. The link between Shakespeare's figure and violence was weakening

as theatre managements began to act more firmly to quash audience misbehavior. Increasingly Shakespeare productions became part of a legitimate
theatre that excluded lower-class audiences because managements regarded
lower-class audience members as the source of disruption. The geography
of the Astor Place theatre separated the audience by class, and such strat-
ification was an important feature of theatre-going in nineteenth-century
America. The Astor Place Riot marks one moment when well-meaning and
public-spirited Americans, including Herman Melville and Washington
Irving, regarded Shakespeare's figure as rightfully class-bound.

CHAPTER 5

How many ages hence . . .

Buntline, one of the leaders in the Astor Place Riot, would also become one of the leaders in the American Party, often called the Know-Nothings. As such he helped persuade a young man in Maryland that this was the political party that could help save America. In 1854, the young man served as a steward for the American Party for a rally, and in 1855 he wrote a friend after the election:

> Things are going on fine in Country, but I am getting tired – the excitement is all over. The Amer^ican Party was elected by 1749 Majority in this County.
>   Three Cheers for Amerrica.
>   Yours truly
>   J Wilkes Booth[1]

His sister Asia also sent a friend a letter in that election season, telling her that "the men are all gone deranged over their politics. We have two small flags crossed over the door. *Know Nothingism* of course . . . I trust, like water, their influence may wash the filth from our country. Yes, I'm a know-nothing too, in its noblest and most ludicrous" (43–44). For his first venture into politics, the Know-Nothing party offered John Wilkes Booth a platform that stressed the importance of race and ethnicity, encouraging hostility to abolitionists and to recent immigrants. "Although the American Party had virtually disappeared by 1860, nativist doctrines remained an important element of Booth's political thinking. He sounded very much like a Know-Nothing when he declared in 1864 that the supporters of Abraham Lincoln were 'false-hearted, unloyal foreigners . . . who would glory in the downfall of the Republic'" (Booth 44). Booth's resistance to the foreign was closely linked to his racism, his belief that Africans and African-Americans were as happy to be enslaved as slaveholders were blessed to own them (see figure 7).

When Booth considered making his first political speech, however, he turned to a foreigner, Shakespeare, for help. As the actor son of a

7 Undated portrait of John Wilkes Booth (1838–65). He poses for the
camera as a successful and handsome young actor.

distinguished, if erratic, English immigrant actor, Junius Brutus Booth,
and the brother to two leading actors, Junius Brutus, Jr., and Edwin Booth,
John Wilkes Booth had been reared to know more about Shakespeare
than politics. Clearly, for John Wilkes Booth, as for Adams and Jefferson,
Shakespeare was no foreigner, but rather part of his family heritage and
part of his American identity. This observation is troubling, when we realize that for Booth "American" included the peculiar institution of slavery.
In late December 1860, Booth planned to speak on the secession crisis;
the speech was probably never delivered and went unpublished until 1997.
The editors who first published it remark that "The speech . . . shows the

influence of the plays of Shakespeare, particularly *Julius Caesar*. The words are sometimes ordered in Shakespearean cadences and driven by the furious, ranting language of the mid-nineteenth-century American theater" (50). They note that Booth had performed Mark Antony's speech in October 1860. Just as Mark Antony began with "Friends, Romans, countrymen," Booth opens with an appeal to "My fellow countrymen." The editors also identify two Shakespearean quotations that Booth uses: "to hold the mirror . up to nature" from *Hamlet* and "he who steals my purse steals trash" from *Othello*. He uses the first of these in his discussion of the press, which he considers one-sided in its coverage of secession, urging journalists to "hold the mirror up to nature," a conventional idea. The second, however, is stranger: still speaking of newspapers, Booth says that while he is himself a northerner, he could speak as a southern man:

It makes me hate my brothers in the north. It severs all our bonds of friendship. It induces our brothers in the north to deny us our rights, to plunder us, to rob us! But he who steals my purse steals trash. It does more than that. It filches from me my good name which not enriches him, but makes me poor indeed. It misrepresents me to the whole world. It induces all without our circle to look upon me as a heathen. It does more than all that: it induces my very servant to poison me at my meals, to murder me in my sleep. (63)

This passage is unclear, as one might expect, given that this speech was John Wilkes Booth's first effort and that the text may be simply a rough draft that was abandoned. Surely there is something odd, however, in a Shakespearean actor quoting the treacherous Iago's speech and then going on to envision a servant–poisoner or the murder of a sleeping victim in order to make a complaint about the press. How is one to understand these violent images, so appropriate to *Othello*, so inappropriate to a discussion of newspapers, particularly given the awareness that Booth must have had of Iago's hypocrisy? One possibility may be that John Wilkes Booth was unwittingly betraying his own misgivings about his argument, sabotaging his own rhetoric by inadvertently recalling the Shakespearean character, "honest" Iago. His family, closely associated with Shakespeare in their theatrical careers, had always eschewed slave-holding because Junius Brutus Booth thought it a contemptible practice, and in this speech, so contrary to that familial position, John Wilkes Booth may express himself badly because of an unconscious discomfort with his own position.

An equally interesting Shakespearean reference has gone unnoted, however, and that is Booth's insistence that the real problem is not the south's policy of slavery, but rather the intransigence of northern abolitionists. He writes, "Now that we have found the serpent that madens us, we should crush it in its birth" (sic, 57). The source is clearly Brutus' soliloquy, as he contemplates the assassination of Julius Caesar:

> And since the quarrel
> Will bear no color for the thing he is,
> Fashion it thus: that what he is, augmented,
> Would run to these and these extremities;
> And therefore think him as a serpent's egg,
> Which hatch'd, would, as his kind, grow mischievous,
> And kill him in the shell.   (2.1.28–34)

Booth's comment about the serpent's egg is a curious one. He uses the reference as if it offered a straightforward condemnation of abolitionists or even an incitement to violence. Yet Brutus is in that speech markedly ambivalent about assassination: the later events of the play prove that his choice was disastrously wrong. John Wilkes Booth knew the play very well, since it was the first Shakespeare play that he learned, according to his sister; he also knew the character's dilemma well, both from Shakespeare's play and from John Howard Payne's *Brutus*, a well-known work in the nineteenth century and one in which he sometimes performed and his father had frequently starred. His choice of such an inappropriate moment from the play for his purpose may again suggest his own ambivalence and even discomfort.

One of Booth's contemporaries was an autodidact who loved Shakespeare (see figure 8). Abraham Lincoln had memorized passages from Shakespeare when he was a boy studying the popular textbook, *Lessons in Elocution*, by the English author, William Scott. By the time he was practicing law in Springfield, Illinois, he owned his own copy of Shakespeare's work, which he often read.[2] He did not, however, see any of Shakespeare's plays on stage until he moved to Washington, D.C. There he frequently attended the theatre, watching James Hackett (who had been one of the co-owners of the Astor Place theatre) as Falstaff, Edwin Booth in *Hamlet*, and even John Wilkes Booth in *The Marble Heart* (Donald 569). Certainly he enjoyed "all sorts of theatrical entertainments," from minstrel shows to contemporary plays, but his favorites were Shakespeare's plays (Donald 569). There was another reason for his playgoing, however, namely relief from the weight of his duties as president. Near the end of the war he told one general who had joined him at the theatre: "I have not come for the play, but for the rest. I am being hounded to death by office-seekers, who pursue me early and late, and it's simply to get two or three hours' relief that I am here" (Harris 55).

8 Portrait of Abraham Lincoln reading with his son Tad. Lincoln was largely
self-educated, like many nineteenth-century Americans, and an enthusiastic reader and
viewer of Shakespeare's plays.

While that comment implies that performance is less serious, less worthy
than reading, his enthusiasm for actors and for Shakespearean performance
was genuine. Indeed, he found himself embarrassed by it when in 1863 he
wrote a letter to James Hackett, one of his favorite performers, who was
especially celebrated for his performance as Falstaff (see figure 9). Praising

9 1859 engraving of James Hackett as Falstaff, one of his more famous roles.
Lincoln's enthusiasm for Hackett's performance as Falstaff made the newspapers
of the day mock the President's knowledge of Shakespeare.

Hackett's performance, Lincoln expressed a desire to meet the actor, and
then went on to comment on Shakespeare. He declared his favorite play to
be *Macbeth*, confessing that he had not read all of the canon. Hackett went
on to publish Lincoln's letter, in a book of essays and correspondence, "and
newspapers had a field day, criticizing the President as would-be dramatic
critic" (Donald 569).

Lincoln was given to quoting the plays as well, but not in his political arguments, as Booth did in his first attempt at a speech. That is not
to say that Lincoln saw nothing political about Shakespeare's works. His
favorite plays were all political tragedies – *Hamlet*, *Macbeth*, and *Richard III*
(Harris 55) – although what seems to have fascinated him was the way each
represented the guilt of a man who murdered for power. Such speeches as

Claudius' "O, my offense is rank," or Macbeth's lines after killing Duncan, particularly appealed to him. In April 1865, Lincoln spent a day with the Marquis de Chambrun. During the afternoon, "Lincoln read aloud to us for several hours . . . Most of the passages he selected were from Shakespeare, especially *Macbeth*." The "Macbeth doth murder sleep" passage in 2.2 drew his attention, and he "began to explain to us how true a description of the murderer that one was; when, the dark deed achieved, its tortured perpetrator came to envy the sleep of his victim; and he read again the very same scene" (Chambrun 35). Within a week, Lincoln was assassinated by Booth. This account is uncanny, a moment when Shakespeare's text and American history seem to combine almost too neatly in a narrative about the perils of high office and the horror of assassination. But this Shakespearean coincidence does not stand alone.

In John Wilkes Booth's first attempt at a speech, a draft not published until 1997, the reference to the speech that Brutus gives in *Julius Caesar* might well be regarded as a reinforcement of Albert Furtwangler's thesis that Booth thought of himself as Brutus, a righteous assassin:

The press would call Booth a Brutus. Booth's own papers would show that he thought of himself as a Brutus. Family records would merge with popular speculation to suggest that here was a frustrated actor confusing art with life, bewildering himself and tearing the world apart by attempting to do in public what he could not do in his career. (9)

Furtwangler suggests that Booth was a madman and an actor who knew he was less able than his brothers. Booth's ambition for heroism is merged with his knowledge of Shakespeare's Roman plays; the Shakespearean material mediates his plans and leads him to assassination. Furtwangler's analysis may need to be modified given material that has recently come to light. As John Rhodehamel and Louise Taper comment, ". . . Booth has often been dismissed as a crazy, drunken actor – the son, after all, of a famously crazy, drunken actor . . . However misguided he may have been, John Wilkes Booth was not a monster. He was a highly successful actor and a Confederate secret agent" (1–2). Other views of Booth are also possible, ranging from that of his sister who considers him a young hero who must have had a moment of madness, to that of Carl Sandburg who calls him an "American Judas," to Michael Kauffman who calls him an "American Brutus" and regards him as a sane and successful actor. I shall examine what Booth himself did and said about Shakespeare to try and discover whether Booth was modeling his actions on those of the Roman Brutus.

An important point in John Wilkes Booth's career is a particular performance, the only time that the three Booth brothers were able to share the stage. On 25 November 1864, Edwin played Brutus, Junius Brutus, Jr., played Cassius, and John Wilkes played Mark Antony at the Winter Garden Theatre for a benefit performance of *Julius Caesar* that raised funds for a Shakespeare statue in New York's Central Park. Again there is an uncanny coincidence if one considers that John Wilkes Booth as Mark Antony entered in 3.1 shortly after his brothers had declaimed:

> CASSIUS ... How many ages hence
> Shall this our lofty scene be acted over,
> In states unborn, and accents yet unknown!
> BRUTUS How many times shall Caesar bleed in sport,
> That now on Pompey's basis lies along,
> No worthier than the dust
> CASSIUS So oft as that shall be,
> So often shall the knot of us be call'd
> The men that gave their country liberty. (111–18)

The idea that Lincoln's assassin might have heard that speech as a call for him to act, to repeat the political murder of an American President in a state unborn and accent yet unknown, is at once startling and yet unnervingly tidy. Once again, however, one needs to note that the uncannily prophetic passage comes within a play that demonstrates how mistaken and ill-advised political assassination is. Incidentally, John Wilkes Booth might just as well have identified more strongly with the character that he played, Mark Antony, who swears vengeance on the conspirators. Or one might guess that he identified with none of the characters, given that he rarely even performed in the play. He seems to have had a walk-on role in an 1857 production, recited Mark Antony's funeral oration in 1860, and performed with his brothers in 1864. As Gordon Samples has remarked, "Much has been said about Booth's love for Shakespeare's characters, Julius Caesar and Brutus, and his crime . . . The fixation on *Julius Caesar* is one which has been built up by reporters for the effect and used by psychiatrists as a plaything" (4). In short, the thrilling theatrical anecdote is misinterpreted if one thinks the production prompted John Wilkes Booth to assassinate Lincoln the following April. That is not to say that the production is unimportant in Booth's career, however, for while *Julius Caesar* and its characters may have had little effect on Booth's work as an actor, the production was of central importance to his career as a would-be Confederate agent.

On the night of the performance, 25 November, "a gang of Confederate saboteurs financed by Confederate headquarters in Canada tried to burn down New York by simultaneously setting fire to more than twenty Manhattan hotels. They failed, but news of the operation sent the city into an uproar the next day" (119). Receiving news of the arson, Junius Brutus, Jr., and Edwin Booth denounced the saboteurs and the Confederacy, while John Wilkes defended them. The brothers' quarrel was a serious one, although they would continue to write to one another. What his brothers did not realize was that in defending the saboteurs, John Wilkes Booth was defending men whom he knew. Booth had spent several days that October in Montreal, in the company of Confederate secret service agents, planning sabotage and possibly an assassination attempt on Lincoln. He may well have had advance knowledge of the arson, although no evidence survives to show he was directly involved. (Indeed, Kauffman questions whether the Confederate agents in Montreal put any trust in him.) On 8 November 1864, Abraham Lincoln was re-elected for a second term. Shortly before the New York performance, John Wilkes Booth wrote two letters, one to his mother and one to the general public, that suggest he had committed himself to some dangerous and demanding task, which might result in his death. It is worth noting neither of these letters makes use of Shakespearean material to describe his politics; if Booth's unease led him to use Shakespearean material inappropriately in 1860, as I have suggested, there is no such use here. Booth suggests he is about to embark on some great project: "I write in haste. I know how foolish I shall be deemed, for undertaking such a step as this . . . Nor, do I deem it a dishonor in attempting to make for her [the south] a prisoner of this man, to whom she owes so much of misery" (Rhodehamel and Taper 126). During the last few months of his life, November 1864 to April 1865, Booth was dedicated to kidnapping or killing Lincoln, although it is unclear whether he had agreed to carry out such a crime at the request of Confederate agents or on his own initiative. Booth's presence at Lincoln's second inauguration, a presence recorded in a nineteenth-century photograph, may have been part of this project. A related plot, and one that Jefferson Davis himself had approved, sent Confederate agents into Washington in an effort to blow up the White House, destroying Lincoln and his Cabinet (Rhodehamel and Taper 121). Booth had received his orders from the Confederacy and knew what he had to do; there was little need for him to feel uncertain or to question his own judgment. No Shakespearean reference appears in John Wilkes Booth's writing until after Lincoln's assassination, and then, abruptly, the references come on. As in the case of the 1860 speech, these touches of Shakespeare sometimes jar because they lack appropriateness to what John Wilkes Booth is saying.

After the assassination, John Wilkes Booth sent a letter to the editors of the *National Intelligencer* in which he sought to justify his actions. In it, the only Shakespearean reference comes at the very end:

When Caesar had conquered the enemies of Rome and the power that was his menaced the liberties of the people, Brutus arose and slew him. The stroke of his dagger was guided by his love of Rome. It was the spirit and ambition of Caesar that Brutus struck at.

> "Oh that we could come by Caesar's spirit,
> And not dismember Caesar!
> But, alas!
> Caesar must bleed for it!"

I answer with Brutus:

> He who loves his country better than gold or life.
> John W. Booth

Again, Booth uses a *Julius Caesar* quotation. His meaning is clearly that Lincoln, like Julius Caesar, has been triumphant in war (Lee's Army of Northern Virginia had just surrendered) and holds power firmly. Booth chooses, as Brutus did, to assassinate a leader for fear he will declare himself a monarch. Yet the ending of the letter is a bit ambiguous: what does Booth "answer with Brutus"? The line that follows is neither Shakespearean nor an answer. Rather his answer was an act: the assassination. He actually wrote this letter three different times, and the other two versions seem to have omitted the Shakespearean passage.

When Booth fled after murdering Lincoln, he met another conspirator, Davey Herold, with whom he traveled for twelve days until he was captured and killed (see figure 10). Booth kept a journal of his thoughts in his pocket diary; he also wrote a draft and fair copy of a letter to a man who had refused to help them. In these texts, one sees several peculiar Shakespearean references. Booth repeats his identification with Brutus in his diary:

After being hunted like a dog through swamps, woods, and last night being chased by gun boats till I was forced to return wet cold and starving, with every mans hand against me, I am here in despair. And why; For doing what Brutus was honored for, what made Tell a hero.

The journal ends with this comments on Herold:

And for this brave boy with me who often prays (yes before and since) with a true and sincere heart, was it a crime in him, if so why can he pray the same I do not wish to shed a drop of blood, but "I must fight the course" Tis all that's left me.

10 A poster that the government issued after the assassination, during the search for John
Wilkes Booth. Booth's is the center portrait, Davey Herold's picture is on Booth's left,
while John Surratt is on the right. Public feeling is shown by the size of the headlines, the
substantial reward, and the language of the poster: the men are called "murderers" and
Lincoln is "beloved." In this emotional atmosphere, Booth fled through Maryland,
writing a defense of himself that has significant Shakespeare references.

The comment about Brutus is a direct reference of the same sort as the ones Booth had made in earlier writing. Less direct is his comment on the boy's ability to pray, but that seems to refer to the belief that guilt blocks one from prayer. One finds this idea in both *Macbeth* and *Hamlet*, two of the most popular Shakespearean plays in nineteenth-century America. Macbeth remarks,

> One cried "God bless us!" and "Amen" the other,
> As they had seen me with these hangman's hands.
> List'ning their fear, I could not say "Amen,"
> When they did say "God bless us!"   (2.2.24–27)

And Claudius laments:

> O, my offence is rank, it smells to heaven,
> It hath the primal eldest curse upon't,
> A brother's murther. Pray can I not,
> Though inclination be as sharp as will.
> . . . but, O, what form of prayer
> Can serve my turn? "Forgive me my foul murther"?
>   (*Hamlet* 3.3.36–39, 51–52)

Booth insists that the boy is able to pray, and implicitly distinguishes Herold from either Macbeth or Claudius, regicides who cannot pray. He does not, however, speak of his own ability to pray, simply commenting that he must fight the course, a direct quotation from *Macbeth*. In it he, like the regicide Macbeth, accepts his fate once his crime is known:

> They have tied me to a stake; I cannot fly,
> But, bear-like I must fight the course.
>   (5.7.1–2)

While the initial reference to Brutus suggests that Booth is proudly defiant of his pursuers, the later references suggest guilt and anxiety. The awareness of his crime may be signaled by the way in which, as he describes himself, his mind produces Shakespearean lines from villains like Claudius and Macbeth who have criminally killed a ruler.

Finally, in the letter rebuking the Confederate sympathizer who fed them and then turned them out, Booth first writes, "I would not have turned a dog from my door in such a condition," and then scorning his hospitality, "The sauce to meat is ceremony; meeting were bare without it." The metaphor about the dog may be a simple proverb, or it may recall the way that characters in *King Lear* express their shock at Lear's daughters' behavior. Kent says, "Why, madam, if I were your father's dog, / You should not use me so" (2.2.136–37), while Cordelia, speaking of what has happened to Lear, says "Mine enemy's dog, / Though he had bit me, should have stood that night / Against my fire" (4.7.35–37). Once again the image may suggest a ruler displaced unjustly and violently, particularly when coupled with the direct quote about ceremony as a sort of sauce. That passage is spoken by Lady Macbeth at the gruesome banquet (3.4) haunted by Banquo's ghost.

The Shakespearean references that Booth makes from time to time do not show a madman, a hero, a Brutus, or a monster. They show a man who would like to persuade himself and others that he is a Brutus, but who fears he is a Macbeth, a Claudius instead. Shakespearean quotations in Booth's mouth become an index to anxiety, guilt, and fear. For example, John Wilkes Booth uses Davey Herold's ability to pray as a sign of the boy's freedom from guilt. Yet the way he alludes to Shakespeare suggests that Booth found himself unable to pray, choked by guilt.

PART II

The Shakespearean Broadway musical

CHAPTER 6

Blackface, blue shows, and beards

Moving from the violence of Lincoln's assassination or of the Astor Place Riots, from the social sorting out of Astor Place or of Barnum's museum, from hostility toward the theatre or toward the English, discord between the upper and lower classes, one arrives at . . . musical comedy. In this chapter I shall argue that as American entertainment split between the legit and variety in the nineteenth century, a complex of things happened. Various forms of American popular entertainment coalesced around the impulses to explore transgressive topics and the desire for respectable amusement. Yet this process of splitting is further complicated by a series of shifts that occurred as the popular entertainment continued to evolve. In brief, the legit drama carried off Shakespeare. Legit's alternative, variety entertainment, cheerfully naughty and light-hearted, nevertheless retained the memory of Shakespeare, especially in minstrelsy and burlesques. Moreover, by infusing European operetta tradtion and English music-hall practice with American entertainment practices and themes, the musical became a distinct form. In American musicals, music and dance (whether the cakewalk, ragtime, klezmer bands, or swing) is blended with the use of a "book" or narrative line (initially weak, but increasingly important), and the shows examine issues of gender and race that mattered to American audiences. "Playing with Shakespeare" fit well into the Broadway musical, allowing its practitioners greater freedom to explore matters frowned upon.

Initially, American theatrical practice was to mix material from legitimate drama and other sorts of entertainments like music, dance, or demonstrations of skill (such as fencing or animal training). Of eighteenth- and early ninteenth-century American theatre, Lawrence Levine remarks, "the play may have been the thing, but it was not the only thing. It was the centerpiece, the main attraction, but an entire evening generally consisted of a long play, an afterpiece (usually a farce), and a variety of between-act specialties," an arrangement that anticipates a vaudeville bill. By the mid-nineteenth century, however, a play and a farce afterpiece formed the bill

79

in the legit theatre, and the afterpiece was fading by century's end. While legit drama included a wide range of plays, from thrillers and melodramas to light comedies, at its center were plays that were serious and artistic. The one playwright who was indisputably legit was Shakespeare.

The comic sketches, singing and dancing, and animal acts that had once accompanied the plays were performed in minstrel shows, vaudeville, and burlesque, the forms that contributed so much to the development of the Broadway musical. Katherine Preston notes, "To put it simply, for the scholar in search of a clear lineage to the forms of the twentieth century, musical theatre in the eighteenth – and even more so in the nineteenth – century is a tangled chaotic mess,"[1] yet one can see the shift that Levine describes between variety and the legit audiences by the early twentieth century. Let me return for a moment to my three exemplary figures.

Barnum's museum included the Fiji mermaid and the Siamese twins, as well as a theatre that occasionally performed Shakespeare in bowderlerized versions, for many Americans early in the nineteenth century retained a distrust of theatre, as well as a desire for amusement and self-improvement. Unexpurgated Shakespeare might have threatened such audience members' sense of what was proper. In his fascinating study of the changes that American entertainment went through during the century, Robert M. Lewis highlights the wide variety of such amusing and improving entertainment. He includes material about dime museums, minstrel shows, circuses, melodramas, burlesques and leg shows, wild west shows, summer amusement parks, and vaudeville programs, all of which were available to Americans in the years between 1830 and 1910. As this list suggests, finding a term that covers such disparate amusements is difficult, especially since the term must be set in opposition to that highly loaded term, "legitimate." I shall use the term "variety," although it is also sometimes applied to the concert saloon shows that preceded vaudeville, because unlike "low-brow" or "popular," "variety" seems to me to describe an actual feature of the entertainment. The *OED* is helpful: its definition of variety is that the word is "Used to designate music-hall or theatrical entertainments of a mixed character (songs, dances, impersonations, etc.). Also applied to things or persons connected with such entertainments."[2]

Like Barnum, many managers of these variety entertainments were concerned that their shows be respectable enough to avoid trouble with the authorities, but entertaining enough to draw crowds. While the variety amusements offered in the eighteenth and early nineteenth centuries were diverse enough to appeal to the general public, managements began to specialize as the century went on. One strategy was to seek a specific sort of audience and to appeal to its tastes. For example, if one sought an audience from a particular class or ethnicity or eschewed an all-male audience, that desire affected the sort of amusement that one might offer. As Snyder comments in his history of New York vaudeville:

The volleys at Astor Place marked the end of the years when New York's diverse peoples could gather easily under one roof. A single theatre could no longer house a people who were becoming increasingly different culturally and economically. The differences between mid-nineteenth-century urban theatres increasingly expressed the social differences between New Yorkers, with drama and opera houses for the rich, cheap Bowery theatres for the poor, and foreign-languages theatres for immigrants.[3]

One motive for that process of change and the drive toward respectability was, of course, a fear of the sort of violence that had exploded in the Astor Place theatre (or, indeed, at Ford's Theatre). Closely related was distaste for the rowdiness of the galleries, filled with the working-class patrons who expressed their feelings toward the performance vocally and on occasion with missiles. From mid-century on, theatre managers began to banish the prostitutes in the third gallery, to shut the bars that sold drinks during performances, and to end the gallery's noisy demonstrations by stopping the show or expelling the offenders. These reforms helped them seek audiences of men and women who were well-to-do or at least middle-class.

After Booth's assassination of Lincoln, however, many feared a public backlash against actors and playhouses. Edwin Booth believed his career was over, and all members of the family feared vigilante attacks. But even actors who had nothing to do with the Booth family came under assault. As Michael Kauffman notes, in the days following the assassination:

Theatrical people were especially vulnerable [to attack]; as one Baltimore man said, "It wasn't safe for an actor to walk the streets." It was commonly assumed that someone in the theater had cleared a path for Booth's escape, and the whole profession was called to answer for that. Even their homes and workplaces were threatened. (Kauffman 238)

In following years one result of such anti-theatricalism, whether elicited by a particular event or by more general moral disapproval, was an increased emphasis on the respectability of the legitimate theatre, as well as a sharper separation between the legit and the variety entertainments. Furthermore, while the Lincoln assassination seems to have shocked the nation so powerfully that the earlier association between Shakespeare and political violence ended in America, non-political violence did not vanish. Lawrence Levine recounts an anecdote to illustrate the situation:

On April 23, 1879 – Shakespeare's three hundred and fifteenth birthday – Edwin Booth was playing the lead role in *Richard II* at McVicker's Theatre in Chicago while in the dress circle a dry goods clerk named Mark Gray sat comparing Booth's performance with the text of Shakespeare's play. By Act V, apparently infuriated at the alterations Booth was introducing, Gray drew his pistol and fired two shots at Booth in an attempt, as one eye witness put it, "to kill the man that could, as he thought, so murder Shakespeare." Gray's action was obviously extreme, but his concern for what actors and their audiences were doing to Shakespeare was widely shared. The attitudes of such as John Quincy Adams, who distinguished in 1836 between "the true Shakespeare" he read in his study and "the spurious Shakespeare often exhibited upon the stage," gained an increasing number of adherents in the second half of the century. (165)

To go to the theatre for amusement sometimes seemed to be a risky business in nineteenth-century America: one might be seated by people who were frighteningly different, one might meet with bullies or drunks, one might be harassed by other audience members. For middle-class women, in particular, theatre-going was uncomfortable and threatening, unless the management had made particular efforts to ensure that women and families could enjoy themselves.

One way of being safe was to attend legitimate plays, but these tickets were expensive, several times the cost of a seat in a vaudeville house. Another way was to bypass burlesque shows or concert saloons for the cleaned-up shows of vaudeville. Ever since the 1860s, when Tony Pastor had presented a vaudeville bill aimed specifically at women and families, and increasingly during the 1890s, as the Keith–Albee organization sought the lucrative middle-class family market for their shows, vaudeville had been made respectable. Earlier forms of variety shows that might be rowdy or violent, such as concert saloons or leg shows, became less and less profitable, while their unrepentant audience attended instead the burlesque shows that shifted from social commentary and mockery to display of female bodies. Yet there was some inconsistent enforcement of decorum standards in vaudeville: as Erdman and Kibler have pointed out, vaudeville managers paid lip service to respectability, but often noticed a marked upturn in box-office earnings with acts that featured scantily clad women.[4]

Early in the nineteenth century, burlesques and minstrel shows had both made extensive use of Shakespearean originals to mock the established order. Burlesques, like those by W. K Northall that mocked Barnum or the Astor Place theatre, were a popular form in which a satirical story was combined with song and dance, as well as plentiful topical allusions. In his essay on Shakespeare in popular American culture, Levine mentions such American burlesque titles as *Bad Dickie, Julius Sneezer, Roamy-E-Owe and Juli-Ate, Hamlet and Egglet, Desdemonum,* and *Much Ado about a Merchant of Venice.* Richard Schoch has studied the phenomenon of the Shakespearean burlesque in his book, *Not Shakespeare,* while Stanley Wells' anthology of sample burlesques from England and America fills five volumes.[5]

I have argued elsewhere that burlesque, like parody, travesty, or pastiche, is a comedy of imitation; all such forms "assume a canon of literature exists, that it can be mocked by irreverent imitation, and that its readers will recognize and welcome such mockery. A burlesque may implicitly criticize its target, but it also thereby reasserts, implicitly, the target's importance."[6] In this respect, burlesque, like much of variety entertainment, is necessarily oppositional to legit theatrical productions, and in burlesque's mockery one may find the negative form of popular cultural attitudes. In the burlesque shows early in the century, as the Shakespearean critic Richard Grant White once commented, "The peculiar trait of burlesque is its defiance both of the natural and the conventional . . . [B]urlesque casts down all the gods from their pedestals" (256). The popularity of burlesques was heightened when the English star, Lydia Thompson, toured in 1868, for her troupe of "British Blondes" took transvestite roles, delighting and horrifying audiences with their revealing costumes. Robert Allen notes, "By March [1869], burlesque had become so prominent a cultural phenomenon that it was the subject of a burlesque. The week of March 29, Tony Pastor staged *Romeo and Juliet; or, The Beautiful Blonde Who Dyed (Her Hair) for Love.*" The result was that gender roles and expectations, always a good topic for popular entertainment, became the central topic in burlesque and variety entertainment generally. Gilbert notes that before 1880 "in beer halls and for-men-only dives, roughhouse turns and afterpieces were smuttily 'blued' to amuse the tosspots, strumpets, dark-alley lads, and slummers who in those days made up variety audiences." Increasingly burlesques would become leg shows, opportunities to display female bodies; inversely burlesque shows paid less and less attention by century's end to mocking legitimate theatre or Shakespeare. Yet the idea of burlesquing Shakespeare continues to pop up in vaudeville acts and ultimately in musical comedies.

Such full-length burlesques were not the only way that Shakespeare entered variety entertainment, since, according to Lawrence Levine, "Nineteenth-century Shakespearean parody most frequently took the form of short skits, brief references, and satirical songs inserted into other modes of entertainment." Levine then repeats several minstrel show jokes:

> Adolphus Pompey is my name,
> But that don't make no difference,
> For as Massa Wm. Shakespeare says,
> A name's of no signiforance.

You know what de Bird of Avon says 'bout "De black scandal an' de foul faced reproach!"

Fust to dine own self be true, an' it must follow night and day, dou den can be false to any man.

When was Desdemona like a ship? When she was Moored. (142)

"It is difficult to take familiarities with that which is not already familiar; one cannot parody that which is not well known," notes Levine, arguing that "The minstrels' characteristic conundrums would not have been funny to an audience lacking knowledge of Shakespeare's works." While Eric Lott does not address that specific point in his study of minstrelsy, he does point to the recurrent presence of Shakespearean burlesques in blackface shows, especially of burlesques of *Othello*, including one by the well-known minstrel T. D. Rice.[7] When these jokes occurred in minstrel shows, with white performers blacked up and referencing Shakespeare, they have a double edge. To be sure, such moments offer racist mockery of black folks who use the Shakespearean text inappropriately, but they also mock elite white folks who prefer the stuffiness of such archaic drama to the good humor and lively music of variety entertainment.

Lott also notes that even in African-American theatres like the African Grove, which tried to present legitimate drama, Shakespeare's plays were interspersed with comic songs and hornpipes (Lott 44). In the 1820s the British comedian Charles Mathews visited what he called the "Nigger's (or Negroe's) theatre in New York," where he heard "a black tragedian in the character of Hamlet" recite "To be, or not to be? That is the question; whether it is nobler in de mind to suffer, or tak' up arms against a sea of trouble, and by opossum end 'em." "No sooner was the word opossum out of his mouth," Mathews reported, "than the audience burst forth in one general cry, 'Opossum! opossum! opossum!'" – prompting the actor to come forward and sing the popular dialect song "Opossum up a Gum Tree."

Presumably the theatre that Mathews visited was the African Grove, while the performer he refers to is Ira Aldridge, star of that company. Alridge had found his opportunities in America so limited that he left for Europe in 1825 where he enjoyed substantial success on the stage, performing with Edmund Kean. Mathews' account of what happened at the African Grove is ridiculously racist:

Finishing his song, this versatile genius, retiring up the stage, is strutting down with one arm akimbo, and the other spouting out in front, just for all the world like a black teapot, bellowing out – "Now is de winter of our discontent made de glorious summer by de sun of New York." And on a person in the boxes telling him he should play Hamlet and not Richard III replies, "Yes, him know dat, but him tought of New York den and could not help talking about it." (quoted in Evans 166–67)

Lott notes that Mathews turned this experience into a blackface skit that he performed despite Aldridge's denial that it had occurred or could have occurred:. Aldridge remarked drily, "The truth . . . is that I never attempted the character of Hamlet in my life, and I need not say that the whole of the ludicrous scene so well and so humorously described by Mr. Mathews never occurred at all" (Lott 46). Yet as both Lott and Evans note, Aldridge did begin to perform "Possum up a Gum Tree" at the request of English audiences, although they do not agree on how one is to understand that performance. Once again, when one looks at nineteenth-century variety entertainment, there is a doubleness when the material is both a mockery of a group and a mockery by a group. In the case of Shakespeare references and burlesques, that double-edged humor often pops up.

As these examples suggest, ethnicity, like sexuality, matters when popular variety theatre performers cite Shakespeare (whether in minstrel show, burlesque, or vaudeville turn) and ultimately the same holds true in musical comedy as I hope to demonstrate. Nadine George-Graves points to the problems that such racist humor posed for African-American performers when she writes:

The ultimate irony was that the emergence of African American people in the theatrical workforce perpetuated degrading stereotypes of black people . . . Although recognized as a grotesque genre and decried by black intellectuals at the time (especially philosopher Alain Locke and sociologist W. E. B. DuBois) for sustaining stereotypes, minstrelsy and the practice of blacking up must nevertheless be understood as the first professional performance opportunities for African Americans, and its participants should be regarded as pioneers. For many black performers, minstrelsy was a way out of hunger, out of the Jim Crow South, and into adventure and other opportunities. (35)

One need only think of Ira Aldridge succumbing to the audience's desire to hear him sing a minstrel song. The anxiety about such racist and ethnic humor affected variety performers as well, both because it threatened their self-respect and because it had an impact on working conditions. Nor was it limited to African-Americans: in burlesques and variety entertainments the Shakespeare jokes were often based on other ethnic identities. *Othello, The Merchant of Venice*, and *Romeo and Juliet* often served as the springboard for humor predicated on stereotypes about Jews, Italians, Irish, or Germans. In a similar way, women in vaudeville sketches might give voice to misogyny.

By the final decades of the nineteenth century, then, Shakespeare's figure was central to legit theatre, yet curiously popular in the evolving forms of variety entertainment. Two developments in variety entertainment took Shakespearean materials in different directions. First of all Tony Pastor helped vaudeville become an increasingly middle-class phenomenon, as we have seen, displacing minstrel shows and burlesques as a popular form. Indeed, Erdman even argues that vaudeville becomes the first mass culture entertainment form. In vaudeville, the patterns established by minstrel shows and burlesques held true. Shakespeare was largely the topic of mockery, and that mockery often dealt with ethnicity or sexuality. Often the point of the joke was a register of how one audience regarded another, how a working-class audience regarded an African-American or elite white audience, for example. A second development, however, was the musical comedy in which Shakespeare's figure plays a rather different role. Let me briefly comment on vaudeville before turning to musical comedy.

There was some use of straight Shakespearean performance in vaudeville, with well-known legit performers (principally actresses) staging famous speeches or scenes. Because vaudeville managers were concerned about presenting themselves as respectable, such performances make sense, for Shakespeare had become, partly through being co-opted by the legit stage, the epitome of respectability. As a rule, such Shakespearean specialty acts did not do well, although, as Kibler notes, these performances were offered as a means of raising the tone of the proceedings: "[Vaudeville] Managers recruited high-brow acts such as grand opera vocalists and Shakespearean actors in the attempt to cater to the "best" and, in their public rhetoric at least, believed the multitude would follow. Their correspondence with other managers, however, reveals an uneven, often hostile, response to artistic acts" (42).

More popular were songs and sketches that referenced Shakespeare or his works for humor. The Library of Congress "American Memory" website includes a collection of theatre playbills and programs in its collection, "The American Variety Stage: Vaudeville and Popular Entertainment, 1870–1920."[8] A quick search of these produces six that include the keyword "Shakespeare," all of which are burlesques or travesties of his plays. Another item in the collection, which does not use the keyword, is entitled "Seven Ages" and is clearly structured on Jaques' speech in *As You Like It*. Such material suggests that vaudeville programs did make occasional use of Shakespeare as burlesques and minstrel shows did, to mock pretentiousness and elitism. Yet the mockery is more muted in vaudeville than in the other forms, in all likelihood because of marketing considerations.

A clear example comes from a vaudeville sketch, "Shakespeares of 1922," which Lorenz Hart and Morrie Ryskin wrote for comedian George Price.[9] It began

> Broadway has a Shakespeare fad,
> Actors all are Shakespeare mad,
> And I'd like to do
> His great plays for you.
> But I'll bring them up to date,
> Five acts you won't have to wait
> Till you hear the best scenes of the dramas.
> And the plays will look like new
> When I add a song or two.
> I'll make Shakespeare seem the cat's pajamas!

The song and monologues that followed appealed to the ways that the audience might regard themselves: as genteel people who admire Shakespeare, as people who think elitism is foolish, and as people amused by lower-class pretentiousness. The connotation of the word "dramas" suggests that Shakespeare is a serious topic, not a comic one, while the rhyming phrase, "the cat's pajamas" reverses the serious tone to suggest the trivial. In the skits that followed, George Price played a garment-trade Shylock, Hamlet the bootlegger's son, Lear evicted from a tenement, Mark Antony the baseball fan, and Romeo wooing Juliet on a fire escape. In each one, Price would announce the character, give a speech that parodies a set piece from Shakespeare, then sing a burlesque of a popular song. Thus his Hamlet declaimed,

To be or not to be, that is the question! Whether 'tis nobler to buy your Gordon's gin, and pay the prices of outrageous bootleggers, or to take arms against this sea of highwaymen, and make your own home brew! To drink, to die (to dream, perchance). Alcohol, aye, there's the rub! Home brew does make cowards of us all.

Mother, you have my father much offended. You made him drink shellac. You are toy queen. Your husband's brother's wife. And, would it were not so, so you my mother.

Beginning with a straight quotation, he moves quickly through topical jokes to puns to nonsense; the skit concludes with Hamlet singing a song about his "Mammy." More sophisticated was King Lear's rendition of the popular song, "April Showers":

> Though April showers may come my way
> They can't grow flowers in bales of hay.
> And when it's raining, I just reflect,
> Because it isn't raining rain at all,
> It's just a stage effect!
> I see a rainbow, and life's worthwhile,
> For I'm insane, bo, that's why I smile.
> I haven't even got a bathtub,
> So I hope the rain is strong
> Whenever April showers come along.

This song demands a knowledgeable audience to get the jokes about Lear ("I'm insane"), as well as the metatheatrical joke that rain is a stage effect. This song invites the audience both to preen itself on cultural sophistication, and to sneer at both the stuffiness of high culture and the vulgarity of low. The audience laughs at Shakespeare's simultaneous presence and absence from the stage, at the pretense that he must be an agent for respectability when such agency is displaced into colloquial jokes.

By the time Price sang his Shakespearean novelty songs in 1922, the world of nineteenth-century variety entertainment was long gone. It was more than seven decades since the Astor Place Riots, and even longer since Barnum had stirred up the English by his offer or non-offer on the birthplace. Moreover, it was over half a century since actors had feared for their livelihoods in the aftermath of the Lincoln assassination.

Like most people in the business, Junius [Booth, actor and manager] assumed that his brother's act would hang like a pall on all their industry and the people in it. But contrary to all predictions, 1866 was the best year yet for the stage. Business was at an all-time high, and some Broadway productions brought in more than double the previous year's receipts. Booth's former manager, William Wheatley, set a new box office record that year with *The Black Crook*, a spectacular musical featuring women in body suits that made them appear naked. (Kauffman 377)

Wheatley was managing Niblo's Garden when Henry Jarrett and Harry Palmer asked him for help. Jarrett and Palmer had planned an elaborate leg show when their theatre burned down. Wheatley suggested incorporating their show with *The Black Crook*, a melodrama–operetta that he was producing. The result, as Robert Allen says, "is part melodrama, part extravaganza, part spectacle, but not at all burlesque" (109). Yet the hybrid show was a smash, running for sixteen months. Today *The Black Crook* is regarded as America's first musical.

The distinction between burlesque and musical is not a minor one. A musical comedy has a book that is, generally, just as important as the musical numbers, which are often slight (unlike opera, in which the musical score is far more important than the libretto).[10] A musical may use incongruity, as a burlesque does, but it does not as a rule mock its source text. Thus burlesques of Shakespeare have tended to make fun of his tragedies or histories (or, as Schoch suggests, to make fun of performances of such plays), but musical comedies can consider less serious genres (as *Boys from Syracuse* does *The Comedy of Errors*) or treat its source with some respect (as *West Side Story* treats *Romeo and Juliet*). While *The Black Crook* did not have a strong book, it did have an elaborate and serious plot line, however muddled that story became with the interspersed dance and spectacular displays of chorus girls in startling costumes. Despite Kauffman's comment that the dancers appeared to be naked, Robert Allen's research suggests that most of the costuming was conventional with the exception of one number, a dance called the "Pas de Demons." In it, dancers wore "close-fitting pantaloons, which stopped at mid-thigh, and a sleeveless bodice, both done in polka dots" (111–12ff.). Certainly audiences were titillated by the demon-dancers, but that alone was not enough to fill the theatre for over a year.

While *The Black Crook* was not intentionally innovative, it is called the first American musical because it brought together features that became musical-comedy conventions: hundreds of chorus girls, extended dancing in scanty costumes, and spectacular effects were allied with a weak libretto. Leigh George Odum quotes the critic for the *New York Tribune*: "The scenery is magnificent; the ballet is beautiful; the drama is – rubbish." Perhaps the most important (and characteristic) feature of a musical is that its success is indicated by its sensational popularity with audiences, who flocked to see it from its opening in September 1866 until it closed in February 1868. The production then toured America for forty years (Odum 22).

The post-bellum years saw American musicals burgeon: audiences loved the way the form combined elements of humor, song, dance, and spectacle. Initially modeled on European operettas, American musicals were soon affected by variety entertainments. By the end of the century, the dialogue, the situations, and most importantly the music and dance numbers were becoming idiosyncratically American. Shows offered dialogue that used slang and jokes about American immigrant groups, race, or women and men. Such writing was much like the humor found in burlesque, minstrel and vaudeville shows. The comedy was interspersed with musical and dance numbers, which combined European operetta form and style with the minstrel shows' appropriated African-American dancing and ragtime or the music of immigrant groups like klezmer bands or Irish ballads. The most popular plot was some form of the Cinderella (or Horatio Alger) tale, while the most popular feature was probably the huge dance numbers. To perform the musicals, producers found chorus girls and dancers trained by vaudeville's rigorous tours. William Gould remarked in 1907, "seven-eighths of the musical comedy stars received their theatrical education and training in vaudeville" (in Stein, 78). Such a show would open in New York, and if it succeeded there go on to extensive tours throughout the country. The American musical quickly became a hodge-podge of influences, coalescing around the dreams of its audience. By the twentieth century it was a liminal form, between the legit and variety.

While a beard can signal masculine identity, that clear signal fades both in slang usage and in theatrical practice. The word "beard" may become a slang synecdoche for an identity as a man, but it may also be used as slang for female pubic hair and serve as a synecdoche for an identity as a woman. This complication – that a beard is a claim about gender identity, but we cannot be quite sure what the nature of that claim is – helps account for Banquo's remark about the witches in *Macbeth*:

> You should be women,
> And yet your beards forbid me to interpret
> That you are so.   (1.3.45–47)

The original actors playing the witches were men, but were understood to represent women; their masculine beards rendered their sexual identity as women uncertain, uncanny. A beard means differently in *Much Ado about*

Nothing. When the character Benedick decides to be in love with Beatrice, he shaves, or rather the actor playing Benedick removes a false beard, so that the actors playing Don Pedro and Claudio may comment on his changed appearance:

D. PEDRO. Hath any man seen him at the barber's?
CLAUD. No, but the barber's man hath been seen with him, and the old
    ornament of his cheek hath already stuff'd tennis-balls. (3.2.43–47)

In this instance, the character's move away from the homosocial soldier's world and into a heterosexual relationship is signaled by the actor's removal of part of his costume, a false beard. Thus the early modern drama enacts the mixture of meaning found in late modern slang usage. In Shakespeare's theatre and in today's world, a beard may serve not only to establish one sort of identity, but also to disguise or complicate identity.[11] Before turning to twentieth-century appropriations of Shakespeare in American book musicals, I shall briefly explore the complications that the term "beard" provides in Shakespeare's case and then turn to an instance when Shakespeare serves as a beard for other playwrights.

In the two portraits that have some claim to authenticity – the Droeshout engraving in the First Folio and the memorial bust in Holy Trinity Church – we see Shakespeare as a working character actor and as a retired man of letters respectively. The Droeshout portrait of Shakespeare (1623) is accompanied by a verse from B. I., almost certainly Ben Jonson, declaring, "This Figure, that thou here seest out, / It was for gentle Shakespeare cut; / Wherein the Grauer had a strife / with Nature, to out-doo the life . . ." In this portrait, we see Shakespeare in his middle years, a time when he was a working actor and sharer in the King's Men. The costume he wears is traditionally said to be that of Edward Knowell in Ben Jonson's 1598 play *Every Man in His Humor*, a role Shakespeare probably played.[12] The subject has some facial hair, a moustache and a little fuzz on the lower lip, but the chin is clean-shaven. By contrast, the tomb bust (*c.* 1614) that represents Shakespeare in retirement has a goatee as well as a moustache. The subject of the bust is older than that of the engraving, but they look quite a lot alike. The beard is one difference: in the bust it suggests a man of substance, a leading citizen virile enough to have a beard and able to keep it trimmed. In the engraving, the actor wears no beard.

It makes sense that a working actor would prefer not to wear a beard because he has to change his appearance to fit various roles, especially if he is in a repertory company as Shakespeare was. After an actor has left

11 (left) The Droeshout portrait of William Shakespeare, from the First Folio (1623). Note that while the portrait shows some facial hair, his chin is clean-shaven.
12 (right) The tomb bust of William Shakespeare, *c.* 1614. A retired Shakespeare adds a beard and moustache.

the stage with its demand for multiple identities, he might well prefer to grow a beard since he no longer needs to shave in order to play a clean-shaven character or one who shaves in mid-action, like the actor playing Benedick who must remove a false beard in *Much Ado*. Beards are not simply facial decoration in the playhouse; they are part of an actor's costume choice. That Shakespeare knew as much is clear from Bottom's speech in *A Midsummer Night's Dream*, when he prepares for his role as Pyramus:

BOTTOM. . . What beard were I best to play it in?
QUINCE Why, what you will.

BOTTOM I will discharge it in either your straw-color beard, your orange-tawny beard, your purple-in-grain beard, or your French-crown-color beard, your perfit yellow. (1.2.90–96)

Even so unsophisticated a character as Bottom knows that different beards allow the actor a choice about how to present a role. Once again, early modern theatrical practice, the beard as part of an actor's kit, can be seen in late modern slang usage. *The American Thesaurus of Slang* (1953) defines a "crossover beard" as "a beard used by an actor to double in a secondary part, or to cross the stage for an entrance on the other side."[13] The beard disguises the performer long enough to let him move through the on-stage action with one identity and then return in another identity.

The "crossover beard" usage may well be related to another slang usage, for a beard is "an unacknowledged agent." J. E. Lighter records this sense both in the context of gambling: "I played horses, using men as betting commissioners, or 'beards' as they were called at the race track" (Lighter 115), and in the context of sexuality, i.e., "an escort or companion of the opposite sex whose presence is intended to conceal a person's homosexuality." (I have also heard this term used in reference to a heterosexual relationship. When a woman with an unwitting husband attended a party to which her male lover had also been invited, the lover brought a date to "beard" for him.) The beard serves as a screen for someone who wants to engage in an activity, but cannot do so openly. The beard screens the proscribed activity from public view, giving the impression of respectability. In this section, I shall set aside "screen" for "beard," a term associated with gay culture and appropriate to the discussion of Shakespearean musicals that will be the focus of this part of my study.

But why focus on musicals? To explain why the Shakespearean musical suits my purposes, I need to consider several factors. Such scholars as Westfall, Dunn, Cartelli, Bristol, and Sturgess have done splendid work in examining Shakespeare's effect on American intellectual, aesthetic, and political concerns, what one might think of as serious areas of thought and action. This study, however, is interested in idiosyncratic ways that American popular culture employs Shakespearean materials. That focus means that I want to examine materials that are less serious, even trivialities, not simply because I enjoy those light topics, but also because it is in such unconsidered trifles that one finds "the way that ordinary people made sense of the world."[14] Musicals are an excellent example of precisely the material that operates in a specific cultural moment to imply the concerns and desires held by the people in the audience. Consider the analysis I have offered of American culture before the twentieth century.

An eighteenth-century American used Shakespeare as an index to concerns about England, I have argued (and this argument is congruent with that made by Sturgess). That usage continued into the early nineteenth century, and Shakespeare's figure was, in some important ways, useful in establishing the American sense of nationhood. Sturgess points in particular to the way that nineteenth-century orators employed Shakespeare in Fourth of July orations. I am rather more concerned with the way that performers found Shakespeare's plays a convenient way to circumvent troubling regulations. Yet I am as concerned with the colonial mantelpieces and newspaper parodies that used Shakespeare as I am by the struggles to set up acting companies. The way that John Quincy Adams employed Shakespeare in his political speeches and thought is of less interest to me than it is to other scholars, like Bristol or Sturgess, because while that practice is certainly characteristic of him, I cannot be sure it is characteristic of many of his countrymen. An upsurge in the number of journalistic re-writings of "To be or not to be" does speak to an increased general awareness of Shakespeare in American culture.

In the nineteenth century, a shift occurs, and Shakespeare's figure becomes used as a way for Americans to define themselves socially, whether as tourists in England, as individuals seeking to mark a particular class status, or as people who love or loathe the English. As the century moves on and Shakespeare becomes increasingly popular, he functions as a talismanic figure who seems able to open the doors of society or justify any position or action, even crime. In my examination of that phenomenon, I have obviously drawn on Bristol's work, though my own concern is with matters far more ephemeral than he treats in his book. Thus I have concentrated on the story of individuals who define themselves or their world in Shakespearean terms that authorized often startling actions. With the twentieth century, however, a new factor enters the history: the explosion of Shakespeare in popular culture or mass culture.

Doug Lanier has drawn attention to the contested nature of the term "popular culture" (4–8), and Richard Burt comments on why students of Shakespeare prefer that term to one that is often more accurate, "mass culture" (3–5).[15] Both scholars draw attention to the importance that film-making has had since the earliest twentieth century, its popularity soon matched by radio and television. Each medium drew on Shakespeare,

introducing his figure to every aspect of American life. Moreover, the con-
comitant print advertising in magazines and newspapers also drew heavily
on Shakespeare's image and plays to sell a wide variety of products. Meanwhile, in genre fiction, Shakespeare may appear as a cultural reference,
his plays may occur as allusions or as sources, or his canon may operate
as an unspoken, often unconscious, even unintended intertext or paratext. To try to map such a huge body of material in any sort of exhaus-
tive fashion would be impossible, although a number of studies have suggested some of the cultural grammar that affects Shakespeare in modern
and post-modern America (Lanier 179–82). In addition to the size of the
field, there is the complication that the modern and post-modern world
is often, and increasingly, international (global, if you will) rather than
national.

Consider, for example, movies. If one looks at the Internet Movie
Data Base (IMDB, http://imdb.com), it soon becomes clear that while
Shakespeare movies have been important throughout the century, they can
hardly be said to be idiosyncratically American. In the summer of 2005,
IMDB listed 97 entries for silent films under the name William Shakespeare
(i.e., those made between *King John* in 1899, the first filmed Shakespearean
play excerpt, and Pickford and Fairbanks' *The Taming of the Shrew*, the
first Shakespeare talking picture in 1929). The IMDB says that of these
97 movies, one is Czechoslovakian, two are Danish, two are Indian, eight
are German, twenty are Italian, nineteen are British, one is a joint British–
Portugese production, fourteen are French, one is a joint French and American production, and twenty-nine are American. Moreover, a film, wherever
the headquarters of its producer, generally includes performers and technical crews of several nationalities. To consider Shakespearean movies to
be any particular nation's preserve is simply silly; Shakespeare on film has
always been an international undertaking.

To find a product of twentieth-century American culture that is national
(rather than international) and popular (rather than elite, folk, or mass)
culture, I have chosen Broadway musicals. Although I shall focus my discussion on their first productions, I should note that the successful shows
tour widely and are revived across the country. Thus musicals, unlike movies
or genre fiction or tourism or any of the many other instances of Shake-
spop or Schlockspeare (terms from Lanier and Burt), fit the criteria I want
to apply as I examine what role the figure of Shakespeare has in American culture. Given that I am focusing on musicals, the term "screen"
becomes less appropriate because it suggests movies, while the term "beard"

suggests both the reality of a theatrical presentation and the importance of "unacknowledged agency."

I would agree that "Long before its kind was manifestly endangered, the Broadway musical took on a protective coloration" (Miller 1998: 1),[16] and add that a musical's protective coloration is not limited to sexual preference. As I hope to show, Shakespeare can also serve as a beard for transgressive desires about race or female independence. Musicals in Miller's reading (and John Clum would agree) serve as a beard for gay experience because they are "a somehow gay genre, the only one mass culture ever produced" (Miller 1998: 16). But the participation of gay writers and performers places them in a position analogous to that of African-American performers in variety theatre: they must seem to assent to stereotypes or values that they may resist in their private lives. Just as the jokes in minstrel shows or vaudeville depended on racist stereotypes, musicals have until recently depended upon a fiction of universal heterosexuality.

If Miller is also correct in seeing "the Broadway musical [as] the unique genre of mass culture to be elaborated in the name of the mother" (Miller 1998: 83), what is one to make of Shakespearean musicals, invoking the literary father? Rather than consider the gay poetics of Shakespeare musicals, it might be more useful to concentrate upon their peculiarity, their queer nature. They invoke the central figure of the legit theatre in a non-legit form, and they grow out of the mockery of the burlesque and minstrel shows, but become musicals by not mocking. Whatever else happens in a Shakespearean musical, he does not become a fabulous diva or a peculiar presence; he remains what he has always been in American theatre, a mainstay of the legit, the respectable stage. Quite apart from questions of gender preference, in musical comedy, Shakespeare plays his role as a beard, an unacknowledged agent, for other dramatists. His presence may indicate illicit desire, but it also indicates how such desires can be powerfully presented, made acceptable. Thus, one could argue that musical theatre, especially musical comedy, is from the outset a culturally queer form. For example, if one considers a hallmark of post-modernism to be the way in which it collapses elite and popular, high and low cultures, what is one to do with musical comedies, which perform that collapse throughout the modernist period, only to go slack and lose power (and then regain it) during the post-modernist period?[17]

A digression is in order here: some might argue that musical comedy is not so much an American phenomenon as it is a local phenomenon, centered on Broadway in New York. Those who regard musicals as necessarily New York- based see the form as one that is threatened: each year for the past few decades, the number of original musicals produced each year has been falling off (though the figures are, if one eliminates revues, comparable to the number of original musicals during some years of the Depression). A different point of view considers musicals as originating in New York, but surviving outside the city in a variety of professional, avocational, and educational venues. From that perspective, musical comedy is a remarkably healthy form, and is more popular than ever across the country. Shakespeareans face an analogous situation, of course: Shakespeare is in some sense a London dramatist whose work can be understood within the conditions that prevailed in that city at a specific historical moment. Yet as any Shakespearean knows, the dramatist is simultaneously a London playwright, the British national poet, and a globally important dramatist. While musical comedy is inevitably and inextricably associated with Broadway, it is also a form that one finds all across America in regional and community playhouses, as well as on the stages of innumerable school auditoriums.

If Shakespeare is the quintessential figure of English theatre, then musical comedy is the quintessential form of American theatre. Of course musical theatre is found world-wide, often with national inflections. Whether one considers satyr play, opera, zarzuela, or Broadway show, the work is clearly musical theatre. The book musical is the kind of musical theatre most strongly associated with Broadway, and the most powerful theatrical form (and export) in America's theatrical history. In a recent essay, Terry Teachout observes:

no other genre remains so central to American theatrical life. Of the twenty "top Broadway shows" listed in the April 23 *Wall Street Journal/Zagat Theater Survey*, a weekly poll of New York theatergoers, sixteen were musicals. Among movies, *Chicago* (2002), the most recent film version of a Broadway musical, won six Oscars, including Best Picture. Most of the best musicals of the 20th century continue to be revived regularly, on Broadway and elsewhere, just as their songs continue to be sung and recorded.[18]

Certainly if one asks a friend to name a "Broadway show," the friend is apt to produce the title of a musical rather than a play by Arthur Miller, Tennessee Williams, or August Wilson. Tourism commercials for New York City feature chorus lines of current musicals, while the export of such musicals (both on national and international tours) generates millions of dollars each year. Yet musicals are not limited to elite tastes, for although the price to the Broadway audience can make them a luxury item, the standard musical shows are also the mainstay of innumerable high school, college, and community theatre companies.

Perhaps the first point I should make is that few Shakespearean musical comedies come along, although more musical comedies draw on Shakespeare than on any other literary figure. Unlike opera, which often uses Shakespeare's plays, book musicals use him relatively rarely. While Shakespeare is certainly present in Broadway musicals, among the many hundreds of musicals that have opened in New York, I have been able to identify fewer than twenty that have been Shakespearean. The relationship each musical has to its Shakespearean base is crucial: the show employs Shakespeare for the sake of incongruity, prestige, or whatever, but simultaneously erases him in order to create enough aesthetic distance for success.

The use of Shakespeare in musical comedy should signal to us that something unusual is happening. When a team writing a musical comedy wishes to push convention in some way, they may invoke Shakespeare as a cultural icon. Under the cover of Shakespeare's beard, they can then explore bawdy heterosexual humor as in *The Boys from Syracuse* (1938). The same process occurs when a musical employs a mixed-race case (*Swingin' the Dream*, 1939), casts doubt on conventional ideas about marriage (*Kiss Me, Kate*, 1948), plays with politics (*West Side Story*, 1957), toys with homosexuality (*Your Own Thing*, 1968), or examines sexual and political freedom (*Two Gents*, 1971).[19] I shall not consider the Shakespearean musicals that flopped: *As You Like It* (1964); *Babes in the Wood* (*A Midsummer Night's Dream*), 1964; *Love and Let Love* (*Twelfth Night*), 1968, *Sensations* (*Romeo and Juliet*), 1970, *Music Is* (*Twelfth Night*), 1976, *Pop* (*King Lear*), 1974, *Rockabye Hamlet*, 1976, *Dreamstuff* (*The Tempest*), 1976, and *Oh Brother* (*The Comedy of Errors*) 1981.[20] Of late, the Shakespearean musicals that succeed are those that are substantially distanced from Shakespeare (*The Lion King* or *Play On!* for example) or those that return to the nineteenth-century's burlesque tradition (*The Bombitty of Errors*, 1999). (Appendix 1 offers information about the production personnel in Shakespearean musicals; Appendix 2 offers cast lists for those musicals that I discuss.)

Alternatively, one might argue not that a production team uses Shakespeare specifically so that they can take risks, but that once Shakespeare has been invoked in a musical comedy, the creative team finds it coincidentally much easier to take risks. My concern is not so much with the order that the process takes for a musical comedy, i.e., whether invoking Shakespeare leads to unconventionality or desire for unconventionality leads to invoking Shakespeare, but rather with the effect. What occurs when Shakespeare is a beard? To understand how musicals use Shakespeare, I shall examine a very early example and use it to sketch the cultural background for the American book musical. Then I shall consider some of the more interesting (and better-known) instances of Shakespeare musicals.

CHAPTER 7

"Mr. Hamlet of Broadway"

In 1908, rumors began to circulate in New York's theatrical circles that the variety stage comedian Eddie Foy planned to change his name to Mr. Edwin Fitzgerald, because he felt he required a more distinguished moniker before venturing into the legit by undertaking the role of Hamlet. When asked about the rumor, Foy would answer:

I have long known that I have the artistic temperament for those roles. I am really a Shakespearean actor, but the managers have kidded me out of it. I shall start with Hamlet, and after that play Touchstone, Lear, and other roles. Of course no artist can be sure of success in Shakespearean drama, but if, as I expect, I do succeed, none will ever hear of me in a comedy as Eddie Foy again.[1]

Despite the remark that "no artist can be sure of success in Shakespearean drama," Eddie Foy could be sure of success on the variety stage, where he had long enjoyed starring roles across the country as a comedian in musical shows and vaudeville. Whether playing a comic chef (*Hotel Topsey Turvey*), jailer (*The Strollers*), or sandman (*Piff Paff Pouf*), a traveling hypnotist (Paracelsus Noodle in *The Wild Rose*), a dog-trainer and would-be earl (Jim Cheese in *The Earl and the Girl*), a head gardener (Artie Choke in *The Orchid*), or Sister Anne in *Mr. Bluebeard*, Eddie Foy was a godsend to management because his shows made money.[2] And Foy required money since he and his third wife (his first two wives had died) were raising a large family: eight children in all. (Foy had one daughter by his first wife and seven children by his third wife. It was the children in the later household who toured as the Seven Little Foys in vaudeville and even became the subject of a Bob Hope film.) When Eddie Foy played on a vaudeville bill, he was a well-paid headliner. Why, then, would Foy try his hand at a role so risky and unremunerative as Shakespeare's Hamlet?

He wouldn't. He couldn't. He didn't. In fact, the rumors were planted during the publicity campaign for his next show, *Mr. Hamlet of Broadway*. In this musical comedy, Foy played Joey Wheeze, a circus clown who winds up at Starvation Inn in Lake Putrid, where he is hired at the last minute to play Hamlet in the place of a non-appearing tragedian. Produced by the Shubert organization and staged by Ned Wayburn, *Mr. Hamlet of Broadway* began touring in September 1908, opened at New York's Casino Theatre on 23 December 1908 and ran for 54 performances during that season. The show then toured from February to April 1909, again toured in a revised form from August 1909 to April 1910, ending with a week in Brooklyn's Majestic Theater (Fields 242–43). The book was by Edgar Smith, with lyrics by Edward Madden and music by Ben M. Jerome. Musical numbers included "The Dusky Salome," "Under the Honeymoon," "The Hornpipe Rag," "When I Was a Kid like You," "Good-bye Mollie Brown," "Waltz Me Away with You Dearie," "A Poor Little Girl like Me," "Mr. Hamlet of Broadway," "Nimble Symbaline," "When We Made the Gallant Charge at Bunker Hill," and "The Man Who Built the Summer Hotel." (Two of these have been recorded.) Throughout the tour of the production, songs were altered, dropped, or added. Thus the song "Hamlet's Ghost," which was in the show in 1908, had disappeared by 1909. When the show was revived for the 1909 season, it had additional songs, including "Beautiful Rose," with lyrics by George Whiting and Carter De Haven and music by Ted Snyder; other added songs were Madden and Jerome's "Everything Depends on Money" and "Down Where the Watermelon Grows."[3]

At first the use of Shakespeare in this musical revue seems incidental, a chance for Eddie Foy to fool around in his characteristic fashion. The names Hamlet and Cymbeline provide song hooks ("Mr. Hamlet of Broadway" and "Nimble Symbaline") and little more. Numbers like "Dusky Salome" or "When We Made the Gallant Charge at Bunker Hill" are substantially less Shakespearean. From Foy's autobiography, however, as well as Armond Fields' recent biography, one learns that the show integrated Shakespeare, that centerpiece of the legit stage, into what would be the most successful variety stage show in which Foy ever starred. Although *Mr. Hamlet of Broadway* uses a Shakespearean burlesque, its unconventional tone makes it arguably the first Shakespearean musical comedy in that it is a show structured much like *Kiss Me, Kate* (1947), using a Shakespearean burlesque within a frame plot that echoes the inset Shakespearean material. Even if one refuses to see the show as a Shakespearean musical comedy, however, its affectionate treatment of *Hamlet* inside a book that does not simply mock Shakespeare makes it an interesting example of how Shakespeare's presence was received on the popular stage at the beginning of the twentieth century.

Mr. Hamlet of Broadway opens at Starvation Inn on Putrid Lake, a sad resort hotel that is going broke, to the chagrin of the inn's landlord Jonathan

Cheatam. Indeed, the residents at the hotel are so disgusted that they are ready to leave, but they settle down after Cheatam promises them anything they ask for. In particular, Cheatam promises a guest, Mrs. Barnaby Bustle, that a well-known New York tragedian will come and play Hamlet to her Gertrude. The peaceful moment allows the Bustles' daughter, Cymbeline (or Symbaline), to enjoy her courtship by Tom Manleigh, who belongs to the local militia company known as the Utica Reds. After word arrives that the great tragedian cannot come, Jonathan Cheatam thinks quickly and engages a clown whose circus is stranded nearby, one Joey Wheeze (Eddie Foy). Accompanied by his trick bear Amelia, Wheeze agrees to fill in as Hamlet. Barnaby Bustle, reluctant to play Claudius, tries to bribe Wheeze to back out of the show, but negotiations fail when Mrs. Bustle bribes the actor to stay. Wheeze remains loyal to the role of Danish prince as the first act ends.

In Act Two, the action shifts to Mount Kalish, where the production of *Hamlet* is being guarded by the Utica Reds. In the course of rehearsing and performing *Hamlet*, Foy found many gags. The show became a series of sketches that featured his comic abilities to entertain the audience: he drilled the militia company, performed a novelty song about nursery rhymes, fought a mock duel, and presented a burlesque version of *Hamlet*, which included this soliloquy's musings on the life of a small-time actor:

> To flee, or not to flee, that is the question
> Whether 'tis nobler in the sun to suffer
> The slings and arrows of outrageous scorching
> Or to fling his claims against a sea of critics
> And, I suppose, offend them;
> To fly, to sneak, to "blow" and by that sneak
> To say, I end the headshakes and the thousand
> Natural wrongs the profesh is heir to.
> To fly, to sneak, and when that sneak I make –
> What meals may come? For where's the grub?
> Oh, who could bear the trips to one-night stands,
> The press' wrongs, the crowds' damned contumely,
> The trains delay, the prongs of despised hotels,
> The insolvency of managers, and the spurn of waiting sheriff
> When your trunk he takes with a bare suitcase;
> This makes me rather play the part I have than fly
> To authors that I know not of.
> What! Ho! Some music!

Using the form of Hamlet's metaphysical contemplation on being, the burlesque substitutes observations about the difficulties that a variety actor

faces: critical sneers, constant traveling, and financial chicanery. To be a
Shakespearean actor is to hold a distinguished place in the legit theatre,
worthy of critical praise, but to be Joey Wheeze, taking the place of that
distinguished actor as Hamlet, means facing contempt, a sea of sneering
critics. He considers escape, not via a bare bodkin, but by sneaking off,
"blowing" the engagement, to escape the acting "profesh's" innate difficulties. The slang he uses here continues with "grub" and "prongs," the insider's
language for the bad food and inconveniences of life on the road as an actor.
As Schoch points out, "In looking . . . at the burlesque's relentless use of
slang, we are looking not at a gratuitous recitation of vulgarities, but rather
at the public performance of a socio-cultural identity through a particular
mode of speech" (Schoch 130). While what he says is true, it is equally true
that American variety performers, who were often highly sensitive about
professional gradations of status, struggled with slang in the theatre. (I am
here treating burlesque and vaudeville as forms that have similar approaches
to social propriety; Foy's training was certainly in vaudeville, although his
success in this soliloquy is in a burlesque.) The legit actor and playwright,
Edwin Royle, recalled a season he had spent in vaudeville, particularly the
prohibition on vulgar slang as defined by the management, namely, "Such
words as Liar, Slob, Son-of-a-Gun, Devil, Sucker, Damn, and all other
words unfit for the ears of ladies and children . . ." (in Stein, 24). Royle
reports that he was caught violating that prohibition, and he was not alone.
Despite the desire of managers and some performers to escape being labeled
vulgar, others knew perfectly well that they were vulgar and that they could
use that vulgarity to good effect in getting laughs. In the instance of Foy's
burlesque soliloquy, the use of such colloquial terms as "grub" and "profesh" or the mild profanity "damned" elicits laughter because the diction
is at odds with the grandeur of the source text, the "To be or not to be"
soliloquy. The language also serves to establish Foy's character as a small-
time actor who would ordinarily be kept well away from any Shakespearean
role.

   This humor is unsophisticated, in keeping with the rest of the play.
Indeed, it is superior wit compared to some gags. For instance, Joey Wheeze
is sad because he has lost his trained bear Amelia, but announces,

I'm a clown, an actor, a bear trainer, and a tin soldier, all in twenty four hours. I
think I had better study up this part if I am going to play it. (Reading) Who can
bear . . . There's a bear in this. Who can foredells bear when he himself can this
quie[t]us make with a bear . . . Holy Smoke, there's a lot of bears in this . . . if
Amelia hadn't escaped last night she could have had a swell part in Hamlet. (Script
from the Shubert Archive, Act 2, page 5)

And Fields points to other such jokes: "At the end of his soliloquy, the King remarked, 'Our Ham is cured,' while Ophelia, with garlands of carrots and turnips in her hair, made it difficult for Hamlet to 'plant' her after she died" (Fields 176–77). The burlesque production of *Hamlet* succeeds, however, and saves the inn, which means the lovers can marry and all live happily ever after.

While a burlesque of *Hamlet* is hardly unusual (most of us have seen a number of such joke versions), Foy's treatment of Shakespeare in his play was reverential. For instance, the publicity stunt was a fair representation of Foy's actual interests: he says in his autobiography that he would have enjoyed playing a straight Shakespearean role. That desire stems from his early days in Chicago, when he had served as a supernumerary for Shakespeare productions. He reports that as a beginning performer, "I appeared as citizen, ruffian, soldier, peasant, or brigand in *Julius Caesar, Coriolanus, Macbeth*, . . ." and in Edwin Booth's 1876 Chicago appearances as Hamlet (Foy and Harlow 71 and ch. 8 passim; Fields 21–22). Later in vaudeville, Foy would imitate Booth's Macbeth as part of a comedy act: ". . . he'd [i.e., Foy] swing a sword menacingly over his head, only to crack himself in the skull, the sword flying offstage. Staggering onto the boards, sword embedded in his body, would be an impaled, astonished 'stagehand'" (Fields 45). Foy also told, with considerable relish, of a production of *Julius Caesar* in which he was persuaded to take part after he had enjoyed some success, but before he became a headliner. Unfortunately, during the assassination of Caesar, one of the other actors looked at Foy and got the giggles, and the infectious laughter spread uncontrollably, ruining the performance. There was enough affection in Foy's feelings toward Shakespeare that he could claim, "I knew Hamlet's lines backwards and forwards, and had . . . often been heard off the stage reciting not only that but other Shakespearean parts by the yard" (Foy and Harlow 298).

Foy had a lifelong fondness for Shakespeare and a fair knowledge of the canon. Moreover, in the first decade of the twentieth century, Foy might well have considered a move away from clowning. In December 1903, he had starred in *Mr. Bluebeard* at Chicago's Iroquois Theater. A defective light set the playhouse on fire, and "Of the 1,900 people in the audience, mostly women and children, at least 600 perished."[4] Foy was backstage with one of his young children as the alarm was given. When Foy realized what was happening, he handed his child to a stagehand and went out on the stage despite his own danger to plead with the audience not to panic, but to exit carefully. Nevertheless, afterwards "trampled bodies were piled ten high in the stairwell area where exits from the balcony met the exit from the main floor." Horrified by the event, Foy left Chicago, performing in vaudeville for a while before moving to New York and signing with the Shuberts to do musical comedies. One unexpected result of the Iroquois Theater fire, as Fields suggests, is that Eddie Foy's gallantry had made him a public hero: had he chosen a different path as a performer, he might well have enjoyed success (155–56). Instead, he chose to continue with comedy.

He did claim to feel some regret when he played *Mr. Hamlet of Broadway*:

In the [Hamlet] burlesque . . . I dressed and made up the part with scrupulous care as to tradition. I used all the grace of voice and gesture that I could command, but the words I spoke were ridiculous parodies of the original lines. At the very last minute I longed – oh, how wistfully! – to play just one scene in the original words, as I had longed to do it thirty years before. (Foy and Harlow 302)

Foy then reports, with great satisfaction, that the critics praised his Hamlet, and he quotes a Philadelphia critic, "For once we see the comedian becomingly garbed, and it was to be noted that he has an admirable stage presence, that his reading is good when he wanted it to be so, and that he has a grace of movement and an authority which are quite compelling" (Foy and Harlow 303). Indeed, the production's poster (also used as the cover for the sheet music) uses a caricature of Foy in the costume that he thought closely resembled Booth's presentation of Hamlet. To my eye there is little resemblance to portraits of Booth, but that is hardly the point. What matters is not the uncanny resemblance (which does not exist), but that Foy dreamed of himself as being like Booth, although his wonderfully comic appearance led him away from the legit stage. His anecdote about how laughter at his looks spoiled the production of Julius Caesar suggests that he was well aware that he would not be taken seriously as a Shakespearean and that he made the best of his features. Usually burlesques from this period are pointed, even hostile toward the legit theatre's production of Shakespeare; Foy made more fun of himself than anyone else.

So were Foy's regrets simply the conceit of a nostalgic comedian convinced he is able to do serious work, a sort of Pagliacci Syndrome or a King of Comedy Crisis? More is going on in this case than the daydreaming of a clown. As the "To flee or not to flee" soliloquy suggests, the burlesque was very much part of the larger plot line, which one might see as an extended consideration of where a performer (whether Joey Wheeze or Eddie Foy) registered in the cultural range that stretched from the legit stage's productions of Shakespeare's tragedy and the variety stage's burlesques of such drama.

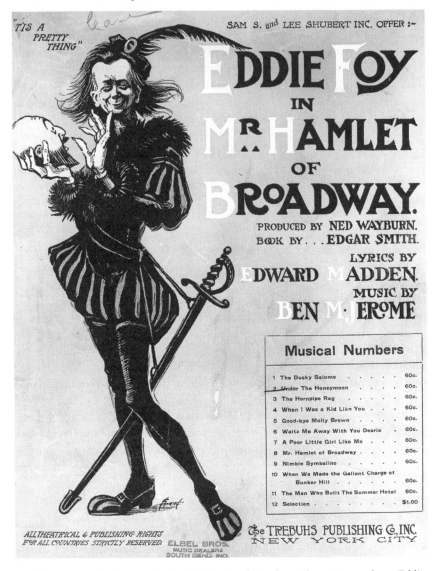

13 The cover to the sheet music for *Mr. Hamlet of Broadway.* The caricature shows Eddie Foy in his Hamlet costume, holding Yorick's skull as he muses "'Tis a pretty thing."

Douglas Gilbert notes the opposition between variety and the legit: "Variety was a curious hit-or-miss activity, a theatrical shot in the dark. It was of the stage, yet distinct from the legitimate theater whose 'Harolds and Arthurs' regarded variety performers as low persons of no moment" (24). Gilbert overstates the situation somewhat, especially in 1908 when *Mr. Hamlet of Broadway* was performed. There was traffic between legit and variety stages, although no one would deny that the legit performer had a higher social rank than the variety performer. Dramatic critic Norman Hapgood told this story to illustrate the distinction in 1901: "A famous American actress, now one of our most popular stars, was, a few years ago, in decided need of money. A vaudeville manager offered her eight thousand dollars to play eight weeks in his houses. She refused" (In Stein, 34). Hapgood goes on, however, to say that "the lines between the legitimate and vaudeville have been shattered of late," although he insists that movement between the two is almost exclusively legit actors stepping down to vaudeville: "Of course, the great majority of vaudeville players have no opportunity to decide which stage they will appear on. They usually lack talent sufficient for success in the drama" (In Stein, 39). A contemporary, Acton Davies, contributed an essay to the first issue of *Variety* (1905) declaring that between the legit and vaudeville, "there is a wide gulf fixed – one of those gulfs which no suspension can ever span. The actor in nearly every instance regards his dip into vaudeville as a vast condescension on his part," and regards vaudevillians as "belonging to an essentially lower orbit, a being of a distinctly cruder grade" (in Stein, 84). That oppositional nature of legit and variety is important to the way that Shakespeare is treated in Foy's musical comedy because the traditional hostility shown by variety burlesques of Shakespeare here gives way to an implicit claim that even the variety performer – who must "fly, sneak, and 'blow'" in his performance – can reasonably play in the Shakespearean dramas that Harolds and Arthurs customarily guarded. A variety comic may even be a weak performer, and "fling his claims against a sea of critics" knowing he'll offend them, but in this show he decides to go on as Hamlet, however inadequately, and by so doing achieves a happy ending for the musical comedy. The idea that *Hamlet*, a mighty mainstay of the legit, has the power to enable lovers to marry, a resort to succeed, and a career to be launched is not the usual sort of message that one might expect from the American variety stage.

Another important feature is that two topics occurring regularly in variety are central to Shakespearean musical comedies: sex and ethnicity. Even in vaudeville, with its drive for respectability, performers had the counterbalance of humor on such risky topics. To be sure, such jokes had to be slipped into acts at times. Edwin Royle's comments on the prohibition against slang, especially against language that was deemed indelicate, "words unfit for the ears of ladies and children," suggest the concern many vaudeville managements felt about the wide perception of their shows as vulgar. Despite impresario B. F. Keith's insistence on rigid social rules in the vaudeville circuit that he ran, most managements were less fussy. Those jokes and epithets – whether dirty or ethnic – survive in American musical comedy.

In *Mr. Hamlet on Broadway* we can see both elements of bawdiness and ethnicity. The song "Goodbye, Mollie Brown" is a comic song that mocks people who are French and English, for example (Shubert Archive script, Act 1, 25–26), while Maude Raymond claiming to be the "Dusky Salome" brags about her "Oriental style" and announces in the song's chorus that, "I want a coon who can spoon to the tune of Salomy, / I'll make him giggle with a brand new wiggle" (Act 2, 9). Neither song refers to Shakespeare. Even a Shakespearean reference could be made into an ethnic joke, however. When Ophelia does her mad scene, she sings

> Tomorrow is St. Patrick's Day
> And in the morning time
> I'll wear my old plug hat and sash
> And be my valentine,

transforming herself into a stereotypical Irish joke. The authors seem to have felt the need for a ghost story that Foy could perform. In some versions of the script, there is a ghost song by Jerome and Madden called "De Ebony Spook," in which we learn of a "Niggar spook" [sic] and how he frightened a preacher so much that "Black Parson Green turned white." Another ghost song sometimes used in the second act, "Hamlet's Ghost," includes clear references to the play:

> He's a most important factor to the young ambitious actor
> He will say the part of Hamlet fits you most
> And he said to one comedian, "Why you're a born tragedian"
> "I ought to know for I am Hamlet's ghost."

The ghost explains that

> "As I flit about first-nighting I have heard you oft reciting
> Those immortal lines 'tis such a pretty thing.
> Shakespeare said I'd recognize you, you're the man he put me wise to
> He had you in mind when he wrote Hamlet's part . . ."

But although the ghost pretends to welcome the actor who (like Foy himself) recites Hamlet's lines so often, he is playing a trick. Despite his encouragement for the actor, the ghost shows a malicious streak in the song's chorus:

> When Hamlet says, "To be or not to be"
> The ghost cries out in fiendish glee
> "I'm hid behind the scenery
> Where the eggs cannot reach me."

The actor who dares attempt Hamlet is greeted with derision and eggs. This song illustrates the dangers inherent in a variety performer attempting the legit role. Others include explicit intrusions of ethnicity and sexuality that may highlight the way that legitimate theatres suppressed the topics, sometimes by erasing them, sometimes by rendering them implicitly. It seems valuable to remember that only two seasons before, Shaw's *Caesar and Cleopatra*, a play written in Shakespeare's shadow that draws attention to both race and sex, had had its premiere in New York, where it was far more successful than it would be in the West End of London. While the highly respectable E. H. Sothern and Julia Marlowe or Robert Mantell struggled to make their Shakespeare productions pay in New York, Foy's comedy was highly successful.[5] *Mr. Hamlet of Broadway* is an early instance of what occurs when the musical comedy looks toward the legitimate stage; like earlier burlesques, the Shakespearean musical will insist that Shakespeare's work must coexist with American formulations of sexuality and racial identity.

Book musicals grew out of, yet stand superior in status to variety entertainment. Like variety, musicals operate in opposition to the legit from mid-nineteenth century on. The place of Shakespearean musicals is tricky from the outset, for in a Shakespearean musical, the creators take over a legit text, then use that play to overtake legit's "Harolds and Arthurs" as performers. What starts out in variety as performers mocking another theatrical style to celebrate their own theatrical form becomes direct competition when book musicals use Shakespeare. In the musical, a show invokes Shakespeare, yet dismisses most aspects of the legit, including the text; moreover, a musical's descent from variety theatre means it usually employs sex and race, partly to sell the show, partly because those topics are more interesting than conventional Shakespearean productions, even when the performers who speak of such topics might themselves be made uncomfortable by them. The Eddie Foy show *Mr. Hamlet of Broadway* fits this pattern, although it is far from the sort of book musical that we recognize today. The credit for the first Shakespearean musical has always gone to *The Boys from Syracuse* (1938), and perhaps knowing what is the "first" is unlikely to alter theatre history in any significant way.

Yet Shakespearean musicals may offer an index to the way that variety theatre regards its rival, the legit stage. If that be the case, then the cheerful way in which *Boys from Syracuse* acknowledges Shakespeare only to dismiss him suggests impertinent self-confidence. The earlier show, *Mr. Hamlet of Broadway*, with the leading comedian's "wistful longing" (the diction is Foy's), shows us a theatrical world that may be less self-confident about the priority of comedy, but that sees no obstacle to claiming Shakespeare as part of its own. Early in the twentieth century, the concern with class identity, so characteristic of the way that nineteenth-century America used Shakespeare's figure, seems to have altered. Foy may regret his exclusion from the legit because he loves Shakespeare, but he is the star of a play that tells its audience to laugh at Mrs. Barnaby Bustle and her social pretensions. In *Mr. Hamlet of Broadway*, Shakespeare is secondary to what really matters: singing, dancing, and fooling around. By the time of *The Boys from Syracuse*, the nineteenth-century concern with social class has very little relevance. To be a Dromio in that show is not to be a slave, but to be a star.

CHAPTER 8

A hit and a flop

Following Foy's musical, the next two shows to use Shakespeare in a central way were staged thirty years later, in 1938 and 1939, the first a success and the second a failure. The contrast between them is instructive. According to Richard Rodgers,

We [Rodgers and Hart] were on a train heading for Atlantic City, where we thought the fresh sea air might help to stimulate some new ideas. For some reason we began discussing Shakespeare, which led to our discovery that no one had ever thought of using one of his plays as the basis of a musical comedy.

The mere fact that it had never been done before was reason enough for us to start thinking that it should be our next project. The problems of *I Married an Angel* were pushed aside as we began tossing around titles of plays. Even *eliminating the tragedies and histories*, we had a pretty large field to choose from (my emphasis).[1]

Burlesque treatments of Shakespeare, like the one that concluded *Mr. Hamlet of Broadway*, have to focus on tragedies and histories because the whole point of a burlesque is to deflate a serious and prestigious work. Moreover, the more serious plays were the ones most often produced on the legit stage – *Hamlet*, *Romeo and Juliet*, and *Richard III* in particular – and hence the ones best known to an audience. In 1938, however, a musical comedy required a book that was light comedy, hence Rodgers' caveat that they should eliminate tragedies and histories.

A show like *The Boys from Syracuse* makes use of a Shakespearean play's shell – the plot line and central characters, dispenses with the language and structure, and seeks to make a distinctively contemporary point. It is less a burlesque than a travesty: the musical does not draw upon a serious work nor does it mock the original directly. Instead, the Shakespeare play becomes a convenient agent to make the playwright's point without either the encumbrance of being "faithful" to or the aim of mocking a text. It borrows the respectability of the figure of Shakespeare and gets rid of the troublesome aspects.

14 ©Al Hirschfeld. The Dromios in *Boys from Syracuse*. Al Hirschfeld represents the twin Dromios, played by Teddy Hart and Jimmy Savo as two bodies with a single face. The performers' strong resemblance helps account for the show's existence.

Rodgers and Hart chose *The Comedy of Errors*, because of the opportunity to link Hart's brother Teddy to the comedian Jimmy Savo. As Rodgers tells it:

one play attracted us from the start, and for a very personal reason. Larry's younger brother, Teddy, was a clever comedian best known for such George Abbott farces as *Three Men on a Horse* and *Room Service*. He was short and dark, and though he looked a great deal like Larry, he was always being mistaken for another gifted comic, Jimmy Savo.

"Why don't we do *The Comedy of Errors*?" Larry said rubbing his hands together as he always did when a good idea hit him. "Teddy and Jimmy would be a natural for the twin Dromios." Nepotism notwithstanding, we both realized that it was an inspired casting idea . . .

(See figure 14.) George Abbott has a similar version of the show's origin: "Larry Hart had a strong protective feeling for his brother, and he got an idea to help Teddy, which he brought to Dick Rodgers and me."[2] Hart recognized that the coincidental resemblance would help his brother's career. In *The Complete Lyrics of Lorenz Hart*, his sister Dorothy quotes him as saying, "Teddy had to be star [sic], and this was the first star part that ever fit him" (133). But Teddy Hart was no beginner, having achieved success in *Three Men on a Horse* (1935) and *Room Service* (1937), both shows that George Abbott had directed.[3]

In this case, Abbott, Rodgers, and Hart had little if any interest in popularizing a giant of English literature or sharing their reverence for Shakespeare. Yet both men knew Shakespeare's plays well enough that Hart could propose the trick casting that would benefit his brother and be immediately understood by Rodgers.[4] Like the Shakespeare routine that Hart and Ryskind had written for the vaudevillian George Price in 1922, Hart's idea of using the *The Comedy of Errors* offers multi-level humor that both appeals to Shakespeare's cultural value and simultaneously mocks it. Because the *Boys from Syracuse* is a book musical and not a burlesque, the final work is one that stands on its own to sustain a full evening in the theatre.

The team wanted to showcase a specific performer (Teddy Hart), to enjoy a substantial profit (the goal of any musical produced in such a competitive and commercial venue as Broadway), and to bend the conventions of musical comedy by writing a show substantially more risqué than any that they had written before. This final claim is speculative, to be sure: how can anyone know that the production was intended to push the boundaries of what was acceptable? Yet a subsequent Rodgers and Hart show, *Pal Joey* (1940), also directed and produced by George Abbott, is widely recognized today as innovative and strong, despite its initial failure on Broadway because it was too frank about sexual mores, including female sexual desire and gigolos.

Abbott began work on the book, while Rodgers and Hart expected that they would join him as collaborators after he had an initial draft. As it turned out, Abbott's rough draft "was so right that they [Rodgers and Hart] withdrew as collaborators" (*"Mister Abbott"* 186). Rodgers remarked, "The book was so sharp, witty, fast-moving, and, in an odd way, so very much in keeping with the bawdy Shakespearean tradition, that neither Larry nor I wanted to change a line" (Rodgers 191). For the 1963 revival, Abbott's book was re-written, principally by adding jokes. According to Abbott,

Twenty-five years later, I was in Florida when an off-Broadway revival of *The Boys from Syracuse* was produced by Richard York. I was delighted to read of its outstanding success, and distressed that some of the reviewers referred to the old-fashioned jokes in the book. But I was puzzled when one of the reviewers cited one of these jokes, a corny pun: "Dozens of men are at my feet." "Yes, I know, chiropodists." This kind of humor is so alien to me that I knew I could never have written it; and when I got back to New York I found that the "old jokes" in the revival were new jokes inserted by Mr. York to "modernize" the script. (187)

Abbott reports that he removed some, but not all of these jokes. The version of the script currently available from the Rodgers and Hammerstein Library uses the revised version, although crediting Fred Ebb rather than York with the additional dialogue.

The Boys from Syracuse had a remarkable production team and cast. The musical opened in November 1938 at the Alvin Theatre, with songs by Rodgers and Hart, book by George Abbott, scenic design by Jo Mielziner, costumes by Irene Sharaff, and choreography by George Balanchine. The show starred Eddie Albert and Ronald Graham as the Antipholi, Jimmy Savo and Teddy Hart as the Dromios, and Muriel Angelus and Marcy Wescott as Adriana and Luciana respectively; a very young Burl Ives took a role as a tailor's apprentice. The show was a big success, running 235 performances, being filmed in 1940, and having a major revival in 1963. In 2003, *Da Boyz*, a hip-hop adaptation of *The Boys from Syracuse* opened in London. (I shall discuss this production in connection with *The Bombitty of Errors* in a later chapter.)

The plot line of *The Boys from Syracuse* is closer to the Shakespearean play than in any other Shakespearean musical. In a comic forepiece, a dancing Tragedy mask and Comedy mask declare, "If it's good enough for Shakespeare, it's good enough for us." To be sure, the musical is more economical with its dialogue, so Shakespearean speeches are often shrunk to a few lines, which makes room for song and dance. Aegeon's elaborate speech about the wreck (*The Comedy of Errors* 1.1.62–103) becomes a four-line account, for instance:

> But on one unhappy day
> We went sailing on the sea.
> This was an unlucky blunder
> For our ship was torn asunder.[5]

Such numbers as "Falling in Love with Love," "Sing for Your Supper," or "This Can't Be Love," took the place of the missing Shakespearean dialogue. Changes in the characters are largely made to emphasize the importance of the Dromios. The role of Luce is substantially expanded, so that the comedienne Wynn Murray who played Luce had the chance for comic numbers with both Dromios (another change that Abbott made was having Luce sleep with her brother-in-law). A sorcerer has been added to the characters, probably as a substitute for Shakespeare's Doctor Pinch, whom the musical cuts. He contributes a few tricks, principally existing to set up a comic dance number in which Dromio of Ephesus asks for a vision of his lost twin and sings, "Big Brother," while the Sorcerer makes Dromio of Syracuse appear so the two can dance.

Despite the similarity of the plot, the show retains few lines of the text of *The Comedy of Errors*. The common claim is that when the two lines, "The venom clamors of a jealous woman / Poisons more deadly than a mad dog's tooth" (5.1.69–70), occurred, Savo popped his head out from behind the curtain to announce to the audience, "Shakespeare!" In his biography of Richard Rodgers, Geoffrey Block records other lines that follow Shakespeare's text closely and inventories the parallel plotlines (97–98, 102–03).

What a Shakespearean will find more interesting than parallels between *The Boys from Syracuse* and *The Comedy of Errors* are two things: both the musical's reflexive lines that demonstrate familiarity with Shakespeare and the changes that make the play's material more suitable for a musical comedy. In the former category, one finds the line Dromio of Syracuse uses to tell Adriana her husband has been arrested: "He's been pinched" (49). For anyone who knows *The Comedy of Errors*, the line works both as a colloquialism and as a reference to the play's character, Dr. Pinch. Similarly, in "This Can't Be Love," the lovers sing of their cousins, Romeo and Juliet (24), while Dromio of Ephesus tells his wife Luce, "Don't be a shrew with a man" (11). More subtle are lines like Adriana's declaration that when she locates her husband, "I'll coo him home sweetly as any dove"; the Merchant's advice, "If anyone asks you any questions, say you don't know the language . . . it's all Greek to you"; or the Sergeant's "My God, if we saw that on the stage, we'd laugh it off the boards" (15, 6, 7). These allusions to *A Midsummer Night's Dream*, *Julius Caesar*, and *Twelfth Night* are slipped in to amuse those who catch them without being pedantic. After he graduated from Rochester, Abbott had, after all, studied to be a playwright in Professor George Baker's famous Harvard drama seminar, so he knews Shakespeare's (and Plautus') work well. That background helps to account for his decision to expand the Courtezan's role (an element found in *Menaechmi*, but not *The Comedy of Errors*) and his displacement of the principal character's adultery to the Dromio brothers (an element from *Amphitruo*). But most such changes were made to fit the musical's form and conventions.

The alteration of the Aegeon/Aegean exposition is such a change, for it means that the book opens with a big production number that launches the show with energy, while laying out the background clearly. The darker tone appropriate to Shakespeare's play will not do in a 1938 musical, nor will ambiguity or confused digressions. Again, the book of the musical clarifies the play: the audience sees how the twins end up in identical costumes when a tailor gives Antipholus of Syracuse a suit made for Antipholus of Ephesus, while at the end Antipholus of Ephesus redeems the lives of his Syracusan brother, as well as his father, a point that Shakespeare omits in his play. The number and size of women's roles grows in the musical, so that the show has a strong chorus and dance ensemble. In particular, the role of Luce, tiny in the original, is much expanded, so that the show can include a comedienne to play off the Dromios and to sing novelty numbers. (Wynn Murray, who played Luce in the original production, had more songs than any other character, Geoffrey Block notes.) The omission of characters like Shakespeare's Dr. Pinch and Balthazar streamlines the text, while adding the Sorcerer permits comic conjuring.

Using the Shakespearean plot line allowed the musical to take more chances with off-color materials than was conventional in 1938. Reading the lyrics today one finds the much-discussed bawdiness tame. Antipholus of Syracuse sings:

> When a man is lonely it is good to know
> There's a red light burning in the patio.
> I wanna go back, go back
> To dear old Syracuse.
> Wives don't want divorces there,
> The men are strong as horses there,
> But should a man philander,
> The goose forgives the gander.

The song's references to the red light that signals a bawdy house or to male infidelity, like the songs that Luce sings that suggest her husband will not have sex with her, seem tame. Antipholus of Ephesus sings "The shortest day of the year, / Has the longest night of the year." Adriana, Luciana, and Luce have a trio, "Sing for Your Supper," that compares a canary to a courtesan and concludes, "Songbirds always eat." These instances are as racy as the lyrics get, although a performer can always convey licentiousness in performance, no matter how innocuous the material.

More interesting is the queer subtext of the lyrics. Clum argues that Hart's lyrics also express closeted gay desire, a fascinating counter-narrative

(58–69), suggesting resistance to the heterosexuality mandated in musicals at this point. Thus one can see as homoerotic the Sergeant's "Come with Me," the song inviting Antipholus to jail:

> Be a guest in a house of rest
> Where the best of fellows can cheer you.
> . . .
> In this, your strictly male house

One may also wonder why the trio, "Sing for Your Supper" includes the lines, "I heard from a wise canary / Trilling makes a fellow willing, / So, little swallow, swallow now." For the most part, Hart's lyrics are clever manipulations of language without a strongly erotic quality, while love is associated with yearning and pain. As Jeffrey Smart comments about Hart's work: "In these lyrics, Hart substitutes surface for substance, revealing that, given the assignment 'this is for the boy and girl to sing,' he was at a loss to define, explore, or plumb heterosexual love or, indeed, any enduring love beyond the lustful and bitter" (Smart 185). The lyrics may include both homosexual and heterosexual desire, but this material seems harmless today. In 1938, however, the show aroused considerable attention from the reviewers, who focused on the naughty lyrics, although they clearly consider them heterosexual.

Critic after critic points to the bawdiness of the show. Burns Mantle remarked on the "lyrics that are coarse, but cute," while Louis Kronenberger commented that it featured "brash, bawdy, witty lyrics." As Brooks Atkinson pointed out in his review in the *New York Times*: "mistaken identity results in ribald complications that suffuse this column in rosy blushes of shame. Some one will have to call out the fire department to dampen down the classical ardors of this hilarious tale . . . Let us pass over their bawdries with decorous reserve, pausing only to remark that they are vastly enjoyable . . ." The review in *Life* magazine, headlined as "Old Shakespearean Comedy Comes to Broadway as Ribald Musical," praised it as a "fantastically funny and bawdy show." The reviews are quite clear: the musical is coarse, brash, bawdy, and ribald, producing blushes of shame.

But by using Shakespeare's play, the creative team knew that their bawdiness was sanctioned by Shakespeare's reputation. For how could anyone object to jokes about adultery, prostitutes, or near incest when they came from the high cultural institution of Shakespeare? Moreover, the show offered the respectable Shakespeare with enjoyable songs, dances, and gags, sugar-coating the cultural. The reviewers often comment on how the musical comedy improves on Shakespeare. Richard Watts, Jr., remarks, "If you have been wondering all these years just what was wrong with *The Comedy of Errors*, it is now possible to tell you. It has been waiting for a score by Rodgers and Hart and direction by George Abbott." Robert Benchley notes the show's Shakespearean connection with the comment that "its surroundings happen to be fairly reeking with class," and Joseph Wood Krutch points to the way that the show "neatly combines a certain contemporary flavor with an unimpeachable appropriateness." (An example of this combination might be the notable Balanchine number for a ballerina *en pointe* and two tap dancers.) Finally, Stark Young in the *New Republic* pronounced that "In general, the whole production seemed to have gusto and a certain freshness along the ancient classic line . . . [the] production is closer to the classic than the Elizabethan tradition could have been." The reviews combine a self-congratulatory recognition of the Shakespearean elements, with a gleeful pleasure in the way that Shakespeare has been erased and the story spiced up.

The production's creators wanted to write a successful book musical, a commercial production with lively songs, dancing, and comedy. They knew that they had to compete with the annuals such as George White's *Scandals*, the Earl Carroll *Vanities*, and the Ziegfield *Follies*; American popular songwriters included such giants as Cole Porter and Irving Berlin, and musicals had attained a height of respectability with the 1935 production of *Porgy and Bess* or the 1931 Pulitzer for drama awarded to the Gershwins' *Of Thee I Sing*. How were they to compete? What they did was straightforward: they included sexual situations and jokes, which would not have otherwise been acceptable, and made the claim that this material was Shakespearean. A similar strategy of using a culturally respectable figure as a cover may lie behind two more successful productions in the 1939 season: *The Hot Mikado* and *The Swing Mikado*. Furthermore, Rodgers and Hart, having pushed the boundaries of convention in *The Boys from Syracuse*, went on to *Pal Joey* (1940), a show that was critically attacked for its vulgarity because of its sexual frankness.

Alan Sinfield discusses the way that such playwrights as Stoppard, Marowitz, Wesker, and Bond "have sought to intervene in the processes of cultural production – in collusion with or defiance of all this work to sustain Shakespeare – by writing new plays manifestly related to Shakespearean texts".[6] When the process of intervention occurs in New York in 1938, however, that dichotomy of collusion or defiance fails as a critical model. In producing *The Boys from Syracuse*, Rodgers and Hart clearly want neither to collude with nor to defy the cultural process that maintains Shakespeare as the centerpiece of English literary culture. Instead, they want to borrow his authority, both to mock it lightly and to use it as a cover for their actual goal: writing a commercially successful musical comedy. Were their aim simply mockery, a wholesale deflation, they would have followed the invariable tactic of the revue burlesque and chosen a tragedy or history to work with. If they wanted to make serious use of the Shakespearean text, they would have used more of it (as the Flying Karamazov Brothers did in their 1987 Lincoln Center production of *The Comedy of Errors*, for example). Rodgers and Hart neither endorse nor reject. Shakespeare exists as an excuse, and nothing else. The strategies for using Shakespeare in cultural projects shift in the world of musical theatre, a world more clearly aligned with popular culture (and the variety stage) than with elite culture and the legit. Less is at stake when a musical comedy invokes Shakespeare. The production team feels little "anxiety of influence," since that yearning to recombine the legit and variety stages had passed in Foy's youth, nor is there much desire for the reforming mockery of social satire (or even the burlesques so popular in the nineteenth century). By the 1930s, Shakespeare's figure appears as an anomaly in musical theatre, but an anomaly sanctioned by past traditions. In twentieth-century popular culture, Shakespeare occupies a place not unlike that he held in the colonial years, when his plays could be produced as "moral lectures" to get around the anti-theatrical laws. Thus, Shakespeare is an agent for license, allowing a show to consider any topic and serving as a convenient plot device to resolve any tangle. But there were limits on the kind of Shakespearean influence that American popular culture could absorb. A second Shakespeare musical was a flop the following year.

The 7 Lively Arts (1924, 1957) is one of the earliest attempts to describe what is important about American popular arts. Its author, Gilbert Seldes, proposed an Academy of the Popular, maintaining

> That Al Jolson is more interesting to the intelligent mind than John Barrymore and Fanny Brice than Ethel;
> That Ring Lardner and Mr Dooley in their best work are more entertaining and more important than James Branch Cabell and Joseph Hergesheimer in their best;
> That the daily comic strip of George Herriman (*Krazy Kat*) is easily the most amusing and fantastic and satisfactory work of art produced in America to-day;
> That Florenz Ziegfeld is a better producer than David Belasco;
> That one film by Mack Sennett or Charlie Chaplin is worth the entire *œuvre* of Cecil de Mille;
> That *Alexander's Ragtime Band* and *I Love a Piano* are musically and emotionally sounder pieces of work than *Indian Love Lyrics* and *The Rosary*;

That the circus can be and often is more artistic than the Metropolitan Opera
House in New York;

That Irene Castle is worth all the pseudo-classic dancing ever seen on the
American stage; and

That the civic masque is not perceptibly superior to the Elks' Parade in Atlantic
City.[7]

Throughout his book, Seldes stresses the vitality of popular art in the 1920s,
as well as its originality and grace. His approach is not anti-intellectual (as
would so often be the case in later criticism of American culture), for he
makes it plain, especially in his concluding chapter about Picasso, that he
values what he calls variously the "high," "fine," and "great" arts, detest-
ing only what he calls "bogus art." The influence of *The 7 Lively Arts* was
substantial. It continued to sell steadily, if never sensationally. In Seldes'
obituary the *New York Times* identified him as "one of the earliest and most
influential writers on the popular arts in America," remarking that this reputation was "built" in part upon *The 7 Lively Arts*, which received prominent
attention (30 September 1970). In 1996, Michael Kammen reiterated that
title by calling his biography of Seldes *The Lively Arts: Gilbert Seldes and the
Transformation of Cultural Criticism in the United States*. What interests me
is that while Seldes mentions such "high culture" writers as Joseph Conrad,
Gabriele D'Annuzio, Charles Dickens, Euripides, John Gay, Henry James,
James Joyce, George Bernard Shaw, he never mentions Shakespeare's name
at all. Seldes may argue that a popular writer can also be an artist – even
a great, high, or fine artist – but Shakespeare, who would seem to provide
an excellent instance, is erased. This absence is particularly odd, given that
in 1939, fifteen years later, Seldes collaborated with Erik Charell to write
the book for a musical comedy version of *A Midsummer Night's Dream*,
entitled *Swingin' the Dream*.

Erik Charell was the man with the idea, according to an article in the *New
York Times* shortly before the show opened (26 November 1939). He was
known in New York for an earlier Broadway musical that he had directed
and produced, *The White Horse Inn*. Moreover, he had enjoyed great success
with an early film, *Congress Dances* (1931), which featured Conrad Veidt as
Metternich in a musical based on the 1815 Congress of Vienna. Charell left
Germany after complaints that he had used too many Jewish performers in
his work, immigrating to America. Seldes had also had stage success with
a modernized version of *Lysistrata* in 1931, and he had produced a radio
adaptation of *The Taming of the Shrew*, so evidently while Charell provided
the idea, Seldes provided the language.

Charell's earlier show had been staged in the Center Theatre, a huge space in Rockefeller Center. As the 1939 *New York Times* article points out: "Since its dedication in 1932, the Center Theatre has housed four ornate and baroque spectacles: 'The Great Waltz,' 'White Horse Inn,' 'Virginia' and 'The American Way.' None of them, can we believe the ledgers, has made money while resident there." The space seated close to four thousand and was eventually turned over to an exclusive repertoire of grand opera and ice spectacles in later years, according to the Internet Broadway Data Base. Its daunting reputation might have given Charell pause, but instead it encouraged him to lower the price of tickets to two dollars so that more swing music fans could attend. He also tried to take advantage of the size with special features for amplification as well as entertainment. Special effects were plentiful, although not designed by Walt Disney, as is sometimes stated. According to one account,

The huge Center Theatre's stage was exploited for various trick and interesting effects, with sets and costumes modelled after Walt Disney's cartoons. Titania made an entrance in a World's Fair "World of Tomorrow" electric wheelchair, a Murphy bed emerged from a tree in the forest; microphones (to help audibility in the cavernous playhouse) sprang up in the shape of caterpillars and snails; and there was a noteworthy scene of plantation life on the lawn of the governor's . . . mansion, with a cast of jitter-bugging celebrants.[8]

Clearly Seldes and Charell had sought "lively art" in the production, and the artists they recruited were lively as well.

It must have been an extraordinary production. Unfortunately, no script for the show survives, and information about its music is often confusing.[9] Opening 29 November 1939, *Swingin' the Dream* closed on 9 December, in less than two weeks. Yet the show offered magnificent performers and gave every promise of being a success. The first time one hears about this show, the usual reaction is a disbelief and surprise. (Certainly, that was my first reaction, and over the years I've introduced a number of people to its history, invariably with that response.) Louis Armstrong, Benny Goodman, and Bud Freeman played. Dorothy Maguire, Butterfly McQueen, and Jackie "Moms" Mabley clowned. Agnes DeMille choreographed the show, which featured specialty dances by the well-known tap dancer Bill Bailey, as well as jitterbugging by the Lindy Hoppers. Let me look at each of these elements in turn – the book, the music, the dancers, and the production as a whole – before discussing its failure. (See figure 15.)

Because no complete script survives, the book is something of a mystery. The reviews say next to nothing about the plot, focusing instead on

15 ©Al Hirschfeld. Drawing of the cast of *Swingin' the Dream*. At the center,
Louis Armstrong with his horn, while Benny Goodman and his clarinet are on the
bottom left. To the right of Armstrong is Butterfly McQueen as Puck, while
Maxine Sullivan is below him.

individual turns. Yet one can speculate, based upon what little the newspaper accounts do say, the materials (such as the program) found in collections like the Billy Rose Theatre Collection at the New York Public
Library, performer memoirs, and a three-page excerpt that Alan Corrigan
has found. While Abbott had largely scrapped Shakespeare's language in his
book for *The Boys from Syracuse*, *Swingin' the Dream* seems to have retained
Shakespeare's language and interpolated big production numbers according to the reviewers. It mixed elements of a swing revue and a reduced
legitimate play.

The show is set around 1890. In the first act, at the Governor's summer residence in a mansion in New Orleans, Governor Theodore (Joseph
Holland) is about to marry Polly (Ruth Ford). Everyone celebrates in an
opening number, "Spring Song," which was one of van Heusen's swing
adaptations of Mendelssohn's familiar piano piece.[10] The Governor's cousin
Egbert (George LeSoir) has a daughter Gloria (Eleanor Lynn) who loves
Alexander (Boyd Crawford), the second secretary to the Governor, even

though Egbert wants her to marry Cornelius (Thomas Coley), the first secretary who is loved by a cousin, Helena. Interspersed with these events, so
clearly drawn from Shakespeare, are the comic scenes and swing numbers
that focus on African-American characters. The production used a number
of specialty singers and dancers, like the Deep River Boys, a gospel group, or
Bill Bailey, who played Cupid. The mechanicals were Bottom the fireman
(Louis Armstrong), Quince the midwife (Jackie "Moms" Mabley), Flute
the iceman (Oscar Polk), Snout the steeplejack (Troy Brown), Starveling
the tailor (Nicodemus), and Snug the cleaner (Gerald de la Fontaine).

In the first scene of Act Two, the characters enter the Voodoo Wood,
where the fairies live. Again, the young lovers' action was largely spoken,
unlike the fairies and mechanicals who sang and danced. The act begins as
Titania's pixies (the Dandridge Sisters) and Jitterbugs (the Lindy Hoppers)
celebrate with "Swingin' the Dream," another van Heusen adaptation of
Mendelssohn. One of the Lindy Hoppers, Norma Miller, recalled their
appearance in

the second act which opened with Goodman playing a number. The applause
seemed to go on forever. Maxine Sullivan was Titania, and we were her little
animals in the forest . . . Maxine had a microphone, since her voice was very soft
and would have been lost without one; they built the mike to look like a snake
coming out of the stage. The Deep River Boys were the giant trees that stood in
the forest. [The dancers' manager] Whitey had one group of us in the trees and
another suspended over the stage. (Miller 146)

Miller describes another number as "a great Bee's number with the choir
singing a cappella with a swinging rhythmic beat." At the end of the scene,
the Jitterbugs danced to Count Basie's "Jumpin' at the Woodside," Titania
reprised "Swingin' a Dream" with the Deep River Boys, and the Benny
Goodman sextet performed "Pick a Rib." Shakespeare's plot and characters
hardly seem needed. The second scene of the second act returned to the
Governor's summer mansion where the working folks perform their opera
"Pyramus and Thisbe," the only part of the show that has survived.

Before discussing the opera, let me note that accounts of the show's music
are as confusing as its book. Charell had approached Alec Wilder about
doing the music, but then brought in Jimmy van Heusen. As Wilder wrote
about van Heusen many years later, "I was inclined, without having more
than met him, to dislike him at this point [in 1939], since I had written an
entire score for this show and had to take it back due to the duplicitous
character of the producer."[11] Goodman did much of the arranging, and
Eddie de Lange wrote the lyrics – save for "Love's a Riddle," which was by

Alex Wilder. One finds the occasional claim that Jimmy van Heusen created all the music, basing all his compositions on Mendelssohn's music for *A Midsummer Night's Dream*, but I cannot find support for that. According to Ross Firestone, van Heusen wrote only half a dozen songs, one of which, "Darn that Dream," has become a standard.[12] Bordman's *Chronicle* credits van Heusen with slightly more of the music: van Heusen and Goodman did "Spring Song," Alec Wilder and van Heusen did "Love's a Riddle," while "Peace Brother," "There's Gotta Be a Wedding," "Moonland," "Comedy Dance," "Dream Dance," and "Darn that Dream" are all by van Heusen. These pieces were performed by the show's orchestra, led by Don Voorhees, while the Benny Goodman Sextet and Bud Freeman's Summa Cum Laude band (in gazebos on opposite sides of the stage) played pieces from their repertoire. According to Freeman, "The two bands played for fifteen minutes before the curtain went up," and then they came in from time to time during the show's original numbers and certainly carried the bulk of the music in the final scene.[13] (If this list of musicians sounds like a particularly rich mix, especially with the addition of Louis Armstrong, it is worth noting that the show's rehearsal pianist was no other than James P. Johnson, father of stride piano and composer of "Charleston," "Carolina Shout," and *Harlem Symphony*.)

The three surviving pages are of the Pyramus and Thisbe scene, and they suggest that the show was a much-condensed and breezy version of the Shakespearean text, supplemented by lots of well-known swing numbers. Thus all of Moonshine's blank-verse lines are condensed to a four-stress couplet:

> This lantern should be the moon that you see,
> And I the man in the moon seem to be.

In the margin next to the speech is written "CHRISTOPHER COLUMBUS," suggesting that the lines were sung to that music, although the bands may have played the song during or after the moment. The previous meeting of Pyramus and Thisbe at the wall suggests that the former is the case. In the margin is the note "CAN'T GIVE YOU ANYTHING BUT LOVE," while Pyramus' and Thisbe's lines are revised to "O kiss me thru the hole of this vile wall, Baby" and "I kiss the wall's hole, not your lips at all, Baby." Clearly the Shakespearean text has been reset to the music for the song. The opera is a straightforward travesty of the Pyramus and Thisbe tale, just as in Shakespeare's original, although it makes its jokes musically rather than poetically. While some songs were used because they fit with lyrics, others were intended as purely instrumental and it seems likely those songs might vary. Following the listing in the show's program, Bordman lists 22 titles, while the surviving script lists 20, but the two lists have only 12 titles in common. To judge from the opera script, then, the musicians could improvise during the show, which makes perfect sense.

The ability to improvise, to vary a set arrangement or play list to take advantage of a player's strengths or ideas at a particular moment, is one of the appeals of swing. Today, for example, Charlie Christian is regarded as important because he helped introduce the electric guitar. But Benny Goodman hired him, according to producer John Hammond, not because of his work on the electric guitar, but because Christian improvised beautifully with Goodman's band on a song he did not know.[14] Such improvisation usually requires that the musicians know each other well, which was certainly the case with both Bud Freeman's and Benny Goodman's bands in *Swingin' the Dream*. Freeman's Summa Cum Laude band had spent months playing together at various clubs. In his memoir, he mentions that their previous job, at Nick Condon's club, had run six or seven weeks (49), before they were recruited to the show, while the magazine, *Jazz Information*, included an item in its December 1939 issue that "Bud Freeman and the Summa Cum Laude Orchestra, late of Nick's and 'Swingin' The Dream,' open Wednesday, (December 10) at the Seven Eleven Bar on 55th Street, east of Fifth Avenue, New York." Benny Goodman's Sextet, the pick of his regular band, also performed together frequently, given the popularity of his band and the regular bookings on radio programs. In fact, at the same time that *Swingin' the Dream* was running, the Benny Goodman band continued to do radio shows and on 22 November, three days after the opening, the Sextet did a long recording session for Columbia Records (the "red label" disks).[15]

Abrupt changes could affect other aspects of the production as well. The choreographer announced for the show was Eugene Loring, but he left the show, just as Alec Wilder had. The producers then hired a largely untried young choreographer, Agnes DeMille, who was giving dance and exercise lessons at the 92nd Street Y, working on occasion as a dancer, and trying to introduce African-American dancers to the world of modern dance.[16] DeMille does not really discuss her experience, but the reviewers generally praised the dancing. To be sure, she may have simply carried out some version of Loring's plans, although we cannot know how much work he had done. One of her biographers refers to her work as "doctoring another choreographer's dances for a show" (Easton 157). Furthermore, some dancers would have gone their own way. Bill Bailey, who played Cupid, was very well known as a tap dancer and would have taken care of his own principal numbers. Similarly the Lindy Hoppers, who worked for Herbert White at the Savoy ballroom and had also performed at the New York World's Fair, were well known for their acrobatic style. White received a production credit, and as Miller reports, "He had his own private dressing room and was consulted on all production matters; he was Mr. Big, and indeed he acted the part."[17] Since Miller says nothing about DeMille, it seems likely that DeMille had little to do with the Lindy Hoppers' numbers. There is a further anecdote, however, that suggests the potential power of the dances in *Swingin' the Dream*. In 1986 Bud Freeman told Leonard Feather:

There was one number for which everyone in the show wore anklets, a sort of African tribal thing with bare feet and the anklets ringing. When Voorhees's orchestra played, they drowned out this gentle sound; but on the band's night off, Benny's sextet accompanied the number. Everyone heard this unique effect of the bare feet and anklets, and there was a three-minute standing ovation. If they'd kept it that way, it could have made the show.

The scene that Freeman describes undoubtedly fell in the second act voodoo wood scene, and his description underscores the way in which the show seems to have been improvised from night to night. The choreography that he describes is compelling, at least to him and – if he is correct about the three-minute standing ovation – perhaps to all. But its main effect is drowned out by the orchestra, which may suggest a choreographer who lacked experience or authority. Freeman's reminiscence clarifies the way that the show's song and dance numbers referenced race.

In his own memoir, Freeman wrote that Charell "had just about the finest talent you could get. Just about everyone in the show became world-renowned. He had Louis Armstrong, Nicodemus, Troy Brown, Oscar Polk, Butterfly McQueen, Bill Bailey, Dorothy Maguire, and Maxine Sullivan. If Charell had known the greatness of the black people he could have had a revue that would still be running" (Freeman 49). The regard Freeman shows for the other performers was not misplaced. Like the production staff, the performers had outstanding reputations. Among the principals, Louis Armstrong and Maxine Sullivan were important in the world of music. Even some singers in the ensemble became known.[18] Muriel Rahn, for example, went on to become a prominent singer, doing concerts for the Armed Forces in World War II and singing the lead in the original production of *Carmen Jones* (1943). Like Rahn, Warren Coleman sang in the ensemble but soon went on to play the villain Crown in the original production of *Porgy and Bess* (1942) and John Kumalo in *Lost in the Stars*

(1949). Another member of the ensemble was Kelsey Pharr, who was still singing professionally in 1952 when he played a male saint in a revival of the Virgil Thompson and Gertrude Stein *Four Saints in Three Acts*.

Bill Bailey (brother to Pearl Bailey) and the Lindy Hoppers are important to the world of dance. But others in the cast were also significant actors. Dorothy Dandridge, as one of the Dandridge Sisters, would go on to considerable success as a leading lady in films, as would Dorothy McGuire.[19] Butterfly McQueen was a notable character actress, whose most famous role is probably Prissie in *Gone with the Wind*. Juan Hernandez, who played Oberon, also performed under the name Juano Hernandez. In addition to work on the New York stage in plays like *Strange Fruit* (1945), he had a career as a supporting player in Hollywood.

The actors who played the working-class characters were quite successful. Like McQueen, Oscar Polk also had a role in *Gone with the Wind*, playing Pork, the O'Hara's house servant, as well as roles in other films. Another performer who moved from the east to the west coast was Nick Stewart, whose performance name was Nicodemus (presumably for the African-American town in Kansas). Although Nicodemus was a clown, afraid of ghosts, Stewart was himself an ambitious and committed artist. After his move to Los Angeles, he played Lightnin' on the television series *Amos 'n' Andy*, using the money he earned to open the Ebony Showcase Theatre in Los Angeles, which produced plays and welcomed African-American performers for over thirty years. Like Polk and Stewart, Troy Brown went west and made a number of films before his death in 1944 (most notably, perhaps, *Nothing Sacred*). Alberta Perkins, who was Peaceful Pearl, took other stage roles, including one in the important 1944 production of *Anna Lucasta*, but also had a career in movies with exclusively African-American casts. Finally, Moms Mabley became a very successful comedienne, performing on the Chitlin' Circuit until the 1960s and in more national venues in the 1970s. Her biographer speculates that her work in the closing scene of *Swingin' the Dream* "provided [her] with an idea that would become standard fare in her routine: satirizing the opera" (46).

The show was preceded with talk about how important it would be. Donald Bogle notes, "During rehearsals, word spread among jazz aficionados and fans that *Swingin' the Dream* was a progressive production that made excellent use of its often underemployed Negro talents" (72). According to a story in the African-American newspaper, the Pittsburgh *Courier*, Louis Armstrong had received simultaneous offers to play in a well-known club, to take the lead in a production of *Young Man with a Horn*, and to play Bottom in *Swingin' the Dream* (31 October 1939, 20): Armstrong thought that *Swingin' the Dream* was the most promising (4 November 1939, 20). Another newspaper, the Washington, D.C. *Afro-American* featured a regular column written by Lionel Hampton, who played vibes in Goodman's sextet. He, too, wrote with excitement about the upcoming show and his high hopes for it (4 November 1939, 20). He also commented that in performing the title number, he realized the quality of the Goodman Sextet: "It's in 'Swingin' the Dream' that the sextette really puts over to you how much wider a scope and opportunity for each man for better playing we now have" (2 December 1939, 24).

If prominent names and promising talk were all that a play needed to succeed, *Swingin' the Dream* would have had a long and happy run. It failed. The production closed December 9, in less than two weeks. The *New York Times* reported that "The salary list of the departed 'Swingin' the Dream' came to $6,136 per week, and that exclusive of whatever Benny Goodman charged. It was observed last week that on the Thursday night before closing, there were standees all over the house, but only $596 in the till. On Saturday night so many tickets were given away you couldn't have bought one if you wished" (17 December 1939, 124). The *Afro-American* reported that the total loss was over $80,000 (23 December 1939), while the *New York Times* said the total lost was over $100,000 (10 December 1939).

Why did the play fail? It is difficult to tell, particularly since the script has disappeared. Richard Watts, Jr., in the *New York Herald Tribune* was dissatisfied with *Swingin' the Dream*, but the cause of his dissatisfaction is not altogether clear. He complained that the show was "just a series of good night-club turns, tossed rather carelessly together and brought to no good end" (Leiter 502). Yet two other critics complained that the show made inadequate use of its popular performers. In the *Post*, John Mason Brown praised the first hour:

For that length of time it is charming. It has great vigor and originality . . . It is at its best and a delightful best that is, when Shakespeare is being pushed offstage by its actors and musicians. It is at its happiest when he is being irreverently dealt with . . . Unfortunately in their second act they turn "Bardolators" at least to the extent of following in too great detail the tedious story of the lovers. When they do this, they may please the school marms, but they silence Mr. Goodman and Mr. Armstrong for too long a while, and they prevent the dancers so admirably directed by Miss de Mille and Mr. White from having their rhythmic say. All of which is something of a major pity. (Hill 115–16)

The fullest review was that of Brooks Atkinson in the *New York Times*. He began, "As between Shakespeare and Goodman, Goodman wins." Like Brown, Atkinson felt that Shakespeare was too dominant in the show:

It would have been better to throw Shakespeare out the window. The pedestrian jest cracked in his name merely stands in the way of a lively raree-show. Every now and then a flare of dancing breaks through the professorial patter, and the Benny Goodman boys perform brilliantly on a piece of music. But the going is heavy through long stretches of the evening. "The Boys from Syracuse" did better by forgetting Shakespeare altogether.

Atkinson recognizes the potential riches of the production, commenting on "the exuberant Armstrong," the "particularly gorgeous" Maxine Sullivan, and the "piping-voiced" Butterfly McQueen, "whose travesty is genuinely comic." He also praises "Bill Bailey who can dance his way in and out of almost any score, the indestructible Rhythmettes, who will not live much longer if they keep prancing at that speed . . ." Yet he complained that the production failed to use its performers effectively. Armstrong always carried his trumpet, but rarely got to use it. Sullivan "sings a number of songs in her cool, limpid style, [yet] none of the music uses her voice with the versatility she has at her command." Most telling is his comment that the play pays "laboriously frisky respects to Shakespeare."

One obvious problem was the failure to use the production staff and performers effectively. There is a bitterness to Freeman's comment that "If Charell had known the greatness of the black people he could have had a revue that would still be running." If Brown and Atkinson are correct, the production insisted on retaining unneeded Shakespearean passages instead of relying on (or allowing) popular performers to entertain. Here I would turn once again to that curious erasure of Shakespeare from *The 7 Lively Arts* and speculate that Seldes felt, perhaps, too much respect for Shakespeare and was diffident about admitting the dramatist to the popular realm. In his 1957 revision, Seldes paused to reconsider his 1924 discussion about serious drama, which mentions *Othello*, and remarks: "I did my case little good by going off into a denunciation of theatrical realism and equating that style with the intellectual drama as a whole . . . There was a lot of pretentiousness going on at the time and I was against it. But I may have been overawed by the critical acclaim which the serious drama was getting, so I pulled my punches" (1957: 269–70). In the entire revision of Seldes' book, he gives no hint that he had himself taken part in a production joining the "high" and the "lively" arts. Might it be that the critic who articulated the vigor of America's popular arts, especially the power of American entertainers, was in fact too intimidated by Shakespeare to allow exciting performers to do their jobs effectively? Or did more of the responsibility fall on Charell's shoulders, as Freeman seems to suggest? (If Charell did dismiss Loring or

Wilder unfairly, that conduct might also have contributed to the show's failure.)

If Shakespeare serves as beard, a cover for the unconventional in Broadway musicals, the situation becomes more complex. When one asks what was unconventional, what element in the show required a beard, then the answer might be the way the show played with both class and race, largely through its use of swing music. As Lewis Erenberg has suggested, swing music was strongly affiliated with progressive social values in the 1930s: "Many music critics, writing in new jazz magazines, praised swing as a national art form created by blacks and adopted by a pluralistic society ... Together, attackers and defenders viewed swing as the center of a national youth culture that transcended class, ethnicity, and race."[20] He describes, for example, a concert at Carnegie Hall in January 1938, about two years before the show opened. Benny Goodman and his orchestra played with several of Duke Ellington's and Count Basie's soloists in a performance that was, as one critic proclaimed, a "howling success." Unlike Paul Whiteman, who had displayed caution by using only white musicians in his famous Aeolian Hall jazz concert the decade before, Goodman included African-American composers and performers and refused to moderate the elements in his music that might shock those unfamiliar with popular music. Instead, the orchestra made full use of improvisation, of performers of all races, and of music that ranged from Ellington's "Blue Reverie" to Sholem Secund's "Bei Mir Bist Du Schoen." Moreover, immediately after the concert, most of the musicians and much of the audience raced across town to Harlem to hear a battle of the bands between the Count Basie and Chick Webb Orchestras. Here was the quintessential swing event, one that received praise for its liveliness, originality, and openness, praise that *Swingin' the Dream* never attained.

The show *Swingin' the Dream* used swing music and jitterbugging. Like *The Boys from Syracuse*, the success of *The Hot Mikado* and *The Swing Mikado*, both of which opened in March 1939, had suggested that incorporating swing and Shakespeare was as promising as swinging Gilbert and Sullivan had been. The impulse to synthesize high and low culture was in keeping with the progressivism associated with swing music during the 1930s, when Goodman's group featured white and black performers, when integrated clubs and concerts embraced music by a wide range of musicians. The response of a critic like Watts, however, may suggest that what audiences wanted was separation, that the effective theatrical material was the popular singing and dancing, while the "high culture" Shakespearean material was dull, unsuccessful. There are various ways to understand this response. The reviews often mention race, and the frequent discussion of swing may be a way of referencing class, as well as a reflection of 1930s racial attitudes. For example, Atkinson, who is not notably racist, refers to "Negro jitterbugs" and "dark-skinned steppers"; other reviewers wrote in similar terms. But the way in which the reviewers discuss the African-American performers is clearly more congruent with the tradition of ethnic jokes in variety shows and burlesques than with the social values that Erenberg argues epitomized the world of swing and its proponents. Thus, the critical dislike of the show may reflect social discomfort at the mingling of races or of classes. But it may equally suggest that the popular music and dance in the working-class or the fairy scenes were superior to the more Shakespearean statehouse and lover scenes. After all, the performers who went on to more distinguished careers are principally those in the swing/jitterbug ranks. Finally, there may be factors governing the response that today make no sense.[21] The venue of the Centre Theatre certainly had some effect, for example, and nothing suggests its effect was good.

Part of the pleasure in a show like *Boys from Syracuse* was that it got away with going past accepted stage conventions by claiming to be Shakespearean, even though it wasn't. Thus *Boys from Syracuse* could make sexual jokes that pushed past the conventions of the time because it simultaneously was and was not a Shakespearean work. A similar process is at work in a show like *Hot Mikado*, which is made funny because it both is and isn't by Gilbert and Sullivan. Gilbert and Sullivan operettas are associated with the D'Oyly Carte Company performers who speak and sing nineteenth-century language with great precision; *Hot Mikado* featured African-American performers, who spoke and sang Gilbert's language to twentieth-century swing versions of Sullivan's melodies. Clearly the pleasure that the audience was intended to receive from *Swingin' the Dream* involved their recognition that performers (including African-Americans and Jews) who epitomized what Seldes had named the lively arts were performing a version of Shakespeare, the epitome of high culture. The problem the reviewers identified was too much Shakespeare and not enough liveliness. An additional problem, I suspect, is that audiences were unable to recognize the double claims of the show – both for the beauty of Shakespeare's play and for the vigor and pleasure of swing. The show used the lively arts, but not enough; it threw away the play text, but only occasionally; it wavered. The audience was not invited to wink at what the play was getting away with or to collaborate in its mischievous use of Shakespeare that was not-Shakespeare. In this case, I would speculate, swing was being used as the beard for Shakespeare.

Errol Hill writes generously of *Swingin' the Dream* in his book, *Shakespeare in Sable*, suggesting that it was one of a number of projects in the 1930s that "proved to be a turning point in the relationship of Afro-Americans to Shakespeare's plays" (118). Until these 1930s productions, he argues, "Black folk attending his plays did so as much out of duty to their cultural uplift as in recognition of the fact that Afro-Americans were as talented as Caucasians and could achieve success in the highest form of dramatic production" (118). In addition to *Swingin' the Dream*, Hill mentions a number of productions sponsored by the Federal Theatre Project, which made a deliberate effort to appeal and respond to "a multi-cultural America" and to "help dispel racial bigotry" (118). Unfortunately the House Committee on Un-American Activity found such an agenda subversive and ended the Federal Theatre Project in 1939.

Whether *Swingin' the Dream* was a tricked-up minstrel show or a subversive challenge to racism probably depends on whether one regards Shakespeare as an integral part of African-American theatre (as a work *like The African Company Performs Richard III* suggests) or as separate from African-American culture and embodying white America's fundamental racism (as burlesques of *Othello*, common in variety theatre, suggest). In any case, the show's failure moots the question. The next musical version of Shakespeare to use "race" was *West Side Story* (1957) with its Puerto Rican Capulets; when Joseph Papp used African-American performers in the musical version of *Two Gentlemen of Verona* (1971), the show aroused little controversy. More recently, *Play On!* with its evocation of the Harlem Renaissance suggests a nostalgic reconstruction of history, and I shall discuss it in a separate chapter.

CHAPTER 9

Brush up your Shakespeare

Once the precedent for using Shakespeare had been established, nothing happened for a decade. Then a successful Shakespeare musical opened, to be followed in another nine years by another. These two shows, *Kiss Me, Kate* and *West Side Story*, drew on Shakespeare with enormous success. In any analysis of Broadway musicals these two shows are invariably discussed as central achievements, both in terms of the individual songwriters (Cole Porter, Stephen Sondheim, and Leonard Bernstein) and in terms of the musical-comedy form.

Kiss Me, Kate opened 30 December 1948, with songs by Cole Porter, a book by Sam and Bella Spewack, choreography by Hanya Holm, and direction by John C. Wilson. It starred Alfred Drake and Patricia Morison. This was the first musical comedy to win the Tony for Best Play. Indeed, the *Journal-American* review was headlined, "A Musical Comedy That Has Everything." The next morning Brooks Atkinson wrote in the *New York Times*:

Without losing his sense of humor, [Porter] has written a remarkably melodious score with an occasional suggestion of Puccini, who was a good composer, too. Mr. Porter has always enjoyed the luxury of rowdy tunes, and he has scribbled a few for the current festival – "Another Op'nin', Another Show," "We Open in Venice," "Too Darn Hot," and "Brush Up Your Shakespeare," which is fresh out of the honky-tonks. All his lyrics are literate, and as usual some of them would shock the editorial staff of The Police Gazette.

But the interesting thing about the new score is the enthusiasm Mr. Porter has for romantic melodies indigenous to the soft climate of the Mediterranean. Although "Wunderbar" is probably a little north of the Mediterranean Sea, the warm breezes flow through it; and "So In Love Am I" has a very florid temperature, indeed.

Today this show is regarded as one of the great musical comedies of the American stage, a milestone production from the Golden Age of Broadway. At the time, however, people expected it to be a flop.

Cole Porter had begun writing successful Broadway musicals in the 1920s. During his career, he would compose some twenty shows. *Paris* in 1928 was his first hit, but the following year he had two: *Fifty Million Frenchmen* and *Wake Up and Dream*. Through the Depression years, his string of successes continued with *Gay Divorcee* (1932), *Nymph Errant* (1933), *Anything Goes* (1934), *DuBarry Was a Lady* (1939), and *Panama Hattie* (1940). Yet in the 1940s nothing that he wrote seemed to work. Porter went from being the songwriter who epitomized sophistication on the New York stage to one who was out of style and unsuccessful.[1]

Moreover, the production team was at odds. Bella and Sam Spewack were having marital problems and had separated; although both of them would work on the book, she did the bulk of the work, and their collaboration was difficult. Later, there would be an extended dispute with the co-producer, Arnold Saint Subber, over the extent of his contribution to the show's creation. According to Saint Subber, the original idea for the show was his. He had watched Alfred Lunt and his wife Lynn Fontaine in a 1935 production of *The Taming of the Shrew* and marveled as they made love on stage, exited, and immediately began quarreling. In various accounts, he would say that he thought then of a musical comedy about a couple who played Petruchio and Katherina on stage and quarreled off. Sometimes the claim is that he took the idea to the Spewacks and asked them to write the book, while sometimes it is that he first approached Thornton Wilder and then turned to the separated Spewacks. The experience of writing the book brought the Spewacks back together, making a tidy close for the Saint Subber narrative. Though the story continues to circulate, Bella Spewack consistently and firmly denied it: while Saint Subber and Ayers may have suggested a musical based on *The Taming of the Shrew*, the idea of using parallel on-stage and off-stage action was always hers. Whoever had the idea first, it was certainly Bella Spewack's idea to enlist Cole Porter.

In the preparations for the show, the company had problems with the personnel. Casting the female lead was a particularly hard process, because she had to be a plausible movie star, a singer who had an imposing range, and an actress with enough presence to hold her own against Alfred Drake. Patricia Morison was in some ways the role that she played: she had begun her career in musicals and operetta, and then she had gone to California in 1939 and made over twenty movies in less than a decade. Even after Morison was chosen, however, Porter had second thoughts because of her relative lack of musical training. Another performer, Harold Lang, made difficulties until his part was expanded. Lang was an excellent dancer who was well known both for his work and for his reputation as a sexual athlete. Yet as Arthur Laurents points out in his memoir,

No one suspected that anyone who partied as much as Harold did and drank so much . . . could be as ambitious . . . Coolly objective about his limitations in ballet, – his body was more perfect for sex – he began howling in vacant lots to strengthen his vocal chords as he took endless lessons: in how to sing off the vocal chord, in acting, speech, tap.[2]

When Lang found out that his role had no solo song, he insisted that he had to have a number by himself. Eventually Porter gave in, quickly writing, "Bianca." Finally, Porter's health was not good, and he wrote the show while in constant pain.[3] The entire rehearsal process was beset with problems, and the common talk along Broadway was that the show would fail. Certainly, the Shuberts, skeptical of its potential and reluctant to tie up a playhouse in a prime location for a failure, booked the show into the New Century Theatre, which was inconveniently located. In the summer of 1950 the musical moved into the Shubert Theatre where it ran for another year.

Small wonder, then, that Richard Watts wrote in his *New York Post* review of *Kiss Me, Kate*, "For Mr. Porter, the new musical comedy must be a particularly gratifying success, since there had been dark rumors abroad that the eminent composer had lost some of his old-time power. There is no sign of any such decline . . ." In the *Herald-Tribune* Howard Barnes said "Porter has written the gayest music and lyrics he has in years," while John Lardner accurately claimed, "Mr. Porter . . . is by way of being the true star of the show." It was a magnificent comeback, which used the agency of Shakespeare to attain success.

Like Shakespeare's *The Taming of the Shrew*, *Kiss Me, Kate* is both framed and reflexive. In *Shrew*, the Induction sets up the story of Christopher Sly, who will watch the wooing of Katherina by Petruchio, in language that calls attention to not only the healing function of art, but also its manifest untruth. In *Kiss Me, Kate*, the outer play concerns the trouble Fred Graham is having with his new musical production of *The Taming of the Shrew*, while within the frame, the audience also sees scenes from *Shrew* that give a somewhat condensed version of Petruchio's wooing of and marriage to Katherina.

The chief problem that Fred Graham faces is his ex-wife, Lilli Vanessi, who will play Katherina to his Petruchio. Backstage at Ford's Theatre in Baltimore, Graham's sedulous attentions to Lois Lane, who will play Bianca, infuriate Vanessi, who storms off, correctly surmising that Graham is pursuing Lane to spite his ex-wife. Led by Vanessi's dresser, Hattie, the company launches into the show's first number, "Another Op'nin', Another Show," that underscores the vagaries of life in musical comedy. After the stage clears, Lane seeks out her partner, Bill Calhoun, who will play Lucentio. He has missed rehearsal, and Lane, who wants to move from variety performances to the legit, hopes to take him with her. She points out his failings in the wistful, "Why Can't You Behave?" He confesses that she is completely right. Further, he has been gambling and, short of funds, has forged Graham's name to an IOU.

In this opening, the book may suggest a parallel to the Shakespearean original, with Graham as the trickster Lord and Vanessi as his dupe, Sly, and with the metatheatricality of the show-within-the-show setting paralleling Shakespeare's play-within-a-play. Yet the musical complicates these ideas. If Graham is the trickster to Vanessi, he is also being duped by Lane, who flirts to advance both her own career plans and her lover Calhoun. And the setting in "Ford's Theatre" does not bode well for American actors, creating a heightened reflexivity. The audience watches a musical about a musical, as well as a modification of theatre history (Shakespeare as Broadway musical recalling another historical assault in a theatre).

The subsequent scenes focus on an interesting variation on musical comedy's usual drive to marriage: backstage scenes show us Vanessi and Graham in their respective dressing rooms, quarrelling in a domestic setting that recalls their formerly married state. Yet she is speaking on the telephone to Hamilton Howell, her current lover (supposedly modeled on Bernard Baruch) who has backed the show, urging him to withdraw his backing, while Graham berates her for her heartlessness. Gradually they calm down and recall an early show they did together. It was schlock, and "Wunderbar," the duet from that show that they nostalgically perform, demonstrates its quality. Complications arise when gangsters intrude on Graham to demand payment of the forged IOU. When Vanessi is given an opening-night bouquet from Graham, it moves her to confess that she is still "So in Love."

The next section moves the action on stage to the musical *Shrew*. A second opening number, "We Open in Venice," begins the action, and the songs in this section often quote from the play. For example, Petruchio sings, "I've Come to Wive It Wealthily in Padua," though Katherina insists, "I Hate Men." Petruchio woos her with "Were Thine That Special Face," a line that actually belongs to Bianca in Shakespeare's play. To this point the interior show has nicely paralleled *The Taming of the Shrew*, but once Vanessi discovers a card in the bouquet and realizes that her ex-husband actually meant to send the flowers to Lois Lane, she begins to attack Graham

16 ©Al Hirschfeld. Drawing of *Kiss Me, Kate*. Fred Graham/Petruchio (Alfred Drake) spanks Lilli Vanessi/Katherina (Patricia Morison).

on stage. Finally, Graham/Petruchio picks up Lilli/Katherina and spanks her as the curtain falls on the interior play's first act.

The musical now moves backstage again, as Vanessi vows to leave the show. When the gangsters return, Graham tells them he will pay them from the show's profits, if they can keep her in the show. On stage, the musical *Shrew* continues with the gangsters playing extras guarding Lilli/Katherina so she cannot escape. The first act of *Kiss Me, Kate* ends with the title song as Petruchio carries his new bride away.

The second act of the show moves quickly, but the opening seems digressive. In the alley behind the theatre, Graham's dresser Paul leads the number "Too Darn Hot." (Both acts of the show open with dressers, played by African-American performers, leading the number.) On stage, Petruchio considers his scheme of taming Katherina by denying her food and sleep and asks, "Where Is the Life that Late I Led?" Backstage, Vanessi prepares to flee with her lover, Howell, while Graham tries to stop her; Lanc and Calhoun quarrel and make up. Suddenly the gangsters learn that their boss has been murdered, so Vanessi leaves, and Graham admits he is still "So in Love," reprising her earlier confession. The interior play is limping along, although it brightens when the gangsters accidentally go on stage and perform, "Brush Up Your Shakespeare." The musical version of *Shrew* is about to end without a shrew, when Vanessi suddenly appears to sing the final speech, "I Am Ashamed that Women Are so Simple." Both Graham and Vanessi acknowledge their love as Petruchio ends the show with a reprise of "Kiss Me, Kate."

How one is to understand this show, or indeed any Shakespearean musical, depends inevitably on the particular aspect that catches one's attention. If judged as an entertaining musical about a man and woman in and out of love, *Kiss Me, Kate* operates in one way, but as a queer show that denies heteronormativity, it works another way, while in a third way of working the show praises marriage, yet shows wedlock as inconvenient and unnecessary. These various approaches suggest how Shakespeare's figure functions in American culture at large or in the specific context of show business. In what follows I want to argue that whatever approach one takes, Shakespeare serves metaphorically as a sort of magic ring granting wishes or as a universal solvent dissolving problems in the fiction. One might see the power that such a metaphor has within the world of the musical also having an uncanny effect on the musical's creators.

"Brush up your Shakespeare," sings a gangster who's hanging around backstage in hopes of collecting an overdue gambling debt; "Start quoting him now . . ."

> Brush up your Shakespeare,
> And the women you will wow.
> Just declaim a few lines from *Othella*,
> And they'll think you're a hell of a fella.
> If your blonde don't respond when you flatter'er,
> Tell her what Tony told Cleopatterer . . .

The number stops the show, *Kiss Me, Kate*, so completely that Cole Porter added several encore verses so that the performers could answer the audience's enthusiastic applause with fresh funny lyrics because "we realized that . . . [it] was a 'boff' number – a show stopper" (McBrien 313–14, also 116). The song encapsulates certain features of Shakespeare on Broadway.[4]

To begin with, the song makes a claim for Shakespeare's value, for high culture, for the legit stage, but puts that claim in the mouths of two lowlifes who acquired their culture during "eight years in the prison library in

Atlanta" and who think him of value because invoking his name permits sexual success. Yet as Lawson-Peebles notes, "These are odd crooks. One faints at the mention of cattle-branding; the other has pretensions to be a tap-dancer" (104). In other words, the song relies upon the audience's perception of a split in culture, a division between high and low, elite and popular. Yet even as it relies on that split, it unsplits culture: the gangsters have spent eight years in a library, the novelty song is by a composer who had had a classical education followed by European musical training. Even the basis of that split – the perception that Shakespeare is worthy and hence of value – is simultaneously undermined and underscored by the displacement of his worth from the respectable (marker of education) to the naughty (seduction). The song slides back and forth because its jokes make it function now as a marker of low and now as a marker of high culture: *we* get its jokes because we know about low and high. Even the song's place in the musical's plot works in this slippery way: the gangsters threaten to stop the show by injuring the male lead; they also take part in the production to stay near him; and they ultimately become the means by which he is able to maintain the production and retain his leading lady: they are enemies to, participants in, and saviors of the Shakespearean play. Finally, they have the power to stop and save the show because, as their show-stopping number demonstrates, in a musical Shakespeare is and isn't Shakespeare: he's naughty, knotty, not-He.

The song uses what Joseph Swain identifies as a Bowery Waltz tempo "to conjure up images of middle-class gentility and sentiment," as well as "outrageous rhyming and increasingly bawdy imagery that Porter derives from Shakespeare's titles" (Swain 134, 136). It begins by simply alluding to Shakespeare's plays and counting on the cleverly forced rhymes to amuse the audience: "Othella / hell of a fella," with its piled up rhyme, for example, or "flatter 'er / Cleopatterer," with a dialect gag. ("Cleopatterer" may also be Porter's homage to P. G. Wodehouse, whose novelty song by that title was a hit in the 1917 show, *Leave It to Jane*.) But as the gangsters' song progresses, Shakespeare's titles turn into increasingly bawdy double entendres, making it clear that the references to the eminently respectable, i.e., Shakespeare, permit the lyric to suggest the startlingly unrespectable:

> If she fights when her clothes you are mussing
> What are clothes? Much Ado about Nussing . . .
> If she says your behavior is heinous
> Kick her right in the Coriolanus . . .
> When your baby is pleading for pleasure,
> Let her sample your Measure for Measure.

Once more the meaning is slippery, as Cole Porter ostensibly endorses the heterosexual and slyly engages the homosexual (McBrien 313 and passim). As Mark Fearnow remarks:

. . . Porter was driven to a level of "codedness" in his work. Far from an artistic flaw, the complexity afforded by this intellectual loop-the-loop became the distinguishing mark of his artistic accomplishment . . . Porter's double life propelled him to a high level of metaphor in his work. Unlike [other homosexual writers of the period], Porter's enormous personal wealth insulated him from much of the suffering and humiliation that social pressure and persecution impressed on less economically advantaged homosexuals of his era. For him, his secret life was a source of guiltless pleasure, and the maintenance of a double life a delightful game. The wit and frivolity of his lyrics illustrate that life attitude and – in their riddles and double meanings – are games in themselves. (147)

To attain the doubleness of meaning, Shakespeare's presence in this lyric is essential, then, because he heightens the incongruity enough that we can laugh, as our recognition of the high-culture titles and the vulgar implications work together to permit the impermissible. In the song, Shakespeare becomes an excuse, a subterfuge that permits the show to get on with what it really wants to do (i.e., amuse and sanction naughtiness) by misdirection. In "Brush up Your Shakespeare," we laugh to show that we are and are not elite, straight, knowing. The song and the show employ Shakespeare's figure in much the same way that *Mr. Hamlet of Broadway* had done: Shakespeare becomes the means to resolve all problems.

 The plot of *Kiss Me, Kate*, is simplicity itself, with its two divorced stars who remain in love. After endless comic squabbling, he asserts himself and tames her. By controlling (with Shakespeare) a pair of itinerant gangsters who have wandered into the production, all live happily ever after. But to say the structure is simple is not to deny the show's effectiveness: the Cole Porter songs remain delightful, the dancing and singing were certainly done well by a gifted cast, and no one can wonder at the show's success. Again the show depends on the joke of Shakespeare done in the American idiom (as in *Boys from Syracuse*), rather than the sort of burlesque within a musical that *Mr. Hamlet of Broadway* offered. (And it is worth noting that *Swingin' the Dream* seems to have been an uneasy amalgam of American idiom and burlesque.) Unlike *Swingin' the Dream*, *Kiss Me, Kate* cited Shakespeare without using him much. Yet it took fewer liberties with the Shakespeare text than *Boys from Syracuse* had, choosing rather to embed bits of Shakespeare in a frame-story about a production of *Taming of the Shrew*. The use of a frame-story is similar to the structure of *Mr. Hamlet of Broadway*, although here the burlesque of Shakespearean elements is reserved for the outer off-stage plot line rather than the inner on-stage Shakespearean plot line. *The Boys from Syracuse* had shown appropriation could succeed, yet *Kiss Me, Kate* was more cautious than its progenitor, insisting on its frame and doing some parts of the Shakespeare comedy straight.

Furthermore, the show was safe in its endorsement of prevailing social attitudes: one may joke about divorce, but marriage is forever; gangsters may be amusing, but their boss must be shot; young men should give up gambling and get married. Porter provided a veneer of sexual sophistication with such songs as "Too Darn Hot" or "Always True to You in My Fashion," but the book of the show undercuts such lyrics to suggest that the respectable way of life was perhaps better, in the same way that its lyrics, ostensibly heteronormative, also engage a homosexual listener. It does so in a flippant manner, however, and spends most of its time on the inconvenience of marriage: marriage, it implies, leads attractive people to bicker, cuts the opportunities for a woman to milk her sugar daddies, forces women to accept bullying and forces men to put up with fools. The notion that one might smack around a partner (Lilli slaps Fred, Fred spanks Lilli, and the gangsters threaten to beat up everyone) seems anachronistic. Thus, it is respectable in its endorsement, but less respectable in its actions. This show uses Shakespeare in a re-vision that is itself institutional as none of the earlier shows were. Swain has analyzed the sophistication and understanding of Porter's settings for Shakespearean texts in "Where Is the Life that Late I Led?" "I've Come to Wive It Wealthily," and "I Am Ashamed that Women Are so Simple" (Swain 129–52). Having cited Shakespeare, however, *Kate* largely ignores him, so that the play may do what it wants to do: skeptically interrogate heterosexual relationships.

Perhaps the most interesting aspect of that interrogation is its malleable vision of gender and sexuality. While critics agree on the show's interest in sexuality, they read its concerns individually. William McBrien and others argue that Porter's songs refer to his life as a gay man who enjoys cruising and rough trade (McBrien 313; see also Clum 72). Richard Burt offers a playfully queer reading of the movie version and its "series of double entendres focusing on Lilli/Kate's ass and Graham/Petruchio's inadequate penis size" (Burt 1998: 172). But the transgressive narrative may also be feminist. Barbara Hodgdon suggests that "If *Kate* vents sadomasochistic fantasies in soft-shoe routines to teach that fighting phallic power can be fun, it also suggests that managing monogamy's double-toil-and-trouble standards is strictly women's business" (548) In conversation, Irene Dash has suggested to me that the show has many positive things to say about female independence. I myself think its gestures toward sexual freedom finally collapse into cynical conservatism. Lois/Bianca tells her lover that "I'm Always True to You, Darling, in My Fashion," despite her clear pleasure in seeing other men and trading her sexual favors for gifts. Lilli/Katherina also enjoys her independence. Divorced (and thus free from sexual restrictions placed on unmarried women in 1948), she is a highly successful actress in both films and plays, courted by a powerful man. If Fred angers her, she can walk. The men too enjoy freedom. Whomever one desires is sexually knowledgeable and available; Fred has no qualms about having both Lois and Lilli. Marriage, the show implies, is no fun. As Fred/Petruchio sings of marriage, "Oh, what a bore at night!" The notion that marriage is dull, limiting, and potentially violent simply fades by the end when Lilli abruptly submits to Fred, both yielding independence for a respectable re-marriage. Behind Shakespeare's beard, the show can say that marriage (or the appearance of compulsory heterosexuality if one is gay, as Cole Porter was) is not ideal, but it then backs down for a safe conventionality, conducting that surrender in Shakespeare's language, via Porter's setting of "I Am Ashamed." Its songs remain standards, its performances were superb, and its book is remarkably conservative.

If *Kiss Me, Kate* was flippant, *West Side Story* (1957) was serious. It has music by Leonard Bernstein, lyrics by Stephen Sondheim, a book by Arthur Laurents, staging and choreography by Jerome Robbins. As in the case of *Kiss Me, Kate*, there are varying accounts of who is responsible for the musical. Indeed, when the Dramatists Guild brought the four creators of *West Side Story* together to talk about the musical, Arthur Laurents pointed to the inevitable disagreements that arise when people remember:

There should be a preface to all this. Several years ago, Harold Prince wrote his theatrical memoirs – rather prematurely, as it turned out. In them, he talked about producing *West Side Story*. The original producer, the one who stuck all the way, was Roger Stevens. Later he was joined by Hal Prince and the late Bobby Griffith. I read Hal's recollections, and I phoned Steve [Sondheim] and told him, "I don't think that's the way it happened. Steve agreed. Today each of us is going to tell it the way each of us remembers it. It's a sort of *Rashomon West Side Story*.[5]

Robbins first proposed the notion of a musical about a contemporary Romeo and Juliet. He said that an actor whom he knew had been cast as Romeo and was having trouble with the part. When the actor asked Robbins how he would suggest doing the play, Robbins began to think about the play in terms of song and dance.[6] Having had the idea in 1949, he then consulted both Bernstein, who considered it "a noble idea," and Arthur Laurents.

Laurents recalls that at this point, "Romeo and the Montagues would be Catholic, Juliet and the Capulets Jewish; the action would occur on the Lower East Side during Easter–Passover" (329). Bernstein also commented in his diary that it could be "a musical that tells a tragic story in musical-comedy terms, using only musical-comedy techniques, never falling into the 'operatic' trap. Can it succeed? It hasn't yet in our country."[7] The matter was one of some interest to Bernstein, who had investigated the relationship between American vernacular music and European classical music in a number of essays and compositions.[8] Laurents too was eager to participate for he had "long wanted to write a musical" (Laurents 329). But the project of *East Side Story*, as it was then called, was repeatedly set aside until 1955, in part because all of the three were in high demand. When they discussed the possibilities, among themselves or with others, they were likely to hear about *Abie's Irish Rose*, a sentimental hit in 1927. Nor were they able to agree on how the various elements ought to be balanced, or even what the dramatic elements ought to be. The plans for the show came to a standstill.

In 1955, a chance meeting between Bernstein and Laurents in Hollywood led to a revival of their interest. Visiting one another at the Beverley Hills Hotel, they sat by the pool and considered whether *East Side Story* would work if the two families were not separated by religion but by ethnicity.[9] They had both seen reports of gang fights between Anglo and Mexican adolescents. For Laurents, that change eliminated the possibility of comparisons to the maudlin *Abie's Irish Rose*, while Bernstein was excited by the potential of Latino music. They talked with Robbins, who was also enthusiastic about the possibilities. As Laurents and Bernstein began their work on the book and music, the team realized that they would need a lyricist, and they recruited Sondheim. Again other creative projects intervened, and finding a producer and financial backing was difficult (as Laurents' story about Prince and Stevens suggests), but finally in 1957 the work was ready to open.

The rehearsals and tryouts were an exciting process, as Robbins worked to bring the collective vision of four creative men into being. The process was demanding for the performers because Robbins decided to employ the Method techniques of the Actors Studio in the musical. The cast was young and relatively inexperienced, including Carol Lawrence, Larry Kert, Chita Rivera, and Ken Le Roy. Insisting on a rehearsal period twice as long as usual, Robbins split them into gangs and forbade the members of the Jets to have anything to do with the members of the Sharks. Sondheim would later say that while he had initially found that approach pretentious, he later realized that it was perfect for this work (Guernsey 52). Various stories can be found detailing tension between Bernstein and Sondheim about creating the lyrics, Laurents and Robbins about directorial changes to the book, Robbins and Bernstein about directorial changes to the music, and everyone about what songs would be included, what songs would be dropped, and where the songs would go.[10] Whatever the quarrels were at the time, on the Dramatists Guild panel, the group agreed that the entire process of creation had been exhilarating, pushing each of them to do excellent work. Robbins said that

> For me what was important about *West Side Story* was in our *aspiration*. I wanted to find out at that time how far we, as "long-haired artists," could go in bringing our crafts and talents to a musical. Why did we have to do it separately and elsewhere? Why did Lenny have to write an opera, Arthur a play, me a ballet? Why couldn't we, in aspiration, try to bring our deepest talents together to the commercial theater in this work? That was the true *gesture* of the show. (Guernsey 54)

What strikes me about this statement is how perfectly suited such ambitions are to the use of Shakespeare. Not only had Shakespeare's plays provided a solid basis for decades of operas, plays, and ballets, but they had also served as the foundations for successful musicals. Furthermore, while a Shakespearean tragedy is an impeccable resource for any "long-haired artist" who has cultural aspirations, *Romeo and Juliet* has the added advantage of having been produced with great success in the *commercial* theatre.

When *West Side Story* opened in New York, the reviews, while not uniformly positive, do comment repeatedly on the show's innovations. In the New York *Daily News*, John Chapman wrote that "The American theater took a venturesome forward step, a bold new kind of musical – a jukebox Manhattan opera – the skills of show business are put to new tests – as a result a different kind of musical has emerged – a perfect production" (quoted in Zadan 25). Other critical comments are that *West Side Story* is "an original project" with "a searching point of view," "an entirely new form." Bernstein's music is praised, as is Robbins' remarkable choreography. Over and over, critics make the point that the show is not at all comic, as if they feel a public duty to warn theater-goers about the tone. Suddenly the comic aspect of Shakespeare appropriation dropped out of the picture; the joke that had sustained *The Boys from Syracuse* or *Kiss Me, Kate* is surrendered as if putting Shakespeare into colloquial American terms no longer amused. (No subsequent Shakespearean musical that has avoided comedy has succeeded, although several have tried.) While such innovation is important, one must also recognize that the show was written to make a profit. It is the features that helped to ensure its commercial success that are seemingly the most high-minded.

Instead of providing laughs, the institution of Shakespeare provided yet another way for the production to establish itself as serious art. Shakespeare did, however, provide aesthetic guidance to Arthur Laurents as he wrote the book: the speed of the story, the tension of the warring factions, the poignancy of the deaths all owe something to Shakespeare's original; while the earthiness of the gang members, like that of Mercutio and the Nurse, provides a needed tartness to the lovers' sweetness. Walter Kerr even commented, "Perhaps the echoes of another 'Romeo and Juliet' are too firm: the people often seem to be behaving as they do because of arbitrary commands from a borrowed plot."

But important differences between the play and musical do exist. Shakespeare's warring families are tragic in part because they are so much alike: in Shakespeare's Verona, no one can distinguish a Capulet from a Montague, a plot device that gets Romeo to the ball where he meets Juliet. The infamous feud has no known basis. In *West Side Story* the feud is based on ethnicity, albeit what now seems a curiously pale imitation of twentieth-century America's racial tension. The action of the musical begins at 5 p.m. with an innovative "Prologue." Instead, of Shakespeare's use of lyric language or the conventional musical overture, *West Side Story* opened with Robbins' choreography, as the two gangs, the Puerto Rican Sharks and the "American" Jets,[11] jockey for control of a playground. The music and movement intensify and build until the entrance of two policemen, Officer Krupke and the plain-clothes Lieutenant Schrank, ends the encounter. Clearly Laurents draws the scene from the opening of Shakespeare's play with the street skirmish between the Capulets and Montagues, until the intervention of the Prince stops the violence (and the way that Baz Luhrman stages the gas-station fight in his film version of *Romeo and Juliet* may owe something to *West Side Story*'s opening scene). The Jets agree that a rumble must settle which gang owns the street, and their leader Riff persuades the others that they will need the older Tony. In the following scene, Riff finds Tony at work at Doc's drugstore and persuades him to come to the dance. Tony explains his reluctance by singing of his sense that "Something's Coming." Here Laurents introduces the hero, but has discarded Shakespeare's identification of Romeo as a conventional melancholy lover, sighing over Rosaline, and instead identifies Tony with hope and the future. Moreover, this protagonist is clearly working-class.

Next the musical shifts to the Sharks to introduce recent immigrant Maria, who is also at work. In the Bridal Shop, she and Anita, who combines the characters of Lady Capulet and the Nurse, talk about the dance, their dresses, and Maria's situation as a newcomer to the city. The entrance of Bernardo and Chino, who parallel Tybalt and Paris respectively, signals another scene-change. The stage direction is ideal for a musical, combining sound and visual effects for a transition:

MARIA Because tonight is the real beginning of my life as a young lady of America!
*[She begins to whirl in the dress as the shop slides off and a flood of gaily colored
streamers pours down. As Maria begins to turn and turn, going off-stage, Shark
girls, dressed for the dance whirl on, followed by Jet girls, by boys from both gangs,
The streamers fly up again for the next scene.]*

This way of introducing the crucial dance scene when Tony and Maria meet draws on what makes musicals most appealing: the special effects of a theatre, dancing, music. In the course of the dance scene, the book offers reminders of the plot's tensions as the two gangs jive or mambo competitively or as Tony and Maria perform a "delicate cha-cha." The appearance of Krupke in the background or the oleaginous cheer of the adult Glad Hand offer a reminder of the isolation of the adolescent gangs. As the scene ends, the gangs have made arrangements for a war council at midnight and Tony sings "Maria," having fallen in love.

The following scene has Tony and Maria sing "Tonight" on the fire escape, in the musical's version of the balcony scene. Their meeting ends as first the Sharks and then the Jets have musical numbers about their concerns ("America" and "Cool"). Finally, the gangs agree to fight and Tony tries to limit the damage by persuading them that the best fighter from each gang should do battle, but no more. In these scenes, the smoothness of the action seems inevitable, and the strong dance and music parallels to *Romeo and Juliet*'s ballroom scene distract one's attention from significant shifts. In the world of *West Side Story*, no figure operates quite like Mercutio (Riff is far closer to Benvolio), while adults are not loving family members, but hostile and ineffectual. While the Shark girls have a strong role to play in the action, both backing and deriding the boys, the Jet girls are far more passive. The only one who has a significant role is the character Anybody's, who seeks to be one of the boys in the Jets, despite their constant harassment. Furthermore, the endless arrangements for the rumble that will conclude the act seem to be fragmented. Instead, of a feud that erupts on little provocation, the characters have a series of small rituals to which they must attend in the world of *West Side Story*. They have to manage to meet, to schedule a war council, and to negotiate the conditions of their fight. This ritualized action offers a number of breaks in the action so that musical

17 ©Al Hirschfeld. Scenes from *West Side Story*. In the foreground Tony (Larry Kert) and
Maria (Carol Lawrence) kneel to vow their love. Behind them Bernardo (Ken Le Roy) and
Anita (Chita Rivera) dance, as do other gang members. The background shows New York
buildings and fire escapes.

numbers can take place, and Laurents carefully indicates in his book the
time for each scene, indicating his awareness of how time functions. While
Shakespeare has managed the time in his play so that events occur in a matter
of a few days, making the impetuousity of events a factor in the tragedy,
Laurents has condensed time even further, to a forty-eight-hour period.
The care with he introduces the various stages of negotiation, however,
obscures the breakneck speed of the action.

The act concludes with scenes from the following day. First, in the Bridal
Shop, Tony and Maria sing "One Hand, One Heart" as a surrogate wedding
to parallel *Romeo and Juliet* 3.4. (Bernstein had orginally written the music
for both this song and "Officer Krupke" for *Candide*.) Next comes a highly
effective musical reprise of "Tonight," sung by dispersed groups, each of
whom eagerly awaits something different. The gang members sing of the
upcoming fight, Anita anticipates Bernardo's eagerness as a lover, and Tony
and Maria reveal their joy at meeting once again. Again, the stage direction

indicates an awareness of the theatrical effect: "*[The lights build with the music to the climax, and then blackness at the final exultant note.]*" With tension at its peak, the scene's blackout offers an abrupt shift to grimness. The setting now is "*A dead end: rotting plaster-and-brick walls and mesh wire fences.*" The fight starts, and once again Tony tries to serve as peacemaker. Riff fights with Bernardo, but Tony's interference gets Riff stabbed. During the free-for-all that follows, Tony stabs Bernardo, as sound and light cues signal the arrival of the police. The curtain falls not on the conventional rousing musical number, but with the sound of a clock "booming." With two corpses on a grim set, the hero in flight, and no feature of a musical, the original audience sat stunned. Small wonder that the reviewers repeatedly talk about how innovative the show is and warn theatergoers not to expect the usual sort of entertainment.

The second act uses the power of that desolate first-act conclusion to elicit a range of responses in three songs. It begins in Maria's bedroom at 9:15, just after the fight. The Shark girls prepare to meet their boys after the fight, and Maria sings, "I Feel Pretty." This comic moment is interrupted by the entrance of Chino who brings word of the deaths, abruptly ending the charm of the number. As Maria is left alone to grieve, Tony climbs the fire escape to tell her his version. Again, the bitterness of events heightens the effect of their love as they sing the duet, "There's a Place for Us," before making love. In the subsequent scene, as the Jets talk about the fight, Officer Krupke enters to question them and they mock him. Once he leaves, their fear turns into a cynical bravado as they sing "Officer Krupke," before Anybody's enters with the news that Chino plans to kill Tony. These scenes provide motivation for the rest of the show. The first suggests that the Shark girls, though loyal to their boys, have ties among themselves. The duet suggests the possibility of a future for Tony and Maria. Finally, however, the comic relief of "Officer Krupke" is darkly cynical about anyone – policeman, judge, psychiatrist, or social worker – who seeks to intervene in their lives or wants to offer hope.

As in the first act, the second has an arc: the opening scenes establish the characters and the world, while the later scenes allow action to play out. The time in these scenes is from 11:30 to midnight. In Maria's bedroom as Tony leaves (in a parallel to Shakespeare's 3.5), the lovers agree to meet at Doc's and run away. When Anita enters, she sings the angry denunciation, "A Boy Like That," which Maria answers with the pleading, "I Have a Love." Eventually Anita joins her in the song. Their confrontation is interrupted by Schrank. Indirectly Maria tells Anita to take Tony word of the delay. The rest of the action takes place at the drugstore. As the Jets guard Tony, who is hiding in the basement, Anita comes in. Rather than listening to her, they cynically jeer, harassing her and nearly raping her, until the adult Doc stops them. Furious, Anita spits out the lie that Chino has killed Maria. Heartbroken, Tony goes into the street, calling for Chino to come and shoot him as well. Just as Maria appears, Chino does shoot him. She begins to sing, "There's a Place for Us," as he dies in her arms. Maria seizes Chino's gun as the rest of the gang members and the police appear. After a speech denouncing them all, she stops Schrank from touching the corpse. Instead, two Sharks and two Jets move forward to lift Tony's body as all exit.

The show does not borrow the ending of the Shakespearean tragedy: Maria is alive as the curtain falls. But neither does the show behave like a conventional musical, which would have ended with a major song. Although the creative team tried to come up with such a song, they could not find one that worked as well as the speech that Laurents had written for her. In the script of *West Side Story*, Shakespeare is kept safely off stage. Although every reviewer commented on *Romeo and Juliet* as a source, no explicit reference is made to Shakespeare or to his play within the book and no playful allusion occurs. The closest that the musical gets to *Romeo and Juliet* is the occasional celestial imagery in some of the song lyrics, which may be traceable to the pattern of such images in the play. Yet because of the serious subject matter and the innovations in musical form, Shakespeare's presence, however occluded, was important, for it guaranteed a measure of aesthetic value.

The show was also, of course, of eminent social respectability in 1957: it stood for tolerance and an end to violence, and it evoked a welter of sentimental response. The sympathetic characters oppose street wars and seek to escape violence; as one reviewer remarked, the show suggests that "the younger generation . . . is not nearly as blackhearted as current news stories might make us believe." Another said, "These are crazy mixed-up kids, but you go with them." Such comments imply that the characters are real, not fictional, and their behavior authentic, not the artifice of a musical. Critics responded to the show as if it took the idiom of the streets and allowed it to soar in song. In fact, Laurents made a special point of inventing the play's slang, so that the show would not be too tightly tied to a particular moment, and of paralleling the Shakespearean characters as best he could. No reviewer says anything about the show's alterations of the *Romeo and Juliet* plot, manufactured slang, or contrived scenes. During the rehearsal process, Robbins had put up clippings from the newspapers that described gang violence in New York, and had reminded cast members, "This is your life." Because he insisted on the performers identifying with the gangs and considering the actual conditions of New York street life, the ensemble was stronger and their work helped make the show more powerful. Yet there are undeniable gaps between what makes a musical seem real and what actually occurs outside the theatre.

An actual case further illustrates the differences.[12] In 1959, Salvador Agron, a Puerto Rican sixteen-year-old who was wearing a black cape lined with red, stabbed two other teenagers and when caught, proclaimed himself indifferent to what he had done. Subsequent investigation revealed that his life was unlike that of the characters of *West Side Story* in its poverty and neglect: Agron had been in and out of detention homes, struggled to read, and was rebelling in part against his stepfather's repressive Pentecostalism. That is not to say that *West Side Story* shows wealth, but certainly no one in the show is from circumstances as grim as Agron's, nor is any character in *West Side Story* as remorseless as Agron was initially. Though sentenced to die, Agron was reprieved and served twenty years before being released. In prison he had been rehabilitated, but within a few years he died of a heart attack. (In 1998 Paul Simon and Derek Walcott wrote a musical based on Agron's life, *The Capeman*, which failed.) Journalists in 1959 and 1960 frequently noted how similar the Agron case was to *West Side Story*, but did not comment on the rather marked differences.

One of the few people who has noted that gap between the stage and the street is Sondheim. He told an interviewer, "*West Side* is about the theater . . . It's not about people. It's about how to tell a story. What was best was its theatricality and its approach to telling a story in musical terms. I had always claimed it would date very quickly" (Zadan 28). While Sondheim finds the roles in the show "one-dimensional," and the plot itself a "melodrama," I would disagree. The roles and plot rest upon a cultural awareness of Shakespeare's play that allows them to be elliptical. There seems little need to compete with Shakespeare in establishing the psychology or actions of Maria and Tony, when a simple citation can allow the audience to fill in any gaps in the musical's presentation of character with a remembered response to the play. I do, however, agree completely that what makes the show unusual is its innovative form, and again the presence of Shakespeare allows the creative team to take liberties in their musical that might otherwise have been too much.

It is as if the presence of Shakespeare blinds the critics to what they are watching. Instead, the response to this new sort of musical, with the brilliance of its music and dancing, is doting and even patriotic. While no one can deny the achievement of the show, one should not ignore its made-ness, its craft. Consider the closing paragraph of Frank Aston's review in the *World-Telegram and Sun*:

"West Side Story" is far more than a Romeo meowing to a Juliet on a fire escape. It is a marvel peculiar to this country. Here we breed evil in our cities, but here we also parade a Bernstein and a Robbins so that a big part of this tortured world may say, "America must be proud of boys like those." And theater-going Americans may reply, "You're darn tootin' we are."

For Aston, the musical becomes an uplifting text that documents what is finest about his world. He recognizes the presence of *Romeo and Juliet* as the source, yet he sneers at the way that Romeo "mews" and insists that what is valuable, marvelous, in *West Side Story* is "peculiar to this country." The show was certainly one that broke ground, but in Aston's review one hears echoes of the things Americans said about Shakespeare just after the Revolution.

For the price of a ticket, a spectator received exceptional entertainment, impeccable cultural antecedents, and a dose of social uplift. Yet they did not have to confront Shakespeare directly (nor for that matter did they have to think very hard about race). Clearly the show was a bargain. I do not want to sneer at what *West Side Story* did to and for its audience, but rather to suggest that its effect was more far-reaching than simply illuminating the problems of gangs or juvenile delinquency. *West Side Story* allowed middle-class whites to feel some identification with lower-class immigrants, but D. A. Miller would extend that process beyond the socio-economic category. Miller suggests that gay men can identify with Maria, celebrating themselves as "pretty, witty, and bright," reveling in both the pleasure of Tony's wooing and the pathos as the heterosexual union is destroyed. His queer reading is, finally, less peculiar than Aston's flag-waving "darn tootin" response. Both analyses, however, testify to the power of the show.

The catholicity of *West Side Story* and cynicism of *Kiss Me, Kate* establish the boundaries for what musicals can do with Shakespeare. In the world of *Kiss Me, Kate*, you need only "Brush Up Your Shakespeare" and you can have any object of desire. In the world of *West Side Story* you simply think of Shakespeare, never speaking of him, and you have the power to experience any class, race, or gender. Once spoken, the word "Shakespeare" allows every act; unspoken, the word allows every identity. And the power of these musicals reaches beyond the characters who people them to transform the people who create the characters. Cole Porter's reputation is magically resuscitated. Jerome Robbins and Leonard Bernstein enter triumphantly into new kingdoms. Stephen Sondheim begins at the top of musical theatre.

Swingin' out of the twentieth century

After *West Side Story*, musicals based on Shakespeare boomed in the 1960s and 1970s, but most of them failed. The rock musical, *Your Own Thing* (based on *Twelfth Night*), succeeded off-Broadway in 1968 and *Two Gents* in 1971. Where could a show based on Shakespeare go next? Earlier musicals had lifted a complete plot to amuse an audience, or borrowed part of a plot to amuse or improve an audience. By the 1960s and 1970s, it seemed that little remained to be done. Lack of opportunity did not, of course, stop anyone: nine Shakespearean musicals failed between 1964 and 1976.[1]

At first glance, rock musicals offered a potentially new approach to Shakespeare. Such musicals were, however, not very successful. With the notable exception of *Hair*, the musical theatre quickly moved away from rock, turning back to pop or going on to Lloyd-Weber. Opening a few months after *Hair*, *Your Own Thing*, with a book by Donald Driver and songs by Hal Hester and Danny Apolinar, combined good humor and topicality.[2] Set in New York, the show examined gender confusions, atypical love relationships, and pop culture, and it did so through innovative staging. *Your Own Thing* featured elements that marked it as a product of its time: in addition to the rock score, it employed slide and motion-picture projections in the show. Thus the slides of such then-topical figures as Senator Everett Dirksen, New York Mayor John Lindsay, and right-wing actor John Wayne, as well as cultural icons like the God of the Sistine Chapel, the Buddha, and Queen Elizabeth I commented in cartoon balloons upon the action. (I shall refer to these projections as the talking heads.) Occasionally, films showed action like a shipwreck or created psychedelic effects. The show was done without interruption on a white-box set with ramps and platforms. While most of the dialogue was original to the musical, occasionally it included speeches from the play.

The action began before the action of *Twelfth Night*, showing the shipwreck of two sibling musicians, Sebastian and Viola. Separated from her brother, Viola lands in Illyria, a fun city, where she laments her loneliness.

The head of Buddha acquires a hand to give her a business card for Orson, manager of the rock quartet, Apocalypse. Since Disease has been drafted, the band cannot play at Olivia's discotheque without a new musician. Disguised as a boy named Charlie, Viola is quickly invited to join the band. She also agrees to take Orson's love letters to Olivia.

The scene now shifts to Sebastian, recovering in a hospital. Remembering his lost sister, he sings, "Come Away, Death." A nurse enters to bathe the patient, not realizing he is a male because of his long hair, but discovers his sex during his bath. She talks of her eagerness to serve as an army nurse and urges Sebastian to enlist and get a haircut. Soon a projection and lighting shift indicate the passage of time: the nurse is off to the army, while Sebastian goes to Illyria. Once again the Buddha hand issues a card sending Sebastian to Orson. When Orson greets him as "Charlie" and hands over a letter to Olivia, Sebastian is puzzled, but happy to oblige.

No sooner has he exited, than Viola is shown talking with the Apocalypse about her lost brother. Borrowing again from *Twelfth Night*, the musicians use Feste's lines to prove Viola a fool for mourning her lost brother. In a rapid-fire series of alternating scenes, Viola and Sebastian carry Orson's letters to Olivia, who woos the messenger, to Viola's horror and Sebastian's delight. The farcical action is quite funny as no one suspects that there are two messengers or understands why the messenger responds inconsistently. Viola manages to deliver the "willow cabin" speech (1.5.268–76), but the musical is quite different from the play because of Sebastian's earlier entrance into the action. Because Viola loves Orson and knows she can do nothing about her feelings, she sings, "She Never Told Her Love," using the *Twelfth Night* passage, "My father had a daughter lov'd a man." (2.4.106–15). She tells Orson that Olivia will never love him and then counsels Orson on his courtship technique in a duet, "Be Gentle." Feeling strangely aroused by the song, Orson exits in confusion and writes to Olivia, renouncing her.

In the next section, Sebastian and Viola continue to miss one another by seconds. First, Sebastian performs with the band and then goes off to meet Olivia. A moment or two later, Viola enters, and Apocalypse makes jokes about the speed of the visit. Olivia's surly stage manager enters with five costumes for the band's big number, "Hunca Munca." After squabbling with the Apocalypse, he exits and they begin an anthem, "The Now Generation," praising fondness for androgynous appearance and revolt from conformity. As the band climbs into their costumes, a modest Viola flees unnoticed, just as Sebastian enters and changes into a costume. Both he and Olivia realize that she is ten years older, but soon decide to ignore the problem because of their willingness to make the relationship succeed. The stage manager leaves employment forms, which Sebastian fills out with facetious answers. Sebastian leaves, just as Viola enters with another letter from Orson. The stage manager returns for the forms, and when he sees what Sebastian has written, he scolds the messenger that he sees, Viola.

Orson has been reading in an attempt to understand his desire for the boy Charlie. He sings "When You're Young and in Love," followed by a fantasy sequence in which various slide projections and tableaux trace homosexual love through history. When it ends, Orson meets Viola and declares his love for the boy. Appalled that she, a heterosexual, has fallen in love with a man who is a homosexual, Viola exits in tears.

The band appears in its star number, "Hunca Munca," with a big dance sequence. During it, Olivia encounters Viola and Sebastian in their costumes and is rejected, then pursued. As Olivia and Sebastian embrace, Orson enters and vows his love for the boy. Sebastian flees, and Viola enters to quit. Finally, Sebastian returns, and all is revealed. As Sebastian and Olivia embrace and Orson assures Viola of his heterosexual desire, both couples agree that they will do their own thing. They exit as Apocalypse ends the show with a final song, "Do Your Own Thing."

The musical increases the number of visits to Olivia, perhaps because eliminating the Sir Toby–Malvolio plot line requires the mistaken wooing in the main plot to take up more of the action. But eliminating the secondary plot has some unexpected effects. For example, the musical suppresses the play's character Antonio in two ways: the nurse is female, not male, and she helps Sebastian without falling for him. That is not to say that the musical is homophobic. In addition to an extended celebration of gay relationships, the dialogue includes passages that depend on a knowledge of gay culture and jokes. When the band has three members, they offer to line up and keeping shifting position so no one will notice.

JOHN: We could call ourselves the Lucky Pierres.
MICHAEL (*Falsetto*): I love it.
DANNY: It's an "In" joke. (Richards 311)[3]

But few straight members of the audience would recognize the joke here. As with the lyrics that Hart and Porter wrote, part of the pleasure in getting such a joke is that very "in-ness," its unavailability to a wide audience. Shakespeare's homoerotic Antonio does not fit in this world, but the aggressive nurse, who is fed up with male sexuality and wants to join the army, does. A similar restraint can be seen about the Now Generation and its mistrust of anyone over thirty. Since the Stage Manager is the role closest to Malvolio's, the small size of the role and his lack of interest in Olivia are notable.

He enters, calling the band "guys" and carrying their "freak suits." Immediately, they attack, calling him, "Establishment," "Barf earner," "Flower cruncher." Their reaction is disproportionately hostile. The show's creators may have sensed that some social boundaries were too great to cross. Olivia is thirty and Orson is about the same age. The Stage Manager is said to be in his mid-forties, which may have seemed an unimaginably distant age. Finally, one reason for the play's commercial success was the way that any truly explosive topics were carefully defused. Thus Orson realizes that he could be a homosexual, agonizes comically over the prospect, defeats his own homophobia, and accepts himself as a fine human being, only to discover that he's been a heterosexual all along. There are no risks in this sort of thing. As Robert Sandla comments in the liner notes to the cast recording, "The show spoke for what it was pleased to call 'the Now Generation,' but there was nothing in it to scare Grandma." The Shakespearean element was there as a pleasant sort of cheekiness, as were the topical jokes about John Wayne, Senator Dirksen, and so forth. An implicit tribute to pop music's British Invasion was intended, and Shakespeare's sanctioning of cross-dressing allowed the production to use the device without shocking anyone. It was very successful, running for 933 performances, and winning the Drama Critics' Circle Award for best musical. But the show has no currency today, and its rock songs sound stale, like commercial pop songs. Shakespeare was largely banished, although two of the songs kept his language ("Come Away, Death" and "She Never Told Her Love"). Nevertheless, the reviewers were well pleased by this tactic. Indeed, Jerry Talmer claimed it was more enjoyable than *Twelfth Night*, and James Davis complained that the show was "a brutal bore when it had to wade through the story" (Sandla 15–16). Today the work seems trite, as Sandla also notes; the language is painfully dated. He quotes as a "pivotal line: 'Love is a gas! It's where it's at! And if your own thing is against Establishment's barf concepts, you can drop out and groove with it.'" Compared to Laurents' invented slang and catchphrases in *West Side Story*, the authentic slang of 1968 seems implausible.

The Two Gentlemen of Verona (1971) was adapted by John Guare and Mel Shapiro, with music by Galt MacDermot and lyrics by John Guare, for Joseph Papp's New York Shakespeare Festival.[4] It featured Carla Pinza, Alix Elias, Raul Julia, Clifton Davis, and Jerry Stiller. *Two Gents* offered a politicized subtext about race and sex in America within a musical version of Shakespeare's text.

When an innovative production is both a critical and a popular success, it may achieve that success by being profoundly conservative in some area, by conforming to the status quo and erasing any possible challenge to that status quo. I want to argue that the New York Shakespeare Festival (NYSF)'s production of *Two Gents* follows that model. It was innovative in a number of ways, and not the least of its innovations is its position as the first NYSF production to transfer to the commercial theatre.

> [NYSF] was enjoying its first success of Broadway. The previous summer, the Festival had turned away thousands of people who had come to see its adaptation of *Two Gentlemen of Verona*. The success of *Two Gents* had come as something of a surprise to Papp. Mired in city politicking, he had not had much to do with it besides introducing director Mel Shapiro and playwright John Guare to *Hair* composer Galt MacDermot and agreeing that the play, since it was going out on the Mobile [theatre unit], could use more than the usual incidental music. Before long MacDermot had written a dozen songs and the play had been transformed into a musical the way *The Taming of the Shrew* had become *Kiss Me, Kate* two decades earlier. This adaptation of Shakespeare, however, was fueled by MacDermot's driving rock music, an exuberant multiracial cast that included Raul Julia, Clifton Davis, Jerry Stiller, and Jonelle Allen . . . (Epstein 260–61)[5]

It included a denunciation of war and a celebration of interracial friendship and love. "It was accessible Shakespeare, a wonderful show in the spirit of the time," recalled Bernard Gersten. "Never had any Shakespeare we had done engendered such a response . . ." (Epstein 261). Its success with audiences was especially important because, thanks to a $400,000 gift from LuEsther Mertz, a board member, and no author's royalties, "all earnings [could] go to the company to be used for the production of other plays at the Public Theater and in Central Park" (King and Coven 215). "The musical ran for eighteen months and the Festival became the first not-for-profit company to move a show to Broadway and retain all its rights" (Epstein 262). Thus the production is notable because of its text, its use of the urban community, and its financing. *Two Gents* integrated popular music and ideas with a canonical text to create a script that spoke vigorously about pacifism, racial tolerance, and equity. Like most of Papp's productions in this period, it challenged the idea that Shakespeare was principally open to a white, upper-class audience, and it cast performers of color in exciting ways. The play's success was also economically innovative as it suggested a new path that the NYSF might take to carry out its programs.

Today the show's treatment of women seems profoundly conservative. Perhaps this attitude grew out of the company's atmosphere. Epstein quotes Elizabeth Swados' description of the NYSF atmosphere:

> "There was David [Rabe] and David Mamet and Tom Babe and they all seemed like Davids to me. They were good-looking, slightly sweaty straight guys – it always

18 ©Al Hirschfeld. *Two Gents*. The couple in front is Proteus (Raul Julia) and Julia (Diane Davila), while the couple behind is Valentine (Clifton Davis) and Sylvia (Jonelle Allen).

seemed like there were at least ten of them, and that they would close doors louder than the women and sit around and talk about war . . ."

The "Davids" cultivated an aggressively heterosexual style, which included tough language, hard drinking in Papp's office and at the nearby Cedar Tavern and a confrontational status toward society. (Epstein 317)

This style is reflected in *Two Gents*. (See figure 18.) Yet this show follows Shakespeare's play more closely than any of the musicals I have discussed save for *The Boys from Syracuse*.

As the show begins, Thurio (the Spirit of Love) runs in, singing "Love in Bloom." The Ensemble follow to sing "Summer, Summer," celebrating the season and love. When the song ends, the Ensemble freeze in place as Proteus and Valentine enter with Speed, who announces that this is "*Two Gentlemen of Verona*: A play by William Shakespeare." He and the Ensemble exit as Valentine delivers an abbreviated version of the play's first speech about his intention to travel to Milan and an invitation to Proteus to join him. Proteus answers not with lines from Shakespeare, but with a song, "That's a Very Interesting Question," which becomes a duet for the two of them: Valentine will travel, but Proteus will stay and love Julia. Seeing Julia and Lucetta enter the garden, Proteus runs away. Using language from the play, the two women talk about Proteus, who now returns above on a balcony to do a reverse serenade of Julia in "Symphony"; the Ensemble join to pass his love letter to her. Receiving the note, Julia tears it up to everyone's disappointment. Alone, she insists, "I'm Not Interested in Love," but Thurio/Spirit of Love enters in pursuit of a young woman, he tosses confetti on Julia in passing, and she realizes that she does love Proteus, that she wants to put the bits of letter back together so she can read it and reply, and that "Thou Hast Metamorphosed Me." She gives her letter to Proteus and for a few moments all is joy. The entry of his father Antonio, who commands Proteus to travel to Milan with the servant Launce, forces the lovers to sing, "What Does a Lover Pack?" They exchange gifts: he gives her pearls, a picture, and his ring, while she gives him her ring. They also make love as Launce sings, "Pearls." An extended departure scene allows Launce to complain about his dog Crab, which he was ordered to give to Julia, Proteus to sing, the Ensemble to join in the farewells.

Throughout the show, Guare and Shapiro use a method that varies from previous musicals by combining songs freely with Shakespearean passages and colloquial language. The Shakespearean speeches tend to come at pivotal moments, underscoring their importance. The colloquial passages and songs are largely comic and often call attention to the character's ethnicity: Proteus, for example, was played by Raul Julia and may use a Spanish phrase, while Silvia's songs often use the conventions of the popular 1960s Motown sound.

The role of the Ensemble is important, for they often intervene in the action. When Julia realizes that she is pregnant, for example, she needs the help of the women in the Ensemble, who dress her and Lucetta as boys to travel to Milan. The entire company joins in a number that shows Valentine and Speed, Proteus and Launce, and Julia and Lucetta all on their various travels; the principals sing, "Follow the Rainbow," while moving and dancing around members of the Ensemble, dressed in black capes and masks, who become obstacles and block their paths. The original production was intended for an outdoor auditorium, and a number like this one reflects that origin by taking advantage of the sort of fluid staging that well suits a Shakespearean work and by using the performers' bodies to form the *mise en scène*.

The show's focus now shifts to Valentine and to topical satire. In Milan, the Duke is having a political rally. He introduces his daughter Silvia and announces her engagement to Thurio, then explains that he has begun a war, but if re-elected he will "Bring All the Boys Back Home." As the crowd celebrates, Valentine sees and loves Silvia. He sings, "Who Is Silvia?" and begins writing her letters, even opening a writing shop. Coincidentally Silvia soon needs help with a letter. She explains, "I'm to Marry Thurio," though she does not love him, and wants to send a message to Eglamour to save her. Together Silvia and Valentine compose the letter, in the duet "To Whom It May Concern Me." His interest is her is obvious, and as she sings, "Night Letter," she asks for his help. He agrees, and soon they have a plan to get her out of her tower. Silvia exits, but soon returns to confess that Eglamour is no longer the man she loves: Valentine is.

When Valentine is alone, he is surprised by the entrance of Proteus, and Valentine confides his plan for abducting Silvia with a rope ladder. Alone, Proteus sings "Calla Lily Lady," in praise of Silvia's beauty. Gradually the song reveals that he is jealous of his friend Valentine, and so as the first act ends, Proteus determines to betray both love and friendship. (It is interesting that his closing speeches about foreswearing Julia and Valentine are largely Shakespearean.)

The second act begins as Proteus places an anonymous phone call to the Duke, warning him about the plan to abduct Silvia. He uses a "Renaissance phone"; like the writing shop or "golden Renaissance/Baroque version of a Schwinn" bicycle that Valentine rides, the material settings and props often act as visual jokes about anachronisms. Their unusual appearance also helps fill in the sense of place usually provided by the scenery that the show's fluid staging eschews. As Proteus speaks, Julia and Lucetta, disguised as boys, arrive and overhear him. Proteus speaks to them, and they tell him, "We Come from the Land of Betrayal." Suspecting nothing, Proteus hires them.

While Silvia waits in her tower, the Duke and Thurio lurk below to intercept Valentine. Catching him easily, the Duke tells him he must be in the army and exiled from the city. Proteus enters to help escort Valentine out of town. Meanwhile, Thurio is doubtful about Silvia's love, while Silvia is furious. Sending Silvia back to her tower, the Duke reassures Thurio as, joined by the Ensemble, they sing "Thurio's Samba," a song that celebrates sex.

This number sets off a spate of special songs. The servants, Launce and Speed, have a song, "Hot Lover." In telling Sebastian/Julia to take a ring to Silvia, Proteus reveals his history with Julia, and she too has a song, the woeful "What a Nice Idea," about her continuing love for him. Finally, when Proteus and the Ensemble serenade Silvia in "Who Is Silvia?" she comes out of her tower to answer scornfully, "Love Me [Not

Your Idea of Me]." Then Silvia, backed by the Black Passion Quartet, does an impassioned number calling for "Eglamour" to save her. The Chinese soldier Eglamour appears, magically defeats the guards and Proteus, and carries Silvia off. The Duke and Thurio enter and the company reprises, "Where Is Silvia?" as the action moves to an army camp in the forest.

The love songs of the previous section now become a series of interrupted or unsuccessful sexual acts. Silvia and Eglamour enter a tent to make love. Valentine enters on guard duty, and sings about the hopelessness of his love for Silvia. No sooner does Valentine exit, than Proteus enters and looks in the tent. Angry that Silvia and Eglamour are together, he chases Eglamour off and then forces Silvia to the ground. Valentine returns and confronts Proteus, who is deeply ashamed. Next Eglamour enters with a Chinese dragon to chase both Valentine and Proteus, but the dragon turns on him and chases him off. Proteus tells Valentine of his shame, so Valentine forgives his friend, offering him Silvia just as Sebastian/Julia enters. Hearing this offer, she faints. All gather round (including the entering Launce, Speed, and Lucetta), and when Proteus recognizes his ring on her finger, her identity is revealed, as is her pregnancy. Lucetta, Launce, and Speed sing about what Julia should do in "Don't Have the Baby," but Julia insists that the child was conceived in love, so she will bear it and tell the child the truth. Proteus relents, and exits with Julia. The Duke and Thurio enter. When Valentine chases Thurio away, an admiring Duke gives Sylvia to Valentine. As they exit, Thurio returns and meets Lucetta for the first time. They fall in love to a reprise of "Thurio's Samba" and exit, as Launce enters to sing "Milkmaid" about the girl he's found and fallen in love with. The show ends with the entire company on stage, dancing, playing (basketball, Frisbees, soap bubbles, yo-yos), and singing, "Love Has Driven Me Sane."

The energy and charm of the close is characteristic of the show as whole. Audiences found it delightful, and it enjoyed great success. Because it began off-Broadway and then transferred, the production was eligible for both Obie and Tony Awards in 1972. It duly won the Obie for Best Direction and the Tony for Best Book and Best Musical. In addition it won Drama Desk Awards for Best Music, Best Lyrics, and Best Book, as well as Best Choreography, Best Costumes, and Outstanding Performances by Raul Julia and Jonelle Allen. Finally, the New York Drama Critics' Circle Award for Best Musical went to the show. In part these awards came from the show's liveliness, but the progressive nature of this musical certainly helped it as well. Shakespeare's function as beard allowed the production to endorse a world in which a performer might be of any ethnicity. Those various identities, Puerto Rican, African-American, or whatever, were incorporated into the script, which celebrated love as a force indifferent to racial or ethnic heritage. Unburdened by hypocrisy, sex was joyful and easily crossed color lines. Moreover, in 1971, it took very little skill to recognize that the production commented on the increasingly unpopular Vietnam War. The Duke is arbitrary and insists on waging an unjust war. The show presents him as ridiculous and cruel, a bully and buffoon.

Two Gents is not unmindful of the women in the play. Among its changes, it has Lucetta go with Julia to Milan to keep her company, not simply to help keep her safe. The women in the Ensemble aid them as they go on their way. Shakespeare's Julia must travel alone and her fear of attack makes her travel in men's apparel; there is more danger in Shakespeare's world. Moreover, Silvia may seem stronger willed in *Two Gents* than in *Two Gentlemen*. When the Duke orders her back to her tower, she refuses vigorously. When Proteus woos her, she tells him that he must love her as a woman, and not as a fantasy.

> Don't tell me to keep my chin up
> Stick a baby in my womb
> I won't be nobody's pin up
> In nobody's locker room

As this lyric indicates, *Two Gents* is plain-spoken about sex. In "Thurio's Samba," one of the big musical numbers celebrating love, the lyric belongs quintessentially to that age of Aquarius:

> Boom chicka chicka chicka
> Fuck fucka wucka wucka
> Cock cocka wocka wocka
> Puss pussa wussa wussa
> Boom chicka chicka chicka
> Fuck fucka wucka wucka wow wow
> Boom chicka chicka chicka
> Fuck fucka wucka wucka
> Cock cocka wocka wocka
> Puss pussa wussa wussa
> Fuck fucka wucka wucka now

One of the stage directions during the "Boom chicka chicka chicka" number remarks that the "Ensemble is down right as if at a revival meeting." It is unsurprising that *Two Gents* caps off all its frankness by having Julia reveal that she is pregnant when she confronts the perfidious Proteus at the end and then consider whether she will have the child or not.

Yet the sexual revolution had a way to go. The production eliminated scenes in Shakespeare's original text that allow women to talk to one another, and it was set in an "aggressively heterosexual" world that denied the reality of rape or violence against women. While Lucetta may join Julia in *Two Gents*, the touching scene between Julia and Sylvia in *Two Gentlemen* is missing completely. Indeed, save for the early scene between Julia and Lucetta, a woman *never* talks to another woman in *Two Gents*; women speak only to men. In *Two Gentlemen*, by contrast, women talking make up some of the play's most memorable scenes. Julia and Lucetta talk together in 1.2 and again in 2.7, Julia comments on what Silvia says in 4.3, and Julia and Silvia talk together in 4.4.

Although Silvia speaks frankly in *Two Gents*, she is considerably less forceful in her actions. The Silvia of *Two Gentlemen* "woos" Valentine "by a figure" as Speed points out, quickly perceives that Proteus is fickle (2.4.90–94), helps plan her unsuccessful elopement with Valentine, and arranges her own escape with Eglamour as a protector against the world's dangers. The Silvia of *Two Gents* has Valentine write a love letter to Eglamour, but quickly shifts her affection to Valentine; allows Valentine to make all the plans for their unsuccessful elopement; and simply calls to Eglamour to come and take her away, sure that he'll think of something. (As with Julia in the earlier scene, she faces little danger; the outlaws have gone in this version.) She may sing that she's "nobody's pin up," but she's nobody's rocket scientist either.

The musical's sexual frankness, however, is the place where it is finally most backward by being least serious. In the scene when Proteus tries to rape Silvia, *Two Gents* retains some of Shakespeare's language from *Two Gentlemen*, but adds business, a song, and stage directions that undercut the moment. Silvia and Eglamour are kissing passionately and about to make love. Proteus sees them and sings first of his frustration, "I want to kiss her mouth," and then, "Now I'm angry." Proteus attacks the lovers, and Eglamour runs away. After dialogue from Shakespeare's play, Proteus announces he will force Silvia and the stage direction says

(And he plops himself on top of her. Starts to kiss her. He removes his glasses. Valentine enters left platform. Crosses down left of Proteus and Silvia. Silvia giggles in delight. They become aware of Valentine. Proteus puts on his glasses.)

The question of how a production of *Two Gentlemen* deals either with Proteus' attempted rape or with Valentine's preference for his friend over his true love is clearly difficult. But to suggest that Silvia first welcomes Eglamour's kisses, then "giggles in delight" at a rape by Proteus, and finally with no qualms marries Valentine just increases the difficulties. This Silvia is a patriarchal fantasy figure: to "fuck fucka wucka wucka" is all that concerns her and the partner doesn't matter. Rape simply becomes rough sex.[6]

Most of the critics who reviewed the production praised its exuberance, its joy, and its accessibility. Peter Schjeldahl is the only reviewer I've found who even mentions the change in the scene, and he thinks it is an improvement:

> While streamlining it here and there, Guare and Shapiro have pretty much preserved the story of 'Two Gentlemen.' . . . [I]n a notoriously implausible scene, Proteus finds and tries to rape her . . . [The] adaptors have hung not only a lot of zestful singing and dancing but, boldly, an up-to-date set of values about love and sex and a number of up-to-the-minute theatrical sallies. Thus Silvia is no longer an upright, lovesick maiden; she has become an ingenuous swinger . . . (*New York Times* 8 August 1971)

Those critics who did complain about the production disliked the way it "at times degenerated into . . . musical-comedy glitter and self-conscious ethnicity",[7] but the implicit dismissal of rape went unremarked. Indeed, one of the few dissatisfied critics was T. E. Kalem, whose hostile review in *Time* was headlined "Cultural Vandalism," yet Kalem does praise one thing in the production: "The musical resembles an animated jukebox and comes alive only in one salty number, delivered by a one-woman heat wave named Jonelle Allen" (13 December 1971). Again the production's hidden conservatism may surface, unless one thinks it humorless to ask why no one comments that making Silvia an African-American also makes her "salty" or a "swinger."

The musical *Two Gents* broke ground by using actors of different races, by integrating rock music with Shakespeare's language, by including an anti-war message. Yet what happens to the women is startling: their roles are reduced, they exist almost exclusively in relation to men, and they enjoy rape. By presenting the sexual attitudes of patriarchal folklore, the production had found a way to persuade the public to sanction its break with other conservative social attitudes.

In the failed productions as well as in the two hits, one can see a disturbing development: the Broadway book musical was beginning to change so radically, just as American popular music was changing, that many students of the field believe the musical is dying out. I remain an agnostic on that question, but certainly the ferment in the larger cultural picture affects the Shakespearean musical. The political tensions of the Vietnam War; the successive successes of rock and roll, rock, and rap; the civil rights and feminist movements all change the materials that the book musical employs. The delicious doubleness of Porter's songs, the creative tension in Hart's lyrics were no longer going to work in the same way. The challenges to propriety posed by *The Boys from Syracuse* were no longer exciting once a Shakespearean musical had included the plot elements of transexuality or the lyric of "Fucka fucka wucka wucka." And the progressive possibilities of swing, with its integrated black and white performers, or the "race war" between Puerto Rican and Polish teenagers simply seem quaint given the multiple ethnicities of *Two Gents* and the new musical possibilities that such multiculturalism brings with it.

The transitional nature of *Your Own Thing* and *Two Gents* is perhaps also indicated by their identity as off-Broadway shows (although *Two Gents* did transfer successfully). In recent seasons several New York productions might be said to be Shakespearean musical comedies, although only one is an indisputable Broadway hit: *Return to the Forbidden Planet* (off-Broadway 1989), *Play On!* (1997), *The Lion King* (1997), and *The Bombitty of Errors* (off-Broadway, 1998). These shows fit the patterns established by earlier productions. Following the musical's origin in variety theatre, they play with gender and ethnicity while using Shakespeare's figure as a beard. Some productions treat Shakespeare fetishistically, as source for transformative power, while others seem to regard him as Other and affectionately burlesque him. Three of these, *Return to the Forbidden Planet*, *Play On!* and *Bombitty* play with gender roles, although none breaks new ground. Three, *Lion King*, *Bombitty of Errors*, and *Play On!* engage the topic of race, although only *Play On!* has a sustained or sustaining message.

The first of these is a musical that really does not fit in this discussion. *Return to the Forbidden Planet* by Bob Carlton originated in England, and was a far greater hit there than in New York, where it toured in an off-Broadway venue; it won the 1990 Olivier Award for Best Musical. But it is not the British origin that sets it apart, nor the off-Broadway venue where it played, but rather its nature, for the show is clearly a return to the burlesque. *Return to the Forbidden Planet* is loosely based on the science fiction movie, *Forbidden Planet*, which is in turn loosely based on *The Tempest*. Interspersed with dialogue from the movie and an additional plot line about Doctor Morbius' long-lost wife, the rocket scientist Gloria, Carlton has added scraps of Shakespearean passages, as well as covers of more than twenty rock and roll standards such as (inevitably) "Gloria" and "We Gotta Get Out of This Place." Hugely popular in the UK, where the Shakespearean burlesque has a continuing and strong presence in popular culture, much of the show's delight depends on the over-the-top melodrama of the science fiction plot and the energetic performance of the cover songs. Because the show returns to the burlesque tradition, there are three targets for mockery: Shakespeare, science fiction films, and rock and roll posturing. In the United States, burlesques of the latter two topics are both more frequent and less compelling. In short, *Return to the Forbidden Planet* may work more effectively in the UK than in the USA because it is predicated on a perversely affectionate mockery of Americana in which Americans cannot fully join.[8]

The Lion King opened in November 1997 and has enjoyed huge success. *The Lion King* (1997) is, of course, a Disney vehicle that has been a commercial hit on Broadway and on tour. Based on a successful feature-length cartoon, *The Lion King's* plot offers a loose analogue to *Hamlet*. The prince of the lions, Simba, exiles himself when his wicked uncle Scar kills his father, Mustafa the king of the lions. Simba returns and with the help of a noble friend (and future mate) Nala, as well as two comic friends Pumbaa and Timon, and a wise monkey Rafiki, overcomes his usurping uncle to assume his rightful place. In the stage production, largely thanks to the work of Julie Taymor, the performers are the animals of the veldt, effectively presented via dance, masks, and puppetry.

Lion King operates like *West Side Story*, in that the story is expected to stand on its own, but retains a link to Shakespeare as a source of potential *gravitas*, held unmentioned and in reserve. It is also like *West Side Story* in its sentimentalizing of the Shakespearean tragedy: the prince Simba, like Maria, lives at the end, in a variation from the Shakespearean original. The creators of *West Side Story* made it no secret that *Romeo and Juliet* was their starting place, but *The Lion King* acknowledges its debt less openly. Although the Disney Corporation mentions the link between *Lion King* and *Hamlet* once on their website, the connection goes largely unremarked, as if it were embarrassing. Perhaps the enterprise of adapting a children's cartoon into a live show that entertains families makes it necessary to disguise the un-amusing source, a Shakespearean tragedy. A tourist who wants to see animals sing and dance to the music of Elton John is not likely to welcome the memory of a gloomy Danish prince speaking archaic English. More to the point, however, is the way in which the Disney Studio seems to have borrowed crucial elements, without acknowledgment, from the Japanese animator Osamu Tezuka.[9]

Moreover, the show may have an implicit racial subtext in its evocation of Africa. Surely some awkwardness attends a work celebrating an African world that depends on a literary text central to the canon of European culture or a cartoon hugely popular in Japan. One need only recall *The Song of the South* to realize that Disney has some experience of making a well-meant gesture that is regarded as patronizing and racist. Thus the element of ethnicity, so often found in Shakespearean musicals, is present and not present, because Shakespeare is firmly suppressed.

Bombitty of Errors was 1999 off-Broadway show in which four white men rapped *The Comedy of Errors* in hip-hop style, taking on all of the roles, playing both women (Betties) and men (MCs), delighting the audiences with bad wigs. *Bombitty* is actually the closest of these recent shows to the Shakespearean original. Here the tactic is to retain the plot and jettison the language: the show makes a value claim for a mass culture form, in this case rap performance, by linking it to Shakespeare, a nice example of using Shakespeare as convenient beard. The potential citation of race, so strongly associated with rap in America, is modified in this show since the original performers and creators were white, and indeed all of the New York reviewers commented on that. On tour, the production changed personnel and the London cast was no longer all-white. (Ironically, the same season that brought *Bombitty of Errors* to London also brought a hip-hop version of *The Boys from Syracuse*. DJ Excalibah developed the project for Stratford East, and after success at the Edinburgh Festival, *Dah Boyz* was brought to the Theatre Royal.)

One way of understanding hip-hop in *Bombitty* is to consider an analogy with the ragtime music that Terence Hawkes has explored. Like the rags of the early twentieth century, the show offers a written version of largely unwritten form that "constitutes a bid . . . for genteel, white, European respectability".[10] The New York reviewers also echoed the old claim that the musical improves on the Shakespearean original, a claim made regularly about Shakespearean musicals since 1938. "For everyone who's tired of belabored Shakespeare revivals that remind us just how dead the playwright is, four recent NYU graduates (Jordan Allen-Dutton, Jason Catalano, Gregory J. Qaiyum and Erik Weiner) have come up with a warmly invigorating adaptation of *A Comedy of Errors*," wrote Drew Pizarro; in *Entertainment Weekly*, Jess Cagle would agree: "Maybe it's a stretch to say that *The Bombitty of Errors* improves on Shakespeare, but this energetic update is a thrill nonetheless." In other words, the shift to a musical comedy is an improvement on the Shakespearean play, evidently because the critic finds it more enjoyable, livelier. In a curious way this recurrent claim is a tribute to the power of Shakespeare's figure, given the reviewers' implicit assumption that Shakespeare is worthy of performance despite the perception that productions of his plays are much less enjoyable than shows with catchy tunes and high-stepping dancers. Obviously a production of a Shakespearean text can be "energetic" and "invigorating" as well as a musical version.

The audience's pleasure is not in the production's vigor alone, but rather in the unlikely juxtaposition of the old white Anglo-American text and the lively African-American music coexisting and connecting. Surely some part of the pleasure is also in the discovery that the audience member can follow one of the two strains: whether the Shakespearean plot or the intricate rhythms and wordplay of hip-hop. (Here the implicit assumption is that few in the audience will be comfortable with both elements.) The Shakespearean musical, in this instance, offers a political position (not unlike that of *West Side Story* or *Two Gents*) that we can defeat racial divisions, we can overcome, we can all get along, while the musical stage allows us to recognize different cultural traditions, which are embraced instead of erased. But like the two earlier musicals or *The Lion King*, *Bombitty* originates in the white community: the show began as a school project at New York University, suggesting not that Shakespeare belongs to all sectors of American culture, but that members of the upper-middle class can become missionaries to take Shakespeare to the masses. Such skepticism seems pedantic, and with good reason: this analysis simply reinscribes the false dichotomies of high/low, elite/popular, white/black.

The creators of *Bombitty* are smarter than that and braver. Since they are comfortable with both hip-hop and Shakespeare, they gambled that other New Yorkers (and later, audiences across America and in London) would welcome the wit of their show. Nor are they isolated: African-American choreographer Rennie Harris has adapted *Romeo and Juliet* into the well-received hip-hop ballet, *Rome and Jewels*; while *The Donkey Show*, a celebration of disco by Diane Paulus and Randy Weiner, is very loosely based on *A Midsummer Night's Dream*. Such works are a definite change: they acknowledge that the creators and performers take great pleasure in the Shakespearean text, but regard it as one resource among many in their own creative projects.

Like Rodgers and Hart, the creators of *Bombitty* chose *The Comedy of Errors* for their vehicle, which makes theatrical sense because of its farcical structure. The enthusiasm with which *Bombitty of Errors* has been received and the fate of the slightly later *Play On!* may indicate, however, that a show that does not attend to its audience's attitudes toward race or class will, like *Swingin' the Dream*, fail.

In some ways *Play On!* operates like *Bombitty*. The show's idea is elegantly simple: use the plot of *Twelfth Night*, re-set it in New York during the

Harlem Renaissance, and supplement freely with Duke Ellington's songs from his swing period. Occasionally a phrase from the play is used, but the language is largely colloquial American. Both *Bombitty* and *Play On!* use Shakespeare to make a status claim for popular music, rap or Duke Ellington. The creators of *Bombitty* present the music aggressively, but retreat into Shakespeare's plot. The creators of *Play On!*, on the other hand, invade Shakespeare like a conqueror (to paraphrase another critic) and make him their own. The show's concern is only incidentally Shakespeare: Ellington and his music matter far more, while the central issue is how an African-American woman can fit herself into the masculine history of the Harlem Renaissance. What the show insists on is racial pride. It suggests repeatedly that African-American history is important and inclusive (although it re-writes that history and Shakespeare's play as firmly heterosexual).

Play On! was a great hit at the Old Globe in 1997 but a tepid non-hit on Broadway in 1997, although it enjoyed regional success and one regional production was included in the prestigious PBS series "Great Performances" (2000). The show slightly alters Shakespeare's plot. A young woman named Vi comes to New York from the country, arriving on "The 'A' Train" determined to make it as a songwriter by learning from the Duke, Harlem's finest song composer. Her uncle Jester tells her she cannot succeed as a woman, so she cross-dresses to gain employment with the Duke, who is having a dry spell. All the Duke can think about is the beautiful night-club singer, Lady Liv, so he laments, "I've Got It Bad and That Ain't Good." The Duke sends Vi-man to woo Lady Liv, and – after managing to get past Liv's club manager, the Rev – Vi-man tries to persuade Liv to care. Liv falls for Vi-man, who has fallen for the Duke, while the respectable Rev yearns for Lady Liv.

By himself, the Rev sings "Don't You Know I Care." Mary, Jester, and Sweets overhear him and tell him that he needs to loosen up because "It Don't Mean a Thing, If It Ain't Got That Swing." Dressed in a yellow zoot suit, Rev sings and dances up a storm with Lady Liv in "I'm Beginning to See the Light." When she rejects him, Rev is heart-broken and returns to his navy-blue manager's suit. Liv pursues Vi-man until the untimely entrance of the Duke. The Duke renounces both Liv and Vi-man, Vi rejects Liv, and everyone is unhappy. The show ends with Vi's revealing her female identity to the Duke by asking him to help her complete "Prelude to a Kiss." Meanwhile Rev and Liv fall in love in a duet "I Want Something to Live For." Everyone lives happily ever after.

The alterations that the show makes to Shakespeare's play are similar to those made by other Shakespearean musicals, since they streamline the plot, providing more room in the production for musical numbers. But these changes have other effects worthy of note. One major plot change, for example, is the elimination of Viola's twin brother Sebastian and his loving rescuer Antonio. Cutting those characters reduces the size of the company, but it also brings a consequent reduction of homoeroticism in the show's subtext. Another change is that Sir Toby and Feste are combined in the person of Jester, who is given a familial connection to the Viola figure rather than to Olivia/Lady Liv. That shift reduces the danger that Vi-man runs, since her secret is known early on by the benevolent Jester, but isolates Olivia more thoroughly than in Shakespeare's play. The sweet country girl has family on whom she can draw; while the sultry singer must stand alone. That alteration affects what may be the most significant change: the Rev, serving as the Malvolio figure, ends up with Lady Liv, rather than as the object of humiliation.

Such changes make sense in terms of African-American culture. The resistance to homosexuality, after all, has been called "the greatest taboo" among African-Americans.[11] Thus, reducing such homoerotic elements as Antonio's declared passion for Sebastian neatly trims the production budget and eliminates social discomfort. The image of the isolated Lady Liv recalls the "tragic mulatto" stereotype, yet reclaims it: this woman has agency and concludes with love as well as her career. As for Malvolio/Rev, surely the idea that a black servant becomes a partner and wins his love is, in *this* cultural context, more bearable than that a black servant is mocked, humiliated, imprisoned, and finally driven away.

Although the idea for the show came from Sheldon Epps, and the joyful choreography from Duke Ellington's granddaughter, Mercedes Ellington, the writer of the book was Cheryl West, a noted African-American play-wright whose dramas *Jar the Floor* and *Before It Hits Home* have enjoyed success and won awards. Her concern clearly was to privilege African-American culture both in her emphasis on the Harlem Renaissance and in her refusal to let a black man be humiliated.

But while the alterations make political sense, does the history that West fictionalizes seem at all likely? Does the show in any way resemble what went on in the Harlem Renaissance or in Duke Ellington's life? Reviews of the New York production pointed to the fantasy feeling of the show. In the *New York Times*, Ben Brantley called *Play On!* a "romantic fable," asking "why not substitute a bygone Harlem, nostalgically remembered as a stylishly self-contained cradle for dazzling musical talent, for the fantas-tical dukedom of Illyria?" Brantley considered West's manipulation of the Lady Liv–Rev relationship clumsily handled, and complained that "This awkwardness wouldn't matter as much if the show could create, as it obviously means to, a fluid, fairy-tale sense of Harlem as a hip Brigadoon." Greg Evans had similar complaints in *Variety*: "'Play On!' maintains (loosely) the Bard's storyline and characters, but replaces complexity with sketch-comedy mechanics," he wrote, adding that "A chance to visit the famed Harlem nightclub [Ellington's Cotton Club] remains, like most of "Play On!," a missed opportunity." Clearly the critics thought the show's events unlikely, but if one considers that 1938 production of *Swingin' the Dream*, the events in *Play On!* seem plausible.

Harlem in the 1930s and 1940s was not simply the source of the hot swing music from Duke Ellington, Dizzie Gillespie, Count Basie, and Louis Armstrong that was fast replacing the sweet jazz played by such popular bands as Guy Lombardo and his Canadians. The Harlem Renaissance was in full swing. African-Americans came to New York from across the nation for its opportunities in education, business, and the arts. Many understood an interest in Shakespeare's works as an indicator of their privileged status as members of the talented tenth. Thus Langston Hughes published a collection of poems, *Shakespeare in Harlem*, while Errol Hill writes of important African-American Shakespearean productions in the Harlem Renaissance. That interest was included in the world of swing, most notably in the interest and affection that Ellington and his collaborator Billy Strayhorn felt for Shakespeare.

As I have already suggested, Lewis Erenberg demonstrates that swing was an agent of remarkable social change, especially in precipitating racial integration. There was popular recognition that the best music and the best dancing in America was African-American, leading to white customers visiting Harlem's clubs (most notably Ellington's Cotton Club) and to the success of New York's first integrated club, Café Society. But if addressing racial inequity was part of the swing movement, and Erenberg makes a compelling case that it was, gender inequity was ignored. When Anita O'Day wanted to be recognized as a musician instead of simply the vocalist, she asked if she could wear a jacket like the men in the band. "She wanted audiences to 'listen to me, not look at me. I want to be treated like another musician,' not a trinket 'to decorate the bandstands.' Soon, however, rumors circulated 'that I preferred ladies to men!'" so O'Day went back to glamour gowns. "Girl" vocalists were not recognized as musicians, nor were women instrumentalists welcomed. Indeed, to get jobs as a pianist, Dorothy Tipton began passing as a man in the 1930s, and did so successfully until her death in 1989, when the coroner informed her startled third wife and three sons that Billy Tipton was in fact a woman. Diane Middlebrooks' recent biography of Tipton, *Suits Me*, makes it clear that women were not easily admitted into the world of swing, although Tipton's case is complicated by personal desires. In *Play On!* when Vi turns herself into Vi-man, the show is not simply imitating Shakespeare: it's imitating life.

Play On! with its evocation of the Harlem Renaissance suggests a nostalgic fantasy to most reviewers, not a reconstruction of history. I've tried to suggest that the show is, in fact, closer to the historical record than its creators probably realized. But in this version of history, Duke Ellington and William Shakespeare are recognized as equals, and swing is a triumphant force in America's culture. And that finally is the fantasy, more's the pity.

If the Shakespearean musicals that I've discussed are instances of idiosyncratically American popular culture, what conclusions can I draw? The most obvious, I would suppose, is the way that American social attitudes make an appearance in the various plots. As concerns about sexuality, gender, ethnicity, and race emerge or shift, those same concerns appear in the shows, making them seem dated to audiences today or making Shakespeare seem prescient to contemporary Americans. A second point worth noting is the importance of Shakespeare's figure as an unacknowledged agent for expressing what would otherwise be too controversial. I suspect that this feature results in the critics who are praising such shows also proclaiming that the musical in question is more authentically Shakespearean than a production of a Shakespearean text. Critics want to be able to find the shows that they enjoy authentic, so they simply proclaim such shows to be so. To them it is important that Shakespeare's plays be congruent with their own values. American culture wants Shakespeare, but what is equally important, Americans want Shakespeare to be enjoyable. A musical allows the illusion of such an American identity. And those who create musicals find Shakespeare's presence useful as more than simply a beard: once Shakespeare is introduced into a plot line, his figure operates as a sort of universal solvent (I almost said *deus ex machina* but hesitate to create that parallel), for Shakespeare is able to resolve every difficulty, open any door, and achieve every dream.

Conclusion

In the early stages of my research for this book, I felt fairly sure that I knew the rough outlines of the narrative, which ran something like this:

All American drama grows out of Shakespeare's work, which forms the ground for American theatre, although Puritan hatred of the stage meant that colonial Americans more often read his plays than staged them. As tensions grew between America and George III's government, Shakespeare became suspect, yet he was also of great importance to America's Founding Fathers in the late eighteenth and early nineteenth centuries. Throughout the nineteenth century, Shakespeare colored much of America's literature and thought. Following a split in American culture between high-brow and low-brow forces, he was an important figure for self-improvement and reform movements. By the twentieth century, however, Shakespeare had become associated with a rather stuffy form of civic and cultural virtue. As modernism came into being, Shakespeare was a figure against whom Americans often rebelled. Thus while his works serve as the source for many Broadway musicals, such productions generally mock his work or simply get it wrong.

I no longer believe any of that narrative, which has proved to be completely incorrect. The ways that Americans use Shakespeare's figure are varied, but the motives for using Shakespeare now seem to me to be both preeminently practical and fantastical. In the former case, practicality includes such occurrences as a touring company producing Shakespeare, because he is respectable, when anti-theatrical forces seek to limit or eliminate performances. That practice occurs in the eighteenth century, but a variant recurs in later periods as well when theatrical companies use Shakespeare as a beard.

By saying that Americans use Shakespeare as a social screen, I have tried to draw attention to the practicality of the way in which Americans use Shakespeare's figure. Just as a screen may hide an untidy corner, so Shakespeare operates to hide any improprieties in the theatrical situation: *Othello* becomes a "moral lecture" rather than an exciting play. While gold-miners used screens to sift out valuable metal in the western United States, easterners were using Shakespeare as an index to gentility, the figure who separated gentlemen from ordinary citizens. Both westerners and easterners, of course, watched Shakespeare's plays, and the pleasure that those plays provided is a significant part of his attraction. In fact, Shakespeare was sufficiently valuable to Americans that he became a sort of screen onto which they projected their desires: one of those desires was that England's national poet be transformed to an American, and in some American minds, he was (and oddly enough, still is). Other instances of the practical would be Barnum's using Shakespeare's figure to publicize his activities, a musical production team's introducing a Shakespearean source to serve as beard for illicit subject matter, or Americans' defending their political position by reference to Shakespeare's plays. Yet one finds desire as well in each of these cases – desire for wealth, attention, and so on – and Shakespeare's figure is repeatedly and fantastically invoked to authorize these American dreams.

Just as the narrative about Shakespeare in America needs to be treated with caution, so have I learned to be skeptical about my assumptions regarding the American dream. This phrase is one that one hears repeatedly, but like Shakespeare in America, it operates in a variety of ways. The American dream is said to be (among other things) the nation's promise of "life, liberty, and the pursuit of happiness," the notion that each generation will be more prosperous than the preceding one, the opportunity afforded to immigrants, the possibility of owning one's own home, the pleasure of pickup trucks, a play by Edward Albee, a professional wrestler named Dusty Rhodes, and a public service organization (the Center for the American Dream). A quick check on any internet search engine reveals many more possibilities. That multiplicity makes sense if the idea of the American dream has been in existence throughout the nation's history. As America has changed, so has the nature of her dreams. Yet the phrase is comparatively recent: the *OED* entry under "American" suggests that "American dream" was coined in the 1930s, and the *American Heritage Dictionary* includes a quotation from writer Anthony Brandt that suggests the term originates during the Depression. The American dream comprises many things, then, but evidently originates in a moment of American history resonant with deprivation and desire. The power of the phrase, I suspect, is that it describes a feature of American culture: an American dream belongs to someone who feels great desire with a knowledge that under the right circumstances that desire can actually be satisfied.

If one desires to change social class, for example, it is relatively easy to do so in America. If one desires to become wealthy, one can find many models in American society. Or if one desires respectability instead of wealth, or notoriety instead of respectability, or the world's largest elephant, the sanctioned death of a rival, or a manufactured history, then American social history offers precedents for attaining those dreams. In this process of fulfilling American desires, Shakespeare has played a role. Because the meaning and use of Shakespeare's figure shifts, it has allowed Americans to swing their dreams.

Central to the process, a process that seems to me to be pragmatic, is the pleasure that Americans have taken in Shakespeare. When Shakespeare offered no pragmatic benefit, Americans largely ignored him. In the eighteenth century, as Americans began considering their nation and that nation's relationship with England, Shakespeare enters American culture as a figure that allows them to discuss the political situation. Until 1750, despite what I once assumed, Shakespeare matters little for America, but as the desire for a national identity swells, so too does the use of Shakespeare in discussions of politics, in playhouses, and in the decoration of homes. In each area, political, theatrical, and domestic, one finds Americans taking great pleasure in using Shakespeare and summoning the authority of Shakespeare to support their positions. During the Federalist and Jacksonian periods, the concern with national identity undergoes a shift, although that concern is not completely erased. Americans begin considering not their national identity, but rather their role in a society, as members of a social hierarchy. That is not to say that politics become unimportant. Surely it is no accident that the best-known of American theatres are Ford's Playhouse and the Astor Place Opera House. In the former, an actor who screened his Confederate espionage behind a performance of *Julius Caesar*, killed a president; in the latter, nationalism and the desire for an American Shakespeare led to a horrifying riot. Nonetheless, as America moves from a desire for nationhood to a desire for social place, Shakespeare also undergoes a shift. His figure becomes a means by which Americans identify themselves socially, as a people of education, culture, and gentility. One finds American writers who make use of Shakespeare, appropriating England's national poet and moving him into American libraries and theatres. Yet his figure is simultaneously linked to darker desires: the wish that violence be sanctioned, that misbehavior be regarded as propriety. By the twentieth century, American concern with one's social position fades, although in *Mr. Hamlet of Broadway* Mrs. Barnaby Bustle's infatuation with Shakespearean performance as an enhancement to her social standing shows that it does not disappear. Instead, a concern with one's personal identity, both ethnic and sexual, comes to the fore. Being accepted into high society had once meant doing anything, even altering one's identity, but in the twentieth century individuals begin to insist on being accepted without change. Rather than obscuring or denying one's ethnic background, Americans insisted on retaining it.

While Shakespeare's cultural presence is much broader in the twentieth century than it had been at the start of the nineteenth, one can focus on a particular area to see that concern with social identity. I have chosen the Shakespearean musical, a relatively infrequent phenomenon that succeeds perhaps once a decade, to trace the way that Shakespeare's claimed presence makes it possible to resolve any problem and achieve any desire in the show. When Shakespeare swings, sexual boundaries collapse, so anything goes. But beyond the show, the presence of Shakespeare alters the social identity of the people who put the show on stage. Shakespeare's figure turns a variety star toward the legit (Eddie Foy), a small-time player to a star (Teddy Hart), a has-been to a fresh success (Cole Porter). African-American performers can claim a part in Shakespeare's figure on the Broadway stage, and what is equally important is that white Americans can use Shakespeare to take part in African-American culture, enlisting Shakespeare as a way to enter the worlds of swing or rap.

Are these transformations actual? I would argue that it doesn't really matter. Such dreams of transformation have their own power. Nor does it matter whether Americans use Shakespeare's figure in a way that is idiosyncratically national. The history that I have related is not history at all, but a narrative of heritage. Heritage, as historian David Lowenthal reminds us, is not history:

> Heritage should not be confused with history. History seeks to convince by truth, and succumbs to falsehood. Heritage exaggerates and omits, candidly invents and frankly forgets, and thrives on ignorance and error. Time and hindsight alter history, too. But historians' revisions must conform with accepted tenets of evidence. Heritage is more flexibly emended. Historians ignore at professional peril the whole corpus of past knowledge that heritage can airily transgress.
>
> Heritage uses historical traces and tells historical tales. But these tales and traces are stitched into fables closed to critical scrutiny. Heritage is immune to criticism because it is not erudition but catechism – not checkable fact but credulous allegiance. Heritage is not a testable or even plausible version of our past; it is a *declaration of faith* in that past.[1]

It strikes me as telling that two of the instances he offers to illustrate his thesis concern visits to Stratford by American authors Washington Irving and Henry James. In two essays, both Irving, early in the nineteenth century, and then James, early in the twentieth century, hear a tour guide fabricating tales from Shakespeare's history and find themselves disturbed. Then they both come to terms with the fabrications, with Irving musing that he is "ever willing to be deceived, where the deceit is pleasant and costs nothing. What is it to us, whether these stories be true or false, so long as we can persuade ourselves into the belief of them?"

America's heritage of enjoying Shakespeare is just such a declaration of faith. In appropriating Shakespeare, dreaming about Shakespeare, and employing Shakespeare to satisfy dreams, Americans have found a genuine heritage, even if it is shaky history. Nor is it a heritage that should be scorned. As Lowenthal points out in another essay, both in England and America, "Custodians of public history, managers of heritage, teachers of schoolchildren, social scientists in general, even some professional historians articulate presentist, pre-historicist, whiggish, and other perspectives quite at odds with sophisticated historical understanding today."[2] Other figures, both in America and elsewhere, evoke similar responses of admiration, appropriation, and misrepresentation.

But what, a pragmatic American might ask, does such a heritage accomplish? Let me conclude with one instance. In 1849, just a few months before the Astor Place Riot, a young American wrote to a friend,

I have been passing my time very pleasurably here, but cheifly [sic] in lounging on the sofa (a la the poet Gray) & reading Shakespeare . . . Dolt & ass that I am I have lived more than 29 years, & until a few days ago, never made the acquaintance with the divine William . . . (Markels 35)

About a week later, he was still musing on his new find:

I would to God Shakespeare had lived later, & promenaded in Broadway. Not that I might have had the pleasure of leaving my card for him at the Astor, or made merry with him over a bowl of the fine . . . punch; but that the muzzle which all men wore on their soul in the Elizabethan day, might not have intercepted Shakespeare from articulation. (Markels 37)

Reading Shakespeare for the first time, he enjoys the experience greatly. Within a short time, however, he begins to dream about the delightful prospect of Shakespeare as an American. Moreover, his imaginary Shakespeare promenades on Broadway, visits at the Astor, and enjoys a glass of punch. The reason for these daydreams, he says, is that Shakespeare would be so improved were he a nineteenth-century New Yorker. This response is funny, of course, but Markels goes on to argue that here is the seed for Herman Melville's preoccupation with Shakespeare, a powerful concern that eventually helped to shape and intensify *Moby-Dick*. Melville, like so many Americans, was swinging an American dream.

Appendix: Production information

For each New York Shakespearean musical, I give the available information about the original production. First the Appendix gives the name of the show and the Shakespeare work that it draws on, then the date it opened and the theatre (indicating if appropriate whether the show was off-Broadway), then the creative personnel (music, lyrics, and book), then the producer and director (in earlier productions, the credit is sometimes "staged by" rather than "directed by"). Then the Appendix lists other important participants, such as the scenic designer, the choreographer, the costumer, the musical director, and (more recently) the lighting and sound designers. Finally, for the seven Shakespearean musicals that receive substantive discussion, I include information about film or audio recordings.

Mr. Hamlet of Broadway, based on *Hamlet*
Opened 23 December 1908 at the Casino Theatre
Music by Ben M. Jerome, lyrics by Edward Madden, and book by Edgar Smith
Produced by Sam S. and Lee Shubert, staged by Ned Wayburn
Scenic designer, Arthur Voegtlin; musical director and conductor, Ben M. Jerome
Two songs from *Mr. Hamlet of Broadway* were included on the record *Music from the New York Stage*, volume II: 1908–1913, Sussex: Pearl, 1993

The Boys from Syracuse, based on *The Comedy of Errors*
Opened 23 November 1938 at the Alvin Theatre
Music by Richard Rodgers, lyrics by Lorenz Hart, and book by George Abbott
Produced and directed by George Abbott
Scenic and lighting designer, Jo Mielziner; choreographer, George Balanchine; costumes, Irene Sharaff; conductor, Harry Levant

The show was made into a Universal Studios Film (1940), directed by A. Edward Sutherland and featuring Allan Jones, Irene Hervey, Martha Raye, and Joe Penner. In 1986 the Canadian Broadcasting Company did a television production, directed by Norman Campbell and featuring Colm Feore, Geraint Wyn Davies, Keith Thomas, Benedict Campbell, Susan Wright, and Alicia Jeffrey. Several sound recordings exist, but not one with the original cast. In 1953 Goddard Lieberson did a cast recording for Columbia Studios, which is available as an Sony CD, 1993. The 1963 Broadway revival cast recording is available as an Angel/EMI CD, 1993. Finally, there is a studio cast recording. DRG, 1997

Swingin' the Dream, based on *A Midsummer Night's Dream*
Opened 29 November 1939 at the Center Theatre, Rockefeller Center
Music by Jimmy van Heusen (with one original song by Alec Wilder), lyrics by Eddie de Lange, and book by Gilbert Seldes and Erik Charell. (The musicians in the show played additional musical numbers by a variety of songwriters each night.)
Produced and directed by Erik Charell, with associate producer Jean Rodney and dialogue director Philip Loeb
Scenic design by Herbert Andrews and Walter Jagemann, choreography by Agnes DeMille, with additional choreography by Bill Bailey for himself and Herbert White for the Lindy Hoppers; costumes by Herbert Andrews; musical directors Don Voorhees and Benny Goodman; conductor Don Voorhees, with the assistance of Benny Goodman and Bud Freeman leading their groups, the Benny Goodman Sextet and The Summa Cum Laude
No recordings exist

Kiss Me, Kate, based on *The Taming of the Shrew*
Opened 30 December 1948 at the New Century Theatre
Music and lyrics by Cole Porter, book by Bella and Samuel Spewack
Produced by Arnold Saint Subber and Lemuel Ayres, directed by John C. Wilson
Musical director Pembroke Davenport, choreography by Hanya Holm, scenic design by Lemuel Ayres, lighting design by Al Alloy
An original cast recording by Columbia in 1948 has been released by Sony on compact disc (1990)
The show was filmed by MGM in 1953, directed by George Sidney with Howard Keel, Katherine Grayson, and Ann Miller. Warner Home

Video has a digital transfer of the film available, while the film sound-track was re-mastered by Rhino in 1996

A 1958 Kinescope version was directed by George Schaefer, with Alfred Drake and Patricia Morison, for the Hallmark Hall of Fame. In 1968 Paul Bogart directed another production, with Carol Lawrence and Robert Goulet for ABC. (The musical director was Ray Charles; the production company was created by Robert Goulet.)

Finally, the 1999 Broadway revival of the show was recorded as a cast album by DRG in 2000. Furthermore, when the revival moved to London, the production was taped and shown on PBS's 'Great Performances' series (Image Entertainment dvd, 2002)

West Side Story, based on *Romeo and Juliet*
Opened 26 September 1957 at the Winter Garden Theatre
Music by Leonard Bernstein, lyrics by Stephen Sondheim, book by Arthur Laurents
Produced by Roger L. Stevens, Harold Prince, and Robert Griffith, directed by Jerome Robbins
Musical director Max Goberman, choreography by Jerome Robbins with Peter Gennaro, scenic design by Oliver Smith, costumes by Irene Sharaff, lighting design by Jean Rosenthal
The original cast recording of the show was produced by Goddard Lieberson for Columbia in 1957, and it has been digitally remastered for release as a Sony compact disc (1998). The film version was made in 1961, directed by Jerome Robbins (until he was dismissed) and Robert Wise for United Artists, with Natalie Wood, Richard Beymer, Rita Moreno, and Russ Tamblyn. A digital release of the film is available from MGM/UA (1998); the film's soundtrack was also released as a Sony compact disc (1992). In 1992, Bernstein also conducted a cast recording of a London revival at the Haymarket Theatre, which is available in a two-disc release from Jay Records. Finally, Leonard Bernstein conducted a concert version of the production, with Kiri Te Kanawa, José Carreras, and others in 1985. The concert was recorded as a two-disc release from Polygram (1990), and a PBS documentary was made about the project (Universal Music and Video, 2002 dvd)

As You Like It
Opened 27 October 1964 at the Theater de Lys (off-Broadway)
Music by John Balanos, lyrics and book by Dran and Tani Seitz

Produced by Lucille Lortel, directed by Val Forslund
Choreography by Joe Nelson, lighting design by Ellen Wittman

Babes in the Wood, based on *A Midsummer Night's Dream*
Opened 28 December 1964 at the Orpheum Theater (off-Broadway)
Music, lyrics, and book by Rick Besoyan
Produced by Sandy Farber and Aaron Schroeder, directed by Rick
 Besoyan
Musical director Natalie Charlson, choreography by Ralph Beaumont,
 scenic and lighting design by Paul Morrison, costumes by Howard
 Barker

Love and Let Love, based on *Twelfth Night*
Opened 3 January 1968 at Sheridan Square Playhouse (off-Broadway)
Music by Stanley Jay Gelber, lyrics by John Lollos and Don Christopher,
 book by John Lollos
Produced by the L. & L. L. Co., directed by John Lollos
Musical director Daniel Paget, choreography by Rhoda Levine, scenic
 design by Barbara Miller, costumes by Ynes, lighting design by Fred
 Allison

Your Own Thing, based on *Twelfth Night*
Opened 13 January 1968 at the Orpheum Theater (off-Broadway)
Music and lyrics by Hal Hester and Danny Apolinar, book by Donald
 Driver
Produced by Zev Bufman and Dorothy Love, directed by Donald
 Driver
Musical direction by Charles Schneider, dance arrangements by
 Charles Schneider, scenic design by Robert Guerra, costumes by
 Albert Wolsky, lighting design by Tom Skelton, technical director
 Richard Thayer, slides by Frank Derbas, and sequences by Michael
 W. Lundstead, film sequences by Michael Morse
An original cast recording of the 1968 production was made for RCA
 Victor, which re-released it on compact disc in 1999

Sensations, based on *Romeo and Juliet*
Opened 25 October 1970 at Theater Four (off-Broadway)
Music by Wally Harper, lyrics and book by Paul Zakrzweski
Produced by John Bowab and Charles Celian, directed by Jerry Dodge

Musical director Jack Lee, scenic design by William and Jean Eckart, lighting design by Beverly Emmons

The Two Gentlemen of Verona
Opened 1 December 1971 at the St. James Theatre (an earlier touring version was part of the New York Shakespeare Festival season in the summer of 1971)
Music by Galt MacDermot, lyrics by John Guare, book by John Guare and Mel Shapiro
Produced by Joseph Papp and the New York Shakespeare Festival, directed by Mel Shapiro
Musical director Harold Wheeler with additional musical staging by Dennis Nahat, choreography by Jean Erdman, scenic design by Ming Cho Lee, lighting design by Lawrence Metzler, sound design by Jack Shearing
An original cast recording of the 1971 production was made by Decca, which re-released it on compact disc in 2002

Pop, based on *King Lear*
Opened 3 April 1974 at the Players Theatre
Music by Donna Cribari, lyrics and book by Larry Schiff and Chuck Knull
Produced by Brad Gromelski in association with William Murphy III, directed by Allen R. Belknap
Musical director Donna Cribari, choreography by Ron Spencer, scenic design and costumes by Pat Gorman, lighting design by Hallam P. Greco

Rockabye Hamlet, based on *Hamlet*
Opened 17 February 1976 at the Minskoff Theatre
Music, lyrics, and book by Cliff Jones
Produced by Lester Osterman Productions and Joseph Kipness in association with Martin Richards, Victor D'Arc, and Marilyn Strauss, directed by Gower Champion
Musical director Gordon Lowry Harrell, choreography by Gower Champion with Tony Stevens, scenic design by Kert F. Lundell, costumes by Joseph G. Aulisi, lighting design by Jules Fisher, sound design by Abe Jacob

Dreamstuff, based on *The Tempest*
Opened 2 April 1976 at the WPA Theatre (off-Broadway)
Music by Marsha Malamet, lyrics by Dennis Green, book by Howard
   Ashman
Produced by WPA New Plays Workshop with Daniel Dietrich as co-
   producer, directed by James Nicola
Musical direction by H. Ross Levy, choreography by Lynne Gannaway,
   scenic design by Dan Leigh, costumes by Marianne Powell-Parker,
   lighting design by Martin Tudor

Music Is, based on *Twelfth Night*
Opened 20 December 1976 at the St. James Theatre
Music by Richard Adler, lyrics by Will Holt, and book by George Abbott
Produced by Richard Adler, Roger Berlind, and Edward Downe, Jr.;
   directed by George Abbott
Musical direction by Paul Gemignani, choreography by Patricia Birch,
   scenic design by Eldon Elder, costumes by Lewis D. Rampino,
   lighting design by H. R. Poindexter

Oh Brother, based on *The Comedy of Errors*
Opened 10 November 1981 at the ANTA Playhouse
Music by Michael Valenti, lyrics and book by Donald Driver
Produced by Zev Bufman and the Kennedy Center with the Fisher
   Theater Foundation, Joan Cullman, and Sidney Shlenker, directed by
   Donald Driver
Musical direction and choreography by Marvin Laird, scenic design by
   Michael J. Hotopp and Paul De Pass, lighting design by Richard
   Nelson, sound design by Richard Fitzgerald

Return to the Forbidden Planet, based on *The Tempest*
Opened 13 October 1991 at the Variety Arts Playhouse (off-Broadway)
Written by Bob Carleton with songs from various people
Produced by Andre Ptaszynski and Don Taffner, directed by Bob
   Carleton
Musical direction by Kate Edgar, scenic design by Rodney Ford, costumes
   by Sally Lesser and Adrian Rees, lighting design by Richard Nelson,
   sound design by Bobby Aitken, film effects by Gerry Anderson

Play On!, based on *Twelfth Night*
Opened 20 March 1997 at the Brooks Atkinson Theatre

Conceived by Sheldon Epps, music and lyrics by Duke Ellington and Billy Strayhorn, book by Cheryl L. West

Produced by Mitchell Maxwell, Eric Nederlander, Thomas Hall, Hal Luftig, Bruce Lucker, Mike Skipper, and Victoria Maxwell, in association with Kerry Davis and Alan J. Schuster, directed by Sheldon Epps

Musical director J. Leonard Oxley, choreography by Mercedes Ellington, scenic design by James Leonard Joy, costumes by Marianna Elliott, lighting design by Jeff Davis, sound design by Jeff Ladman

The Lion King, based on *Hamlet*

Opened 13 November 1997 at the New Amsterdam Theatre

Music by Elton John, lyrics by Tim Rice, book by Roger Allers and Irene Mecchi from the screenplay by Irene Mecchi, Jonathan Roberts, and Linda Woolverton; additional music and lyrics by Lebo M, Mark Mancina, Jay Rifkin, Julie Taymor, and Hans Zimmer

Produced by Disney, directed by Julie Taymor

Musical director, Joseph Church, choreography by Garth Fagan, scenic design by Richard Hudson, costumes Julie Taymor, lighting design by Donald Holder, sound design by Tony Meola

The Bombitty of Errors, based on *The Comedy of Errors*

Opened 12 December 1999 at 45 Bleeker (off-Broadway)

Music by J.A.Q., lyrics and book by Jordan Allen-Dutton, Jason Catalano, Gregory J. Qaiyum and Erik Weiner

Produced by Daryl Roth, Michael Lynne, Q Brothers, and Hal Luftig; directed and developed by Andy Goldberg

Scenic design by Scott Pask, costumes by David C. Woolard, lighting design by James Vermeulen, sound design by One Dream Sound, Sunil Rajan

The Donkey Show, based on *A Midsummer Night's Dream*

Opened 18 August 1999 at Club El Flamingo (off-Broadway)

Conceived by Randy Weiner; created by Diane Paulus and Randy Weiner, music from various artists

Production supervisor David Gilman in association with Project 400 Theater Group, directed by Diane Paulus and Randy Weiner, stage manager Jim Athens

Costumes by David Woolard, lighting design by Kevin Adams, sound design by Brett Jarvis, specialty choreography by Maria Torres

Notes

INTRODUCTION

1 Alexis de Tocqueville, *Democracy in America*, ed. Richard D. Heffner (New York: Mentor, 1956), 174.
2 Ralph Waldo Emerson, *Representative Men, Essays and Lectures* (New York: Library of America, 1983), 250.
3 David Bevington and Jay Halio, eds., *Shakespeare: Pattern of Excelling Nature* (Newark: University of Delaware Press, 1978).
4 One of the earliest analyses is Leo Marx, "Shakespeare's American Fable," in *The Machine in the Garden* (London and New York: Oxford University Press, 1964), 34–72, which uses *The Tempest* to consider the earliest accounts of America. While Marx has relatively little to say about Shakespeare's figure in American culture, others discuss it extensively. See, for example, the books by Michael Bristol, *Shakespeare's America, America's Shakespeare* (London: Routledge, 1990); Esther Dunn, *Shakespeare in America* (New York: Macmillan, 1939); Charles Shattuck, *Shakespeare on the American Stage* (Washington, D.C.: Folger Press, 1976, 1987); Kim Sturgess, *Shakespeare and the American Nation* (Cambridge University Press, 2004); and Alfred Westfall, *American Shakespearean Criticism, 1607–1865* (New York, H. W. Wilson, 1939). (The book by Sturgess reached me after I had written my book, but I have tried to indicate the points where we agree or disagree in interesting ways.) I shall use the Riverside Shakespeare as the edition for citations from Shakespeare's plays.
5 Shakespeare's importance in Emerson's work has been widely considered, for Shakespeare and his work not only provided Emerson with endless allusions and examples, but also with the mysterious fact of the dramatist's greatness for which Emerson tried to account. Among the most recent studies are these: Sanford Marovitz, "Emerson's Shakespeare: from Scorn to Apotheosis" in Joel Myerson, *Emerson Centenary Essays* (Carbondale: Southern Illinois University Press, 1982), 122–55; or Len Gougeon, "Emerson and Furness: Two Gentlemen of Abolition," *American Transcendental Quarterly* 41 (1979): 17–31. Bristol's book offers an exemplary analysis of Shakespeare in American literary circles, while Julian Markels discusses Melville in *Melville and the Politics of Identity: From "King Lear" to "Moby-Dick"* (Urbana: University of Illinois Press, 1983). Less has been done on Whitman, but see Stephen Brown, "The Uses of Shakespeare

in America: a Study in Class Domination," in Bevington and Halio, 230–38 or Joann Kreig, *Walt Whitman: Here and Now*, (Westport, Conn.: Greenwood Press, 1985).

1 Phyllis Hartnoll, *The Oxford Companion to the Theatre* (London: Oxford University Press, 1967, 4th edn. 1983). Cf. Felicia Londre in vol. 2 of *The History of World Theater* (New York: Continuum/Frederick Ungar, 1991); Walter J. Meserve, *An Emerging Entertainment: The Drama of the American People to 1828* (Bloomington: Indiana University Press, 1977), esp. chs. 1–2; Garff Wilson, *Three Hundred Years of American Drama and Theatre*, 2nd edn. (Englewood Cliffs, N.J.: Prentice-Hall, 1982), "Prologue." Of course writers of such books are often aware of other versions of history, but are constrained by the limits of the form. Hartnoll does, after all, substantially modify her account of Shakespeare's place in American drama in the fourth edition of the *OCT* (1983), while Felicia Londre and Daniel J. Watermeier's *History of North American Theatre* acknowledges a variety of cultural influences on American theatre.

2 The term "orature" is from Joseph Roach, *Cities of the Dead: Circum-Atlantic Performance* (New York: Columbia University Press, 1996).

3 Elizabeth Wright, Louise Burkhart, and Barry D. Sell are in the process of preparing four Nahuatl texts from 1640 in a scholarly edition, which will be the second volume in the Nahuatl Theater Series for the University of Oklahoma Press; the texts include Nahuatl versions of Pedro Calderon de la Barca's *El gran teatro del mundo*, Lope de Vega's *La madre de la mejor*, Antonio Mira de Amescua's *El animal profeta y dichosa parricida San Julian*, and "an *entremes* of uncertain authorship" (Wright, 1). *OCT* claims translations to the Incan language Quechua as well, but does not give a source for that information.

4 Among the earliest important Spanish-language playwrights from the Americas, for example, are Ruiz de Alarcon, Eusebio Vela, and Sor Juana. I have sought information about the early Spanish language theatre in America from a number of sources. Among these is one particularly rich item: a special issue of *Theatre Arts Monthly* on Mexican theatre, edited by Miguel Covarrubio, 22 (1938). Other sources include Marilyn Ravicz, *Early Colonial Religious Drama in Mexico* (Washington D.C.: Catholic University of America Press, 1970); Rudolfo Usigli, *Mexico in the Theater*, trans. Wilder P. Scott (University, Miss.: Romance Monographs no.#18, 1976); Guillermo Lohmann Villena, *El Arte Dramtico En Lima Durante El Virreinato* (Madrid: [Estades, artes grficas] 1945). I must confess, however, that I have been unable to date the first production of a play by Lope de Vega in the Americas, although his work was known in Mexico by the 1590s and was produced by the end of the sixteenth century after the playhouse was established.

5 Marc Lescarbot wrote the masque; a translation was published in 1927. As Georgianna Ziegler has pointed out to me, in Lescarbot's *History of New France* he contrasts native performance traditions to those of the French.

6 For information on Canadian drama, see Eugene Benson and L. W. Conolly, eds., *Oxford Companion to Canadian Theater* (Toronto: Oxford University Press, 1989) and William Toye, ed., *The Oxford Companion to Canadian Literature* (Oxford University Press, 1983); according to Toye's entry, "Drama in French," the conflict between Monsignor de Saint Vallier and Governor Frontenac was resolved when the Bishop offered the impecunious Governor £100 to cancel his production.

7 David Hackett Fischer, *Albion's Seed* (New York: Oxford University Press, 1989), 55. For the word "nostalgia," Susan Bennett, *Performing Nostalgia* (London, New York: Routledge, 1996).

8 Jeffrey Richards, *Theater Enough* (Durham, N.C.: Duke University Press, 1991) argues that American ambivalence toward the actual theatre and fascination with the *theatrum mundi* trope similarly affects both the Anglican South and the Congregational New England (179). I would modify that argument somewhat, although I suspect he is correct in his analysis of the theatrical aspects of the Great Awakening (201–08). See also Patricia Bonomi's *Under the Cope of Heaven* (New York: Oxford University Press, 1986) on the Great Awakening.

9 Margot Heineman, *Puritanism and Theatre* (Cambridge University Press, 1980), 22. See also Louis B. Wright, "The Reading of Plays during the Puritan Revolution," *Huntington Library Bulletin* 6 (November 1934): 73–108. Both Jeffrey H. Richards and Jean-Christophe Agnew, *Worlds Apart* (Cambridge University Press, 1986), discuss the prevalence of classical play texts in early Puritan libraries.

10 Meserve 15–23; Hugh Rankin, *Theater in Colonial America* (Chapel Hill: University of North Carolina Press, 1960), 5–8; Odai Johnson and William Burling, *The Colonial American Stage* (Madison, N. J.: Fairleigh Dickinson Press, 2001), 92–94. Vernon Jones found the reference to *Ye Bare and Ye Cubbe* (1665), "The Theatre in Colonial Virginia," *The Reviewer* 7 (1925): 81–88. Most histories continue to use the date of 1703 when Tony Aston (or Ashton) gave performances, probably solo dramatic readings, in Charleston and New York, as the beginning of America's professional theatre.

11 Gary Taylor, *Reinventing Shakespeare* (New York: Oxford University Press, 1989); Margreta de Grazia, *Shakespeare Verbatim* (Oxford: Clarendon Press, 1991); Grace Ioppolo, *Revising Shakespeare* (Cambridge, Mass.: Harvard University Press, 1991).

12 Richard Beale Davis, *Intellectual Life in the Colonial South* (Knoxville: University of Tennessee Press, 1978), 2: 509.

13 James Hart, *The Popular Book* (New York: Oxford University Press, 1950), 28.

14 See Richards, *Theater Enough*, "Puritans thought plays to be appropriate reading" (118–19). Richards gives many instances; Wright's article on "The Reading of Plays" is also useful.

15 Dunn 20–24. She mentions only one other Shakespeare quotation in a commonplace book. E. E. Willoughby, "The Reading of Shakespeare in Colonial America," *PBSA* 30 (1936): 48, is also relevant.

16 Dunn 24. William Schiede, "The Earliest First Folio in America?" *Shakespeare Quarterly*, 27 (1976): 332–33, suggests that the tradition of Cotton Mather's First Folio stems from the fact that his granddaughter, Hannah Mather Crocker, married Samuel Parker in 1802. Parker owned the earliest First Folio in America; its presence can be dated to 1791. Sturgess calls the Cotton Mather Folio tale a myth and points out the likelihood that Virginians would be the first Americans familiar with Shakespeare (122–23).

17 Richard Beale Davis, *A Colonial Southern Bookshelf* (Athens: University of Georgia, 1979).

18 Both Charles Shattuck and Cedric Gale, "Shakespeare on the American Stage in the Eighteenth Century" (Diss.: New York University, 1945) mention other possibilities for the first performance of Shakespeare. In 1729/30 a production of *Romeo and Juliet* was announced in New York; although there is no evidence this production took place, Johnson and Burling think it may well have gone forward (107). Gale also records a 1737 performance of "The Song of Mad Tom" in Charleston, which could be a piece from *King Lear*.

The usual credit for the first professional American productions of Shakespeare goes to Lewis Hallam's company, an attribution that Shattuck would "simply accept," although Gale prefers the Murray–Kean 1750 productions in New York or the Robert Upton 1751 productions, also in New York. My own preference is for the Murray–Kean Company, which performed in New York, Maryland, and Virginia, and built the first American playhouse in Williamsburg. Neither Shattuck nor Gale pays much attention to productions of English stage plays in Jamaica, which clearly preceded those on the mainland, as Richardson Wright demonstrates in *Revels in Jamaica, 1682–1838* (New York: Dodd, Mead, 1937).

When all is said and done, the question of which company deserves credit for the first Shakespeare productions in America is far less important or interesting than the questions of why Shakespeare productions came so late to the New World or why they suddenly became so popular.

19 Robert Myers and Joyce Brodowski, "Rewriting the Hallams: Research in 18th-Century British and American Theatre," *Theatre Survey* 44 (2000): 1–22.

20 Jared Brown, *The Theatre in America during the Revolution* (Cambridge University Press, 1995), 4. Cited as J. Brown.

21 For information about Revolutionary performances, I supplement J. Brown, Johnson and Burling, Gale, Shattuck, and Rankin with Thomas Clark Pollock, *The Philadelphia Theatre in the Eighteenth Century* (Philadelphia: University of Pennsylvania Press, 1933); Kenneth Silverman, *A Cultural History of the American Revolution: 1763–1789* (New York: Crowell, 1976); and John Ripley's performance history of *Coriolanus, Coriolanus on Stage in England and America 1609–1994* (Madison, N.J.: Fairleigh Dickinson Press, 1998): 208–210.

22 See David Shields, *Oracles of Empire: Poetry, Politics, and Commerce in British America, 1690–1750* (University of Chicago Press, 1990).

23 Hanford Henderson and Marian Carson detail these items. Henderson discusses a particular mantelpiece in "Shakespeare in Marble in Colonial

America," *Shakespeare Quarterly* 12 (1961): 156–57. Carson surveys catalogues and advertisements in "Shakespeare in Early American Decorative Arts," *Shakespeare Quarterly* 12 (1961): 154–56. Although it does not fit into the years before the Revolution, Carson does include an example that is tantalizing: a sampler prepared by a young American named Anne Hathaway in 1797 that quotes two lines from *Titus Andronicus*:

> Fair Philomel, she but lost her tongue
> And in a tedious sampler sewed her mind.

24 My discussion of such references draws on the following items: Hennig Cohen, "Shakespeare in Charleston on the Eve of the Revolution," *Shakespeare Quarterly* 4 (1953): 327–30; Peter Rawlings, *Americans on Shakespeare, 1776–1914* (Aldershot, Hants.: Ashgate, 1999); Maurice Morgann, "An Essay on the Dramatic Character of Sir John Falstaff," in *Shakespearian Criticism*, ed. Daniel A. Fineman (Oxford: Clarendon Press, 1972); Douglas Wilson, ed., *Jefferson's Literary Commonplace Book*, The Papers of Thomas Jefferson, 2nd ser. (Princeton University Press, 1989); as well as the work by Dunn. Bristol is invaluable, and his discussion of how Shakespeare serves Adams' political ends is fascinating, 51–59.

25 My account of the production draws on a number of sources. For the company's repertoire, see Johnson and Burling. The author of the 6 September 1770 poem is said to be William Eddis by Charles Coleman Sellers, *Charles Willson Peale* (New York: Scribner's, 1969), although both Shattuck in *Shakespeare on the American Stage* and Lillian Miller in *The Selected Papers of Charles Willson Peale and His Family*, 5 vol., ed. Lillian Miller et al. (New Haven: Yale University Press, 1983–2000), argue that the poet was Boucher. Other works I have consulted include *New Perspectives on Charles Willson Peale: A 250th Anniversary Celebration*, ed. Lillian B. Miller and David Ward (University of Pittsburgh Press for the Smithsonian Institution, 1991) and William Dunlap, *A History of the American Theatre* (New York: Burt Franklin, 1963 rpt. of 1832 edn.).

26 The notion that Nancy Hallam's attractiveness might move an Annapolis gentleman to make the purchase may be strengthened if one regards the use of the grotto as erotic. Jonathan Prown and Richard Miller, "The Rococo, the Grotto, and the Philadelphia High Chest," in *American Furniture*, ed. Luke Beckerdite (Foxpoint, Wis.: Chipstone Publications, 1996).

CHAPTER 2

1 For information about the Jubilee, see Christian Deelman, *The Great Shakespeare Jubilee* (New York: Viking, 1964), or Martha Winburn England, *Garrick's Jubilee* (Columbus, Ohio: Ohio State University Press, 1964).

2 Quoted in Van Carl Kussrow, "On with the Show: A Study of Public Arguments in Favor of Theatre in America during the Eighteenth Century" (Diss.: Indiana University, 1959), 37 spelling retained in extract. I have also found useful Paul Langford's essay, "Manners and Character in Anglo-American Perceptions,

1750–1850," in *Anglo-American Attitudes: From Revolution to Partnership*, ed. Fred M. Leventhal and Roland Quinault (Aldershot, Hants.: Ashgate, 2000).

3 I have drawn on a number of sources for my treatment of the Adams and Jefferson visit to Stratford-upon-Avon. First of all, I have looked at their own accounts: Thomas Jefferson, *The Papers of Thomas Jefferson*, ed. Julian P. Boyd et al. (Princeton University Press, 1950–2000), vol. 9; and John Adams, *Diary and Autobiography of John Adams*, ed. L. H. Butterfield (Cambridge, Mass.: Belknap Press of Harvard University Press, 1961), ser. 1, vol. 3. In addition, I found useful Edward Dumbauld, *Thomas Jefferson, American Tourist* (Norman: University of Oklahoma Press, 1946) and David McCullough, *John Adams* (New York: Simon & Schuster, 2001).

4 See Walter Meserve, *Heralds of Promise: The Drama of the American People during the Age of Jackson, 1829–1849* (New York and Westport, Conn.: Greenwood Press, 1986), especially chapter 1.

5 Louis Wright, *Culture on the Moving Frontier* (Bloomington: University of Indiana Press, 1955), 74.

6 In his book, Westfall 168–85 says the earliest American edition of a single play (an adaptation of *The Comedy of Errors*) was published in 1787 (he lists American editions to 1865, 168–85), while Edwin Wolf II says the 1795–96 edition published in Philadelphia was the earliest. ("A signed American Binding on the First American Edition of Shakespeare," *Shakespeare Quarterly* (12) (1961), 153–54). Sturgess reprints the title page and preface from the 1795 edition.

7 Penny's journal was published in 1970, under the title *North to Lake Superior*, ed. James L. Carter and Ernest H. Rankin (Marquette, Mich.: John M. Longyear Research Library, 1970). I first learned of it from a posting by Ron Dwelle on the Shakespeare Conference, Shaksper-L, 27 February 1997.

8 For Shakespeare's fortunes in the western United States, I have used both Helene Koon's *How Shakespeare Won the West: Players and Performances in America's Gold Rush, 1849–1865* (Jefferson, N.C.: McFarland, 1989) and Jennifer Carrell's "How the Bard Won the West," *Smithsonian* 29 (1998): 98–102, 104, 106–07.

CHAPTER 3

1 "P. T. Barnum," *American National Biography Online*, 25 October 2005, http://www.anb.org/articles/home.html. I have, of course, also examined Barnum's own account of himself: *Struggles and Triumphs* (Buffalo: Warren, Johnson, 1872), cited as *S&T*, as well as *The Humbugs of the World* (New York: Carleton, 1866). For an overview of Barnum's career, I found Philip Kunhardt, et al., *P. T. Barnum, America's Greatest Showman* (New York: Knopf, 1995), especially useful. The most interesting cultural studies analysis of Barnum that I have found is James Cook's *The Arts of Deception: Playing with Fraud in the Age of Barnum* (Cambridge, Mass.: Harvard University Press, 2001).

2 Robert Lewis, *From Traveling Show to Vaudeville* (Baltimore: Johns Hopkins Press, 2003): 4–5.

3 Joe Vitale, *There's a Customer Born Every Minute* (New York : AMACOM, 1998), 12 and chapter 7. I was curious where Vitale found this epithet, but he gives no source. In Irving Wallace's popular biography of Barnum, *The Fabulous Showman* (New York: Knopf, 1959), however, I stumbled across this sentence: "On a recording of Barnum's voice reissued in 1940 Professor William Lyon Phelps called Barnum 'the greatest psychologist who ever lived . . . the Shakespeare of advertising.'"

4 It is, perhaps, worth noting that Barnum's account of what he found at the birthplace, including the exaggerated accounts of the guides, seems curiously close to the account that Washington Irving gives. One might suspect that Barnum was plagiarizing, but a third account, that of Henry James, is also quite close to what both Barnum and Irving say. The accounts by Washington Irving and Henry James can be found in the Rawlings anthology.

5 The account about Barnum was available on 17 July 2002 at this URL, http://www.stratford.co.uk/birthplace/barnum.html, but has subsequently been removed.

6 The text I quote is part of an internal information memo that Mairi Macdonald prepared for the Birthplace Trust Library. In the summer of 2002, I met with her and she very generously offered me a copy and told me I could publish it.

7 Sturgess does believe he made the effort to buy the birthplace (182–83), while I suspect he may have thought about it without acting, and then later have embellished his plans to create a good story.

8 Mark Twain, *Following the Equator*, ed. Shelley Fisher Fishkin (Oxford University Press, 1996).

9 The "Jumbo" episode, of course, occurred in 1881–82, long after the birthplace was saved.

10 Quoted in Rawlings, 159. According to Rawlings, this anonymous essay is a review of Thomas De Quincy's *Biographical Essays* that was published in the *Literary World* 7 (1850).

11 W. K. Northall, *Before and Behind the Curtain*, New York: W. F. Burgess, 1851), 165–66.

CHAPTER 4

1 Richard Moody, *The Astor Place Riot* (Bloomington: Indiana University Press, 1958); citations to "Moody" will be to this book. More work is needed on Forrest's life; however, Moody's biography, *Edwin Forrest: First Star of the American Stage* (New York: Knopf, 1960) remains essential.

2 Alvin Harlow, *Old Bowery Days* (New York: D. Appleton, 1931), 264.

3 H. M. Ranney, *Account of the Terrific and Fatal Riot . . .* (New York, 1849), 16.

4 Dennis Berthold, "Class Acts: Melville's 'The Two Temples,'" *American Literature* 71.3 (1999): 430; Berthold offers a fascinating investigation of Melville's role. Barbara Foley's essay is also useful in providing background for the riots: "From Wall Street to Astor Place: Historicizing Melville's 'Bartleby,'" *American Literature* 72 (2000): 87–136.

5 Peter Holland, "Touring Shakespeare," in *The Cambridge Companion to Shakespeare on Stage*, ed. Stanley Wells and Sarah Stanton (Cambridge University Press, 2002), 202.

6 Lawrence Levine, "William Shakespeare and the American People," in *The Unpredictable Past* (New York: Oxford University Press, 1993), 168.

7 Bruce McConachie, "The Theatre of Edwin Forrest and Jacksonian Hero Worship," in *When They Weren't Doing Shakespeare*, ed. Judith Fischer and Stephen Watt (Athens: University of Georgia Press, 1989), 4. McConachie also points to Macready's interest in such political dramas (4).

8 John Velz and Frances Teague, *One Touch of Shakespeare* (Washington, D.C.: Folger Press, 1986), 275.

CHAPTER 5

1 *"Right or Wrong, God Judge Me"*: *The Writings of John Wilkes Booth*, ed. John Rhodehamel and Louise Taper (Urbana: University of Illinois Press, 1997), 43. I have also consulted Asia Booth Clarke, *John Wilkes Booth: A Sister's Memoir*, ed. Terry Alford (Jackson: University Press of Mississippi, 1996). Histories of Wilkes Booth and the Lincoln assassination seem innumerable, but these have been useful to my research: Lloyd Lewis, *The Assassination of Lincoln: History and Myths after Lincoln* (Lincoln: University of Nebraska Press, 1994); Philip Van Doren Stern, *The Man Who Killed Lincoln: the Story of John Wilkes Booth and His Part in the Assassination* (New York: Literary Guild of America, 1939); Gordon Samples, *Lust for Fame: The Stage Career of John Wilkes Booth* (Jefferson, N.C.: McFarland, 1982); Albert Furtwangler, *Assassin on Stage* (Urbana: University of Illinois Press, 1991); Michael Kauffman's recent *American Brutus* (New York: Random House, 2004).

2 David Donald, *Lincoln* (New York: Simon and Schuster, 1995), 569; Donald has the fullest treatment on Lincoln's reading. Hackett's *Notes, Criticism, and Correspondence upon Shakespeare's Plays and Actors* (New York: Benjamin Blom rpt. 1864 edn., 1968) has Lincoln's letters about Shakespeare. Marquis Adolphe de Chambrun offered his "Personal Recollection of Mr. Lincoln," *Scribner's Magazine* 13 (1893): 35. William C. Harris, *Lincoln's Last Months* (Cambridge, Mass.: Belknap Press of Harvard University Press, 2004) is helpful on the Hackett contretemps.

CHAPTER 6

1 "American Musical Theatre before the Twentieth Century," in *The Cambridge Companion to the* Musical, ed. William A. Everett amd Paul R. Laird (Cambridge University Press, 2002), 3. While I regard variety as the more important precursor to book musicals, others would argue that operetta is more important. See, for example, Alan Jay Lerner, *The Musical Theatre: A Celebration* (New York: McGraw-Hill, 1986), or Mark Steyn, *Broadway Babies Say Goodnight* (New York: Routledge, 1997).

For variety entertainment history, Lawrence Levine's generative essay, "William Shakespeare and the American People," sometimes called "High Brow, Low Brow," is useful, as is Ray B. Browne's "Shakespeare in American Vaudeville and Negro Minstrelsy," *American Quarterly* 12 (1960), 374–91. I have also found *American Vaudeville as Seen by its Contemporaries*, ed. Charles W. Stein (New York: Knopf, 1984), a collection of first-person recollections, an invaluable resource for understanding early twentieth-century variety performers.

2 To call some entertainments "legitimate" and others "popular" implies that Shakespeare and other drama was unpopular, while melodrama or burlesques are in some way bastard forms. To divide the kinds of entertainment into elite and high-brow versus low-brow suggests that the well-to-do and upper-class never enjoyed vaudeville or circuses, while the working-class or poor never enjoyed opera or Shakespeare. I can do nothing about "legitimate" since the term is too widely accepted, but I choose to use "variety" because it does not offend my common sense as the other terms do.

3 Robert Snyder, *The Voice of the City: Vaudeville and Popular Culture in New York* (New York and Oxford University Press, 1989), 5.

4 Andrew Erdman, *Blue Vaudeville: Sex, Morals, and the Mass Marketing of Amusement, 1895–1915* (Jefferson, N.C.: McFarland, 2004) and M. Allison Kibler, *Rank Ladies: Gender and Cultural Hierarchy in American Vaudeville* (Chapel Hill: University of North Carolina Press, 1999).

5 Stanley Wells, *Nineteenth-Century Shakespeare Burlesques* (Wilmington, Del.: M. Glazier, 1978) and Richard Schoch, *"Not Shakespeare": Bardolatry and Burlesque in the Nineteenth Century* (Cambridge University Press, 2002).

6 In Alex Preminger, T. V. F. Brogan, et al., *The New Princeton Encyclopedia of Poetry and Poetics* (Princeton University Press, 1993), s.v. Burlesque, 152. Also relevant are Richard Grant White's "The Age of Burlesque," *Galaxy* (August 1869): 256–66; Robert C. Allen, *Horrible Prettiness: Burlesque and American Culture* (Chapel Hill: University of North Carolina Press, 1991); Douglas Gilbert, *American Vaudeville: Its Life and Times* (New York: Dover Books, 1963 rpt. of 1940 edn.).

7 On the history of minstrel shows, Browne and Levine's studies have been followed by Nicholas Evans' discussion of Ira Aldrich's association with minstrel stereotypes, "Ira Aldridge: Shakespeare and Minstrelsy," *American Transcendental Quarterly* 16 (2002):165–87, as well as the very important study by Eric Lott, *Love and Theft: Blackface Minstrelsy and the American Working Class* (New York and Oxford University Press, 1993). Finally, on the doubled sensibility of minstrel performances, see Nadine George-Graves, *The Royalty of Negro Vaudeville: The Whitman Sisters and the Negotiation of Race, Gender, and Class in African-American Theatre, 1900–1940* (New York: St. Martin's Press, 2000).

8 The American Vaudeville Stage site is http://memory.loc.gov/ammem/vshtml/vshome.html (27 October 2005).

9 *The Complete Lyrics of Lorenz Hart*, ed. Dorothy Hart and Robert Kimball (New York: DeCapo, 1995), 28–29. In the sketch the phrase "toy queen" may be a reference to the melodrama *Frou-Frou* (1870), by Augustin Daly. It was made

into several silent films, the most memorable of which was *Toy Wife* (1938) with Luise Rainer.

10 For a good general discussion, see *The Cambridge Companion to the Musical*, especially in the "Preface" where the editors define terms. Although American musicals are said to have begun with *The Black Crook* in 1866, the *integrated* book musical is generally said to begin in 1915 with the Princess Theatre show, *Nobody's Home*, although it was certainly building on what had happened in other shows. On *The Black Crook*, see Leigh George Odum, "'The Black Crook' at Niblo's Garden," *Drama Review* 26 (1982): 21–40, as well any history of the Broadway musical.

11 A full discussion of Renaissance practice *vis à vis* stage beards can be found in Will Fisher's essay, "Staging the Beard: Masculinity in Early Modern English Culture," in *Staged Properties in Early Modern English Drama*, ed. Jonathan Gil Harris and Natasha Korda (Cambridge University Press, 2002), 230–57.

12 Samuel Schoenbaum, *Shakespeare's Lives* (New York: Oxford University Press, 1970), 13.

13 *The American Thesaurus of Slang*, ed. Lester V. Berrey and Melvin Van den Bark (New York: Crowell, 1953), s.v. Beard; see also J. E. Lighter, *Random House Historical Dictionary of American Slang* (New York: Random House, 1994).

14 Robert Darnton, *The Great Cat Massacre and Other Episodes in French Cultural History* (New York: Vintage, 1985), 3.

15 Douglas Lanier, "Introduction," *Shakespeare and Modern Popular Culture* (Oxford University Press, 2002), 1–20; Richard Burt, "To e- or not to e-? Disposing of Schlockspeare in the Age of Digital Media," *Shakespeare after Mass Media* (New York: Palgrave, 2002), 7. For the terms "intertext" and "paratext," and the distinction between them, see Eric Mallin, "'You Kilt My Foddah': or, Arnold, Prince of Denmark," *Shakespeare Quarterly* 50 (1999): 128–29.

16 D. A. Miller, *Place for Us: Essay on the Broadway Musical* (Cambridge, Mass. and London: Harvard University Press, 1998), 1. Another useful book for my theoretical approach is John M. Clum, *Something for the Boys: Musical Theater and Gay Culture* (New York: St. Martin's Press, 1999). Finally, among the work that has influenced me are books listed in the bibliography by Geoffrey Block, Gerald Bordman, David Ewen, Martin Gottfried, Mark Grant, Otis Guernsey, Robert Lawson-Peebles, Kim Marra and Robert Schanke, Ethan Mordden, Richard Norton, Joseph Swain.

17 For this feature of post-modernism, see Andrew Milner, *Literature, Culture, and Society* (New York University Press, 1996), 56, or *The Columbia Dictionary of Modern Literary and Cultural Criticism*, ed. Joseph Childers and Gary Hentzi (New York: Columbia University Press, 1995), s.v. Postmodernism. Shakespeare's central position in the legitimate theatre is underscored by the *OED*'s definition of "legit" as "the legitimate drama: the body of plays, Shakespearian or other, that have a recognized theatrical and literary merit . . . Also in other collocations. So as sb., an actor of legitimate drama." The first instance the *OED* offers is from the late eighteenth century.

The idea of queer theory is still quite new, since Teresa de Lauretis introduced the term in 1991. A particularly useful introduction for critics who are also feminists is Kathy Rudy's "Queer Theory and Feminism," *Women's Studies* 29 (2000): 195–216.

18 Terry Teachout, "Is Musical Comedy Dead?" *Commentary* 117 (June 2004): 47.

19 The actual title of the Guare play is *Two Gentlemen of Verona*, but I shall generally refer to it as *Two Gents* to keep confusion between the early modern dramatic text and the twentieth-century musical at a minimum.

20 There are others that I do not discuss, because they were straightforward burlesques like Anna Russell's *Hamletto* (1956) or George Greanias' *Hello Hamlet!* (1969 and regularly revived at Rice University).

A number of regional theatres do musical adaptations, such as the Source Theatre's 2003 production of *Titus, the Musical*, the Georgia Shakespeare Festival's *Shrew: The Musical* (1993, revived 1999), or Chicago Shakespeare Theatre's *Hamlet, the Musical!* (2000). For some reason, *Hamlet* is particularly popular, having almost as many musical incarnations as the comedies. Unless these shows have made it to New York, I do not include them, but the topic of regional musical versions crops up regularly on the Shaksper-L listserve, which is searchable.

Other Shakespeare musicals include the rock musical film *Catch My Soul*, also known as *Santa Fe Satan* (*Othello*, 1973), and Bob Carlton's UK burlesque *Return to the Forbidden Planet*. Carlton has also done a musical version of *Macbeth* entitled *From a Jack to a King*, but I have not found details on it. Although Shakespeare's Juliet is mentioned in Rodger and Hammerstein's *Me and Juliet* (1953), it is in no other way Shakespearean; *The Fantastiks* has parallels to *Romeo and Juliet*, but is certainly based on Edmond Rostand's *Les Romanesques* (1894).

In *American Musical Theatre: A Chronicle* (Oxford University Press, 2001), Gerald Bordman mentions the shows I have named as well as such other works as an 1877 operetta, *Marjolaine* (based on *Cymbeline*), an 1895 burlesque, *Hamlet II*, and various revues (ranging from sketches in *The Passing Show of 1915* to *Shakespeare's Cabaret* in 1981).

CHAPTER 7

1 Eddie Foy and Alvin Harlow, *Clowning through Life* (New York: E. P. Dutton, 1928), 298. Other information about Foy's life comes from Armond Fields, *Eddie Foy: A Biography of the Early Popular Stage Comedian* (Jefferson, N.C.: McFarland Press, 1999).

2 In *American Musical Theatre*, Bordman notes "that Foy had touched on Hamlet before, singing 'Hamlet Was a Melancholy Dane' in the star-crossed *Mr. Bluebeard* (21 January 1903)," 289.

3 The two recorded songs are "Goodbye, Mollie Brown" and "Dusky Salome," *Music from the New York Stage*, vol. 2: 1908–13 (Sussex: Pearl, 1993). This record is quite hard to locate, and I am grateful to music historians at Indiana University,

Thomas Mathiesen, Jeff Magee, and Peter Schimpf, who sent me information
about the recording.

    Information about "Beautiful Rose" is from The Tunesmiths Database
http://www.nfo.net/.cal/ts6.html, consulted on 17 January 2001. The other
added songs are named in Fields, 179. I am grateful to the Shubert Archive,
particularly Mark Schwarz, for allowing me to examine scripts, programs, and
other documents relating to the production and its tours.

4 My information on the fire is from Foy's autobiography, checked with Marshall Everett, *The Great Chicago Theater Disaster* (Chicago and Philadelphia:
Publishers Union of America, 1904), as well as the splendid Chicago
Public Library website on the Iroquois Theatrical Fire: http://cpl.lib.uic.
edu/004chicago/disasters/iroquois_fire.html, consulted 25 October 2005.

5 On the theatrical season, see Gerald Bordman, *American Theatre*, vol. 1, 1869–
1914 (New York and Oxford University Press, 1994), 594–95, 648–49. Bordman
includes only the legit stage in this reference work, so Foy and his show go
unmentioned in it, although Bordman of course covers *Mr. Hamlet of Broadway*
in *American Musical Theatre*.

CHAPTER 8

1 Richard Rodgers, *Musical Stages: An Autobiography* (New York: Random House,
1975), 190–91.

2 *"Mister Abbott"* (New York: Random House, 1963), 186.

3 Abbott is also credited as co-author of *Three Men on a Horse* and producer for
Room Service and *The Boys from Syracuse*. In short, the production team knew
each other very well.

4 One must also wonder if Hart had seen the 1923 jazz production of *The Comedy
of Errors* by the Ethiopian Art Theatre. It seems unlikely, but possible. Errol
Hill describes *The Comedy of Errors* production, *Shakespeare in Sable* (Amherst:
University of Massachusetts, 1984), 98–101.

5 I use *The Complete Lyrics of Lorenz Hart* as my source for all citations from
Hart's lyrics. Also useful is Frederick Nolan, *Lorenz Hart – A Poet on Broadway*
(New York: Oxford, 1994) and Richard Rodgers, *Musical Stages*. The libretto
for *The Boys from Syracuse* was published in New York: Rodgers and Hammer-
stein Library, 1978, while the vocal score was published separately (New York:
Chappell, 1965).

    I have also consulted the books on Rodgers by Geoffrey Block, particularly
his biography, *Richard Rogers* (New Haven: Yale University Press, 2003), Meryle
Secrest's *Somewhere for Me: A Biography of Richard Rodgers* (New York: Knopf,
2001), and Jeffrey Smart's "Lorenz Hart: This Can't Be Love," in Kim Marra
and Robert A. Schanke, *Staging Desire: Queer Readings of American Theater
History* (Ann Arbor: University of Michigan Press, 2002), 167–93.

6 Alan Sinfield, "Making Space: Appropriation and Confrontation in Recent
British Plays," in *The Shakespeare Myth*, ed. Graham Holderness (New York:
St. Martin's Press, 1993), 130.

7 Gilbert Seldes, *The 7 Lively Arts*. (New York: Sagamore, revision of the 1924 1st edn., 1957), 309. The closest thing to a mention of Shakespeare comes in a section when Seldes, denouncing contemporary "serious drama," excludes "the *Medea* of Euripides and the tragedy of *Othello*" from his remarks (315).

8 Samuel Leiter, *Encyclopedia of the New York Stage 1930–40* (Westport, Conn.: Greenwood Press, 1989), 502. The Center Theatre was one of two theatres in Radio City at Rockefeller Center (the other being the Music Hall); it seated 3,700 and was demolished in 1954, according to Alan Balfour, *Rockefeller Center: Architecture as Theater* (New York: McGraw-Hill, 1978) 97.

9 I have found no mention of the script in performers' memoirs nor have I located a full script after checking the principal repositories for Seldes' papers (the New York Public Library's Billie Rose Library, the University of Pennsylvania library since Seldes established the Annenberg school there, or the Beinecke and Houghton libraries). The biographer of Seldes, Michael Kammen, says he has never seen a script, although "Marian Seldes gave me access to his surviving papers, and nothing remotely close was there" (private communication 18 July 2003). Alan Corrigan has found a few pages of a script in the Jimmy van Heusen papers at UCLA, and he was kind enough to share these with me. For his article about the manuscript and a reproduction of the pages, see "Jazz, Shakespeare, and Hybridity: a Script Excerpt from *Swingin' the Dream*," *Borrowers and Lenders* 1 (2005), 9 September 2005 http://atropos.english.uga.edu/cocoon/borrowers/index.

10 The decision to swing the "Spring Song" was not completely original. Tommy Dorsey recorded a swing version as one of his *Early Jazz Sides: 1932–1937* (reissued as a compact disc by Allegro in 2004).

11 Alec Wilder, *American Popular Song: The Great Innovators, 1900–1950* (New York: Oxford University Press, 1972), 444. The producer that Wilder mentions is clearly Charell, although Jean Rodney (later Jean Kintner) is listed as the associate producer.

12 Ross Firestone, *Swing, Swing, Swing: The Life and Times of Benny Goodman* (New York and London: W. W. Norton, 1993), 274. He gives more details about the production, 274–76. While Firestone reports the mistake that "Walt Disney provided artwork" he has also interviewed a number of the people involved, including Gilbert Seldes' daughter Marian Seldes, who was taken to the show as an eleven-year-old. The show's one hit: "Darn that Dream" sold more than 200,000 copies in sheet music by the end of 1940.

13 Bud Freeman and Robert Wolf, *Crazeology, the Autobiography of a Chicago Jazzman* (Urbana: University of Illinois Press, 1989), 50. Leonard Feather also discussed the production with Freeman, as he reports in *The Jazz Years: Earwitness to an Era* (New York: Da Capo, 1987).

14 John Hammond and Irving Townsend, *On the Record* (New York: Ridge Press, 1977).

15 "Swing Dream Has Rude Awakening," *Jazz Information* 1. 14 (14 December 1939), no page; and D. Russell Connor and Warren W. Hick, *BG On the*

Record: A Bio-Discography of Benny Goodman (New Rochelle, N.Y.: Arlington House, 1969).

16 For Loring as choreographer, see *New York Times* article by Vandamm, 26 November 1939, p. 132. I have taken the account of DeMille's life from Carol Easton's *No Intermissions: The Life of Agnes DeMille* (Boston: Little, Brown, 1996) and from DeMille's memoirs, *Speak with Me, Dance with Me* (Boston: Little Brown, 1973) and *Dance to the Piper* (Boston: Little, Brown, 1952). It's worth noting that Loring and DeMille shared space in a studio at about this time, so Loring may have recommended DeMille.

17 Norma Miller with Evette Jensen, *Swingin at the Savoy: The Memoir of a Jazz Dancer* (Philadelphia: Temple University Press, 1996), 145. Another Lindy Hopper, Naomi Waller, supposedly fought with DeMille, however; Terry Monaghan makes that claim in an online article about the Savoy Ballroom, writing "Agnes de Mille, the Dance Director, however did not take kindly to Naomi's embellishments of her chorus line choreography, or at least pretended not to whilst taking careful note and including them subsequently" (URL http://www.savoyballroom.com/nets/dafloor1/socdance/waller.htm, 20 August 2005).

18 I have drawn on the databases at the Internet Movie Database and the Internet Broadway Database sites, as well as Errol G. Hill and James V. Hatch, *A History of African American Theatre* (Cambridge University Press, 2003). For Mabley, see Elsie A. Williams, *The Humor of Jackie Moms Mabley: An African-American Comedic Tradition* (New York and London: Garland, 1995). The one "mechanical" I have not traced is the Snug, Gerald De La Fontaine, who came to the show from a play done by the WPA's Negro Theater Unit, but has left no further record.

19 Donald Bogle's *Dorothy Dandridge* (New York: Amistad, 1997) explains that Armstrong had first worked with Maxine Sullivan and the Dandridge Sisters in the 1938 movie, *Going Places*. When Armstrong returned to New York, he invited Sullivan and the Dandridge Sisters to join him in a nightclub act, and it seems likely that once he signed for *Swingin' the Dream* he proposed that they be cast.

20 Lewis A. Erenberg, *Swingin' the Dream: Big Band Jazz and the Rebirth of American Culture* (University of Chicago Press, 1998), 38.

21 Consider, for example, John Hammond's 1935 *Downbeat* attack on Duke Ellington's music as lacking guts because it was "unnegroid" and vapid. One factor in Hammond's criticism was Ellington's refusal to integrate his orchestra with white musicians. See Erenberg, 144–45.

CHAPTER 9

1 For information about Cole Porter's career, I have used William McBrien, *Cole Porter, a Biography* (New York: Alfred A. Knopf, 1998); Mark Fearnow's "Let's Do It: the Layered Life of Cole Porter," in Marra and Schanke; and Robert Kimball, ed., *Cole* (New York: Holt, Rinehart and Winston, 1971).

2 Arthur Laurents, *Original Story By* (New York: Knopf, 2000), 47.

3 Much of the information about the production problems of *Kiss Me, Kate*, comes from McBrien, chapter 16, "The Champ Is Back" and the chapter on *Kiss Me, Kate* in Geoffrey Block's *Enchanted Evenings* (Oxford University Press, 1997).

4 After I had written my initial analysis, I read that of Robert Lawson-Peebles, "Brush Up Your Shakespeare: the Case of *Kiss Me, Kate*," in *Approaches to the American Musical*, ed. Robert Lawson-Peebles (University of Exeter Press, 1996), 89–107. His reading of the film makes many of the same points that I do about the musical on stage, and I am delighted that I have the opportunity to include his comments here. Other critics whose work on *Kiss Me, Kate* has been useful are Richard Burt, *Unspeakable ShaXXXpeares: Queer Theory and American Kiddie Culture* (New York: St. Martin's Press, 1998); Barbara Hodgdon, "Katherina Bound; or, Play (K)ating the strictures of Every day Life," *PMLA* 107 (1992), 538–53; and the superb musical analysis of Joseph Swain, *The Broadway Musical: A Critical and Musical Survey* (New York and Oxford University Press, 1990).

5 The panel discussion was published in Otis Guernsey's *Broadway Song and Story* (New York, Dodd, Mead, 1885), 40–54. I have consulted a wide variety of other sources including memoirs and biographies of the production team, who have all been much written about. Especially useful is Arthur Laurents' autobiography; Deborah Jowitt, *Jerome Robbins: His Life, His Theater, His Dance* (New York: Simon and Schuster, 2004); Joan Peyser, *Bernstein: A Biography* (New York: Billboard, 1998); and Craig Zadan's *Sondheim & Co.* (New York: Harper and Row, 1986). Block's *Enchanted Evenings* was also a very useful resource. Finally, for background on the production process I have used Keith Garebian's *The Making of "West Side Story"* (Oakville, Ontario and Buffalo, N.Y.: Mosaic Press, 1998).

6 According to Jowitt, in "Robbins' 'tale of an actor friend' [it] has been assumed that the actor was Robbins' then-lover, Montgomery Clift" (267). Yet Jowitt argues that in fact the actor was Kevin McCarthy, cast to play Romeo on the television program *Omnibus*, and that McCarthy consulted not Robbins but Clift, who then told Robbins about the experience.

7 The Bernstein quotation is reprinted from Garebian 30, but first appeared in Bernstein's *Findings* (New York: Simon and Schuster, 1982). As a number of people have pointed out, parts of Bernstein's diary were evidently written well after the fact.

8 His 1939 bachelor's thesis at Harvard, "The Absorption of Race Elements in American Music," considered precisely these issues, and was later reprinted in *Findings*. See Garebian 26–27.

9 Again, there is disagreement about what happened. Jowitt remarks, "Judging by a letter dated July 19 from Laurents to Bernstein, which included a skeleton outline, the plot shift had begun before the legs-in-the-pool moment" (268).

10 In addition to the disagreements about what credit is due whom, everyone does agree that Bernstein's refusal to accept any credit as the show's co-lyricist was an extraordinary act of generosity.

11 The label is from Laurents, who says "the Jets are an anthology of what is called 'American'" in his opening stage direction. There were a number of attempts to change the opening, making it more violent, but the team finally felt that the current scene worked better than any alternative (Zadan 24).

12 See Richard Jacoby, *Conversations with the Capeman* (Madison: University of Wisconsin Press, 2004).

CHAPTER 10

1 Rick Simas, *The Musicals No One Came to See* (New York: Garland, 1987).

2 The script was published as a paperback by Dell in 1970, but is now out of print. It is also included in Stanley Richards, *Great Rock Musicals* (New York: Stein and Day, 1979), 289–378. Robert Sandla's liner notes to *Your Own Thing* (New York: RCA Victor, 1999) are excellent. Virtually nothing else has been written about the show save for reviews.

3 On the Lucky Pierre joke, see Gregory Bredbeck, "B/O – Barthes' Text/O'Hara's Trick," PMLA 108 (1993): 268–82.

4 The script was published by Holt, Rinehart, and Winston in 1973; it too is anthologized in Richards, 67–167. I have also drawn on Helen Epstein's biography, *Joe Papp: An American Life* (Boston: Little, Brown, 1994), and Christine E. King and Brenda Coven, *Joseph Papp and the New York Shakespeare Festival: An Annotated Bibliography* (New York: Garland, 1988).

5 Jerry Stiller was not in the opening-night cast, although two members of the Ensemble, Jeff Goldblum and Stockard Channing, have enjoyed considerable fame.

6 I remember seeing and being delighted by this production of *Two Gents*: the concerns I am raising here were not concerns I thought about in the early seventies. Yet I do not think that the attitudes of the play are simply a reflection of the cultural mores at that time. Had anyone asked me or most members of the audience whether ignoring the existence of rape was acceptable, we would have denied it vehemently. The weight of the production's innovations, the pleasure of seeing a Shakespearean production that spoke to our concern about the war, and the freshness of seeing an enactment of racial harmony was so great, that the audience welcomed the exuberantly happy ending. The political content about race and peace were so innovative that the production's treatment of women went unnoticed.

7 Robert Brustein, *The Culture Watch: Essays on Theatre and Society 1969–1974* (New York: Knopf, 1975), 186.

8 The show operates in much the same artistic territory as *The Rocky Horror Picture Show*, which was also more successful on the London stage than the American, although *Rocky Horror* is a notorious smash in American movie culture. Richard Burt's comments about Shakespeare's presence in *Scary Movie* suggests that were *Return to the Forbidden Planet* to be filmed, it might well succeed with an American audience (Burt 2002, 22–23).

9 For information on the controversy, I have found helpful the links gathered at http://www.cs.indiana.edu/~tanaka/Tezuka_Disney/ (18 July 2004).
10 Terence Hawkes, *That Shakespeherian Rag: Essays on a Critical Process* (London: Methuen, 1986), 89.
11 I take the epithet from Delroy Constantine-Simms and his anthology, *The Greatest Taboo: Homosexuality in Black Communities* (Los Angeles: Alyson Books, 2001), with contributions from bell hooks, Henry Louis Gates, and *Rolling Stone*'s Touré.

CONCLUSION

1 David Lowenthal, "Fabricating Heritage," *History and Memory* 10 (1998): 7–8.
2 David Lowenthal, "The Timeless Past: Some Anglo-American Historical Pre-conceptions," *Journal of American History* 75 (1989): 1265.

Bibliography

For the most part, I have not included items from newspapers, such as reviews. One can access these through the Lexis–Nexis database, as well as the standard reference works, *The New York Times Theater Reviews* (published biennially) and *The National Theatre Critics' Reviews* (published annually).

PRINTED SOURCES

Abbott, George. *"Mister Abbott."* New York: Random House, 1963.

Abbott, George, Richard Rodgers, and Lorenz Hart. *The Boys from Syracuse*. New York: Rodgers and Hammerstein Library, 1978.

The Boys from Syracuse (vocal score). New York: Chappell, 1965.

Adams, John. *Diary and Autobiography of John Adams*. Ed. L. H. Butterfield. Ser. 1, vol. 3. Cambridge, Mass.: Belknap Press of Harvard University Press, 1961.

Agnew, Jean Christophe. *Worlds Apart: The Market and the Theatre in Anglo-American Thought, 1550–1750*. Cambridge University Press, 1986.

Allen, Robert C. *Horrible Prettiness: Burlesque and American Culture*. Chapel Hill: University of North Carolina Press, 1991.

The American Thesaurus of Slang. Ed. Lester V. Berrey and Melvin Van den Bark. 2nd edn. New York: Crowell, 1953.

Ames, Fisher. *Works of Fisher Ames as Published by Seth Ames*. Ed. W. B. Allen. Indianapolis: Liberty Classics, 1983.

Bailyn, Bernard. *The Ideological Origins of the American Revolution*. Cambridge, Mass.: Belknap Press of Harvard University Press, 1967.

Balfour, Alan. *Rockefeller Center: Architecture as Theater*. New York: McGraw-Hill, 1978.

Banfield, Stephen. *Sondheim's Broadway Musicals*. Ann Arbor: University of Michigan Press, 1993.

Barnum, P. T. *The Humbugs of the World: An Account of Humbugs, Delusions, Impositions, Quackeries, Deceits and Deceivers Generally, in All Ages*. New York: Carleton, 1866.

Struggles and Triumphs, or Forty Years' Recollections. Buffalo: Warren, Johnson, 1872. Cited as *S&T*.

Bennett, Susan. *Performing Nostalgia: Shifting Shakespeare and the Contemporary Past*. London, New York: Routledge, 1996.

Benson, Eugene and L. W. Conolly, eds. *Oxford Companion to Canadian Theatre (OCCT)*. Toronto: Oxford University Press, 1989.

Bergreen, Laurence. *Louis Armstrong: An Extravagant Life*. New York: Broadway Books, 1997.

Bernstein, Leonard. *Findings*. New York: Simon and Schuster, 1982.

Berthold, Dennis. "Class Acts: Melville's 'The Two Temples.'" *American Literature* 71.3 (1999): 429–61.

Bevington, David and Jay Halio, eds. *Shakespeare: Pattern of Excelling Nature*. Newark: University of Delaware Press, 1978.

Block, Geoffrey. *Enchanted Evenings: The Broadway Musical from "Show Boat" to Sondheim*. Oxford University Press, 1997.

   Richard Rogers. New Haven: Yale University Press, 2003.

Block, Geoffrey, ed. *The Richard Rodgers Reader*. Oxford University Press, 2002.

Bogle, Donald. *Dorothy Dandridge, a Biography*. New York: Amistad, 1997.

Bonomi, Patricia. *Under the Cope of Heaven*. New York: Oxford University Press, 1986.

Booth, John Wilkes. *"Right or Wrong, God Judge Me": The Writings of John Wilkes Booth*. Ed. John Rhodehamel and Louise Taper. Urbana: University of Illinois Press, 1997.

Bordman, Gerald. *American Theatre*. 3 vols. New York and Oxford University Press, 1994.

   American Musical Theatre: A Chronicle. 3rd edn. Oxford University Press, 2001.

   Oxford Companion to American Theatre. 2nd edn. New York: Oxford University Press, 1992.

Bredbeck, Gregory. "B/O – Barthes' Text/O'Hara's Trick." PMLA 108 (1993): 268–82.

Briggs, Berta N. *Charles Willson Peale: Artist and Patriot*. New York: McGraw-Hill, 1952.

Bristol, Michael. *Shakespeare's America, America's Shakespeare*. London: Routledge, 1990.

Brown, Jared. *The Theatre in America during the Revolution*. Cambridge University Press, 1995.

Brown, Stephen J. "The Uses of Shakespeare in America: a Study in Class Domination" in Bevington and Halio: 230–38.

Brown, T. Allston. *A History of the New York Stage from the First Performance in 1732 to 1901*. 3 vols. New York: Benjamin Blom, 1964 rpt. of 1903 edn.

Browne, Ray B. "Shakespeare in American Vaudeville and Negro Minstrelsy." *American Quarterly* 12 (1960): 374–91.

Brustein, Robert. *The Culture Watch: Essays on Theatre and Society 1969–1974*. New York: Knopf, 1975.

Burt, Richard, ed. *Shakespeare after Mass Media*. New York: Palgrave, 2002.

   Unspeakable ShaXXXpeares: Queer Theory and American Kiddie Culture. 2nd edn. New York: St. Martin's Press, 1998.

Burton, Humphrey. *Leonard Bernstein*. New York: Doubleday, 1994.

Carrell, Jennifer Lee. "How the Bard Won the West." *Smithsonian* 29 (1998): 98–102, 104, 106–07.

Carson, Marian. "Shakespeare in Early American Decorative Arts." *Shakespeare Quarterly* 12 (1961): 154–56.

Cartelli, Thomas. *Repositioning Shakespeare: National Formations, Postcolonial Appropriations.* New York: Routledge, 1999.

Chambrun, Marquis Adolphe de. "Personal Recollection of Mr. Lincoln." *Scribner's Magazine* 13 (1893): 35.

Clarke, Asia Booth. *John Wilkes Booth: A Sister's Memoir.* Ed. Terry Alford. Jackson: University Press of Mississippi, 1996.

Clemens, Samuel. S.v. Mark Twain.

Clum, John M. *Something for the Boys: Musical Theater and Gay Culture.* New York: St. Martin's Press, 1999.

Cohen, Hennig. "Shakespeare in Charleston on the Eve of the Revolution." *Shakespeare Quarterly* 4 (1953): 327–30.

Collins, James Lincoln. *Benny Goodman and the Swing Era.* New York: Oxford University Press, 1989.

Columbia Dictionary of Modern Literary and Cultural Criticism. Ed. Joseph Childers and Gary Hentzi. New York: Columbia University Press, 1995.

Connor, D. Russell and Warren W. Hick. *BG On the Record: A Bio-Discography of Benny Goodman.* New Rochelle, N.Y.: Arlington House, 1969.

Conrad, Christine. *That Ballet Man.* London: Booth-Clibborne Editions, 2000.

Constantine-Simms, Delroy, ed. *The Greatest Taboo: Homosexuality in Black Communities.* Los Angeles: Alyson Books, 2001.

Cook, James W. *The Arts of Deception: Playing with Fraud in the Age of Barnum.* Cambridge, Mass.: Harvard University Press, 2001.

Covarrubio, Miguel, ed. *Theatre Arts Monthly* 22 (1938).

Culp, Ralph Borden. "Drama-and-Theater as a Source of Colonial American Attitudes toward Independence, 1758–1776." Diss.: Cornell University, 1962.

Daly, Charles P. *The First Theater in America.* New York: The Dunlap Society, 1896.

Darnton, Robert. *The Great Cat Massacre and Other Episodes in French Cultural History.* New York: Vintage, 1985.

Davis, Lee. *Bolton and Wodehouse and Kern: The Men Who Made Musical Comedy.* New York: Heineman, 1993.

Davis, Richard Beale. *A Colonial Southern Bookshelf: Reading in the Eighteenth Century.* Athens: University of Georgia Press, 1979.

Intellectual Life in the Colonial South 1585–1763. 3 vols. Knoxville: University of Tennessee Press, 1978.

Intellectual Life in Jefferson's Virginia. Knoxville: University of Tennessee Press, 1972.

De Chambrun, s.v. Chambrun.

Deelman, Christian. *The Great Shakespeare Jubilee.* New York: Viking, 1964.

De Grazia, Margreta. *Shakespeare Verbatim.* Oxford: Clarendon Press, 1991.

DeMille, Agnes. *Speak with Me, Dance with Me.* Boston: Little, Brown, 1973.

Dance to the Piper. Boston: Little, Brown, 1952.

de Tocqueville, s.v. Tocqueville.

Dictionary of American Biography. 20 vols. New York: Scribner, 1928–36.

Donald, David Herbert. *Lincoln*. New York: Simon and Schuster, 1995.

Dorsey, Tommy, *Early Jazz Sides: 1932–1937*, Allegro compact disc, 2004.

Driver, Donald with Hal Hester and Danny Apolinar. *Your Own Thing*. New York: Dell, 1970.

    Your Own Thing. In Richards, *Great Rock Musicals:* 289–378.

Dumbauld, Edward. *Thomas Jefferson, American Tourist*. Norman: University of Oklahoma Press, 1946.

Dunlap, William. *History of the American Theatre and Anecdotes of the Principal Actors*. New York: Burt Franklin, 1963 rpt. of 1832 edn.

Dunn, Esther Cloudman. *Shakespeare in America*. New York: Macmillan, 1939.

Durham, Weldon. *American Theatre Companies 1749–1887*. Westport, Conn.: Greenwood, 1986.

Easton, Carol. *No Intermissions: The Life of Agnes DeMille*. Boston: Little, Brown, 1996.

Emerson, Ralph Waldo. *Representative Men*. In *Essays and Lectures*. New York: Library of America, 1983.

England, Martha Winburn. *Garrick's Jubilee*. Columbus, Ohio: Ohio State University Press, 1964.

Epstein, Helen. *Joe Papp: An American Life*. Boston: Little, Brown, 1994.

Erdman, Andrew L. *Blue Vaudeville: Sex, Morals, and the Mass Marketing of Amusement, 1895–1915*. Jefferson, N.C.: McFarland, 2004.

Erenberg, Lewis A. *Swingin' the Dream: Big Band Jazz and the Rebirth of American Culture*. University of Chicago Press, 1998.

Evans, Nicholas M. "Ira Aldridge: Shakespeare and Minstrelsy." *American Transcendental Quarterly* 16 (2002): 165–87.

Everett, Marshall. *The Great Chicago Theater Disaster*. Chicago and Philadelphia: Publishers Union of America, 1904.

Everett, William A. and Paul R. Laird. *The Cambridge Companion to the Musical*. Cambridge University Press, 2002.

Ewen, David. *American Musical Theater*. New York: Holt, Rinehart and Winston, 1970.

Falk, Robert. "Shakespeare in America to 1900." *Shakespeare Survey* 18 (1965): 100–20.

Fearnow, Mark. "Let's Do It: the Layered Life of Cole Porter." In Marra and Schanke: 145–66.

Feather, Leonard. *The Jazz Years: Earwitness to an Era*. New York: Da Capo, 1987.

Fields, Armond. *Eddie Foy: A Biography of the Early Popular Stage Comedian*. Jefferson, N.C.: McFarland Press, 1999.

Firestone, Ross. *Swing, Swing, Swing: The Life and Times of Benny Goodman*. New York and London: W. W. Norton, 1993.

Fischer, David Hackett. *Albion's Seed*. New York: Oxford University Press, 1989.

Fisher, Will. "Staging the Beard: Masculinity in Early Modern English Culture." In Harris and Korda: 230–57.

Fliegelman, Jay. *Declaring Independence: Jefferson, Natural Language, and the Culture of Performance*. Stanford University Press, 1993.

Foley, Barbara. "From Wall Street to Astor Place: Historicizing Melville's 'Bartleby.'" *American Literature* 72 (2000): 87–136.

Ford, Worthington Chauncey. *The Boston Book Market 1679–1700*. New York: Burt Franklin, 1972 rpt. of 1917 edn.

Foy, Eddie and Alvin Harlow. *Clowning through Life*. New York: E. P. Dutton, 1928.

Freeman, Bud and Robert Wolf. *Crazeology, the Autobiography of a Chicago Jazzman*. Urbana: University of Illinois Press, 1989.

Furtwangler, Albert. *Assassin on Stage: Brutus, Hamlet, and the Death of Lincoln*. Urbana: University of Illinois Press, 1991.

Gale, Cedric. "Shakespeare on the American Stage in the Eighteenth Century." Diss.: New York University, 1945.

Garebian, Keith. *The Making of "West Side Story."* Oakville, Ontario and Buffalo, N.Y.: Mosaic Press, 2000.

Gassner, John and Edward Quinn, eds. *The Reader's Encyclopedia of World Drama*. New York: Thomas Crowell, 1969.

George-Graves, Nadine. *The Royalty of Negro Vaudeville: The Whitman Sisters and the Negotiation of Race, Gender, and Class in African-American Theatre, 1900–1940*. New York: St. Martin's Press, 2000.

Gilbert, Douglas. *American Vaudeville: Its Life and Times*. New York: Dover Books, 1963 rpt. of 1940 edn.

Gottfried, Martin. *Broadway Musical*. New York: Harry Abrams, 1980.

Gougeon, Len. "Emerson and Furness: Two Gentlemen of Abolition." *American Transcendental Quarterly* 41 (1979): 17–31.

Grant, Mark. *The Rise and Fall of the Broadway Musical*. Boston: Northeastern University Press, 2004.

Guare, John and Mel Shapiro. *Two Gentlemen of Verona*. New York: Holt, Rinehart, and Winston, 1973.

Two Gentlemen of Verona. In Richards, *Great Rock Musicals*: 67–168.

Guernsey, Otis. *Broadway Song and Story: Playwrights, Lyricists, Composers Discuss Their Hits*. New York: Dodd, Mead, 1985.

Hackett, James Henry. *Notes, Criticisms, and Correspondence upon Shakespeare's Plays and Actors*. New York and London: Benjamin Blom, 1968 rpt. of 1863 edn.

Hall, David D. "The Uses of Literacy in New England, 1600–1850." In Joyce et al.: 1–47.

Halliday, F. E. *Shakespeare, a Pictorial Biography*. New York: Crowell, 1956.

Hamilton, Alexander. *The Papers of Alexander Hamilton*. Ed. Harold C. Syrett, et al. 27 vols. New York, Columbia University Press, 1961–79.

Hammond, John and Irving Townsend. *On the Record*. New York: Ridge Press, 1977.

Harbage, Alfred. *Annals of English Drama: 975–1700*. Rev. Samuel Schoenbaum. Philadelphia: University of Pennsylvania Press, 1964.

Harlow, Alvin F. *Old Bowery Days: The Chronicles of a Famous Street*. New York: D. Appleton, 1931.

Harris, Jonathan Gil and Natasha Korda, eds. *Staged Properties in Early Modern English Drama*. Cambridge University Press, 2002.

Harris, William C. *Lincoln's Last Months*. Cambridge, Mass.: Belknap Press of Harvard University Press, 2004.

Hart, James D. *The Popular Book: A History of America's Literary Taste*. New York: Oxford University Press, 1950.

Hart, Lorenz. *The Complete Lyrics of Lorenz Hart*. Ed. Dorothy Hart and Robert Kimball. New York: Decapo, 1995.

Hartnoll, Phyllis, ed. *The Oxford Companion to the Theatre*. 3rd edn. London: Oxford University Press, 1967; 4th edn. 1983.

Hawkes, Terence. *That Shakespeherian Rag: Essays on a Critical Process*. London: Methuen, 1986.

Heineman, Margot. *Puritanism and Theatre: Thomas Middleton and Opposition Drama under the Early Stuarts*. Cambridge University Press, 1980.

Henderson, Hanford. "Shakespeare in Marble in Colonial America." *Shakespeare Quarterly* 12 (1961): 156–57.

Hill, Errol. *Shakespeare in Sable: A History of Black Shakespearean Actors*. Amherst: University of Massachusetts Press, 1984.

Hill, Errol G. and James V. Hatch. *A History of African American Theatre*. Cambridge University Press, 2003.

Hodgdon, Barbara. "Katharina Bound: Or, Play (K)ating the Strictures of Everyday Life," *PMLA* 107 (1992), 538–53.

Hodgkinson, John. *Narrative of his Connection with the Old American Company*. New York: J. Oram, 1797.

Holland, Peter. "Touring Shakespeare." In Wells and Stanton: 194–211.

Horn, Barbara Lee. *Joseph Papp: A Bio-Bibliography* Westport, Conn.: Greenwood Press, 1992.

Hughes, Langston. *Shakespeare in Harlem*. New York: Knopf, 1942.

Ilson, Carol. *Harold Prince: From Pajama Game to Phantom of the Opera*. Ann Arbor: UMI Research Press, 1989.

Ioppolo, Grace. *Revising Shakespeare*. Cambridge, Mass.: Harvard University Press, 1991.

Jacoby, Richard. *Conversations with the Capeman: The Untold Story of Salvador Agron*. Madison: University of Wisconsin Press, 2004.

Jay, John. *The Correspondence and Public Papers of John Jay*. Ed. Henry P. Johnston. 4 vols. New York: B. Franklin, 1970.

Jefferson, Thomas. *Jefferson's Literary Commonplace Book*. Ed. Douglas L. Wilson. The Papers of Thomas Jefferson, 2nd ser. Princeton University Press, 1989. See under Wilson.

  The Papers of Thomas Jefferson. Ed. Julian P. Boyd et al. 28 vols. Princeton University Press, 1950–2000.

Johnson, Claudia. "That Guilty Third Tier: Prostitution in Nineteenth-Century American Theatres." *American Quarterly* 27 (1975): 575–84.

Johnson, James Weldon. *Black Manhattan*. New York: Arno Press, 1968.

Johnson, Odai and William J. Burling. *The Colonial American Stage, 1665–1774: A Documentary Calendar*. Madison, N.J.: Fairleigh Dickinson Press, 2001.

Jones, Vernon. "The Theatre in Colonial Virginia." *The Reviewer* 7 (1925): 81–88.

Jowitt, Deborah. *Jerome Robbins: His Life, His Theater, His Dance*. New York: Simon and Schuster, 2004.

Joyce, William L., et al., eds. *Printing and Society in Early America*. Worcester, Mass.: American Antiquarian Society, 1983.

Kammen, Michael. *The Lively Arts: Gilbert Seldes and the Transformation of Cultural Criticism in the United States*. New York: Oxford University Press, 1996.

Kauffman, Michael. *American Brutus: John Wilkes Booth and the Lincoln Conspiracies*. New York: Random House, 2004.

Kibler, M. Allison. *Rank Ladies: Gender and Cultural Hierarchy in American Vaudeville*. Chapel Hill: University of North Carolina Press, 1999.

Kimball, Robert, ed. *Cole*. New York: Holt, Rinehart, and Winston, 1971.

King, Christine E. and Brenda Coven. *Joseph Papp and the New York Shakespeare Festival: An Annotated Bibliography*. New York: Garland, 1988.

Koon, Helene Wickham. *How Shakespeare Won the West: Players and Performances in America's Gold Rush, 1849–1865*. Jefferson, N.C.: McFarland, 1989.

Krieg, Joann. *Walt Whitman: Here and Now*. Westport, Conn.: Greenwood Press, 1985.

Kroll, Richard W. F. *The Material Word: Literate Culture in the Restoration and Early Eighteenth Century*. Baltimore: Johns Hopkins University Press, 1991.

Kunhardt, Philip, Jr., Philip Kunhardt III, and Peter W. Kunhardt. *P. T. Barnum, America's Greatest Showman*. New York: Knopf, 1995.

Kussrow, Jr., Van Carl. "On with the Show: A Study of Public Arguments in Favor of Theatre in American during the Eighteenth Century." Diss.: Indiana University, 1959.

Langford, Paul. "Manners and Character in Anglo-American Perceptions, 1750–1850." In *Anglo-American Attitudes: From Revolution to Partnership*. Ed. Fred M. Leventhal and Roland Quinault. Aldershot, Hants.: Ashgate, 2000.

Lanier, Douglas. *Shakespeare and Modern Popular Culture*. Oxford University Press, 2002.

Laurens, Henry. *The Papers of Henry Laurens*. Ed. Philip M. Hamer. 10 vols. Columbia: South Carolina Historical Society by the University of South Carolina Press, 1968–85.

Laurents, Arthur. *Original Story By*. New York: Alfred A. Knopf, 2000.

Laurents, Arthur, Leonard Bernstein, and Stephen Sondheim. *West Side Story*. In *Romeo and Juliet and West Side Story*. New York: Dell, 1965.

Lawrence, Greg. *Dance with Demons: The Life of Jerome Robbins*. New York: G. P. Putnam's Sons, 2001.

Lawson-Peebles, Robert, ed. *Approaches to the American Musical*. University of Exeter Press, 1996.

"Brush Up Your Shakespeare: the Case of *Kiss Me, Kate.*" In Lawson-Peebles: 89–108.

Lee, Richard Henry. *The Letters of Richard Henry Lee.* Ed. James Curtis Ballagh. 2 vols. New York: The Macmillan Company, 1911–14.

Leiter, Samuel. *Encyclopedia of the New York Stage 1930–40.* Westport, Conn.: Greenwood Press, 1989.

Lerner, Alan Jay. *The Musical Theatre: A Celebration.* New York: McGraw-Hill, 1986.

Lescarbot, Marc. *Histoire de la Nouvelle-France, suivie des Muses de la Nouvelle-France.* Ed. Edwin Tross. 3 vols. Paris: Librairie Tross, 1866.

Neptune's Theatre: The First Existing Play Written and Produced in North America, 1606. Translator, Edna B. Holman. New York: Samuel French, 1927.

Levine, Lawrence. "William Shakespeare and the American People: a Study in Cultural Transformation," in *The Unpredictable Past: Explorations in American Cultural History.* New York: Oxford University Press, 1993: 139–71.

Lewis, Lloyd. *The Assassination of Lincoln: History and Myths after Lincoln.* Lincoln: University of Nebraska Press, 1994.

Lewis, Robert M. *From Traveling Show to Vaudeville.* Baltimore: Johns Hopkins Press, 2003.

Lighter, J. E. *Random House Historical Dictionary of American Slang.* New York: Random House, 1994.

Little, Stuart. *Enter Joseph Papp: In Search of a New American Theatre.* New York: Coward, McCann, and Geoghegan, 1974.

Littlefield, George E. *Early Boston Booksellers.* New York: Burt Franklin, 1969 rpt. of 1900 edn.

Livingston, William. *The Papers of William Livingston.* Ed. Carl E. Prince et al. 5 vols. Trenton: New Jersey Historical Commission, *c.* 1979–1988.

Londre, Felicia. *The History of World Theater,* vol. 2. New York: Continuum/Frederick Ungar, 1991.

Londre, Felicia and Daniel Watermeier. *The History of North American Theatre: The United States, Canada, and Mexico from Pre-Columbian Times to the Present.* New York: Continuum, 1998.

Lott, Eric. *Love and Theft: Blackface Minstrelsy and the American Working Class.* New York and Oxford: Oxford University Press, 1993.

Lowenthal, David. "Fabricating Heritage." *History and Memory* 10 (1998): 5–24.

"The Timeless Past: Some Anglo-American Historical Preconceptions." *Journal of American History* 75 (1989): 1263–80.

Madison, James. *Papers of James Madison.* Ed. Galliard Hunt. 9 vols. New York: G. P. Putnam, 1900–10.

Mallin, Eric. "'You Kilt My Foddah': or, Arnold, Prince of Denmark." *Shakespeare Quarterly* 50 (1999): 128–29.

Markels, Julian. *Melville and the Politics of Identity: From "King Lear" to "Moby-Dick."* Urbana: University of Illinois Press, 1993.

Marovitz, Sanford E. "America vs. Shakespeare: from the Monroe Doctrine to the Civil War." *Zeitschrift fur Anglistik und Amerikanistik* 34 (1986): 33–46.

"Emerson's Shakespeare: from Scorn to Apotheosis." In Myerson: 122–55.

Marra, Kim and Robert A. Schanke. *Staging Desire: Queer Readings of American Theater History*. Ann Arbor: University of Michigan Press, 2002.

Marx, Leo. *The Machine in the Garden: Technology and the Pastoral Ideal in America*. London and New York: Oxford University Press, 1964.

Mason, George. *The Papers of George Mason, 1725–1792*. Ed. Robert A. Rutland. 3 vols. Chapel Hill: University of North Carolina Press, 1970.

McBrien, William. *Cole Porter: A Biography*. New York: Knopf, 1998.

McConachie, Bruce. "The Theatre of Edwin Forrest and Jacksonian Hero Worship." In *When They Weren't Doing Shakespeare*. Ed. Judith L. Fisher and Stephen Watt. Athens: University of Georgia Press, 1989.

McCullough, David. *John Adams*. New York: Simon & Schuster, 2001.

McNamara, Brooks. *The New York Concert Saloon: The Devil's Own Nights*. Cambridge University Press, 2002.

Mellers, Wilfrid. "West Side Story Revisited." In Lawson-Peebles: 127–36.

Meserve, Walter J. *An Emerging Entertainment: The Drama of the American People to 1828*. Bloomington: Indiana University Press, 1977.

Heralds of Promise: The Drama of the American People during the Age of Jackson, 1829–1849. New York and Westport, Conn.: Greenwood Press, 1986.

Middlebrooks, Diane. *Suits Me: The Double Life of Billy Tipton*. New York: Houghton Mifflin, 1998.

Miller, D. A. *Place for Us: Essay on the Broadway Musical*. Cambridge, Mass. and London: Harvard University Press, 1998.

Miller, Lillian B. and David C. Ward. *New Perspectives on Charles Willson Peale: A 250th Anniversary Celebration*. Pittsburgh: University of Pittsburgh Press for the Smithsonian Institution, 1991.

Miller, Lillian B. and David C. Ward, et al., eds. *The Selected Papers of Charles Willson Peale and His Family*. 5 vols. New Haven: Yale University Press for the National Portrait Gallery, Smithsonian Institution, 1983.

Miller, Norma with Evette Jensen. *Swingin at the Savoy: The Memoir of a Jazz Dancer*. Philadelphia: Temple University Press, 1996.

Milner, Andrew. *Literature, Culture, and Society*. New York University Press, 1996.

Moody, Richard. *The Astor Place Riot*. Bloomington: Indiana University Press, 1958; citations to "Moody" will be to this book.

Edwin Forrest: First Star of the American Stage. New York: Knopf, 1960.

Mordden, Ethan. *Broadway Babies: The People Who Made the American Musical*. New York: Oxford University Press, 1983.

Make Believe: The Broadway Musical in the 1920s. New York: Oxford University Press, 1997.

Morgann, Maurice. "An Essay on the Dramatic Character of Sir John Falstaff." In *Shakespearian Criticism*. Ed. Daniel A. Fineman. Oxford: Clarendon Press, 1972.

Morison, Samuel Eliot. *The European Discovery of America: The Northern Voyages A.D. 500–1600*. New York: Oxford University Press, 1971.

The Founding of Harvard College. Cambridge, Mass.: Harvard University Press, 1935.

Myers, Robert and Joyce Brodowski. "Rewriting the Hallams: Research in 18th-Century British and American Theatre." *Theatre Survey* 44 (2000): 1–22.

Myerson, Joel. *Emerson Centenary Essays*. Carbondale: Southern Illinois University Press, 1982.

Nathans, Heather. *Early American Theatre from the Revolution to Thomas Jefferson; Into the Hands of the People*. Cambridge University Press, 2003.

Nolan, Frederick. *Lorenz Hart: A Poet on Broadway*. New York: Oxford University Press, 1994.

Northall, W. K. *Before and Behind the Curtain: or, Fifteen Years' Observation among the Theatres of New York*. New York: W. F. Burgess, 1851. In *American Culture* microfilm series, reel 45.3.

Norton, Richard C. *A Chronology of American Musical Theater*. 3 vols. Oxford University Press.

Odell, George C. D. *Annals of the New York Stage*. New York: Columbia University Press, 1927.

Odum, Leigh George. "'The Black Crook' at Niblo's Garden." *Drama Review* 26 (1982): 21–40.

Penny, Charles W. *North to Lake Superior, the Journal of Charles W. Penny, 1840*. Ed. James L. Carter and Ernest H. Rankin. Marquette, Mich.: John M. Longyear Research Library, 1970.

Peyser, Joan. *Bernstein: A Biography*. Rev. edn. New York: Billboard, 1998.

Pollock, Thomas Clark. *The Philadelphia Theatre in the Eighteenth Century*. Philadelphia: University of Pennsylvania Press, 1933.

Preminger, Alex, T. V. F. Brogan, et al. *The New Princeton Encyclopedia of Poetry and Poetics*. Princeton University Press, 1993.

Preston, Katherine. "American Musical Theatre before the Twentieth Century." In Everett and Laird: 3–28.

Prown, Jonathan and Richard Miller. "The Rococo, the Grotto, and the Philadelphia High Chest." In *American Furniture*. Ed. Luke Beckerdite. Foxpoint, Wis.: Chipstone Publications, 1996.

Rankin, Hugh F. *Theater in Colonial America*. Chapel Hill: University of North Carolina Press, 1960.

Ranney, H. M. *Account of the Terrific and Fatal Riot at the New-York Astor Place Opera House, on the Night of May 10th, 1849; with the Quarrels of Forrest and Macready, Including All the Causes Which Led to That Awful Tragedy! Wherein an Infuriated Mob Was Quelled by the Public Authorities and Military, with its Mournful Termination in the Sudden Death or Mutilation of More than Fifty Citizens, with Full and Authentic Particulars*. New York: 1849.

Ravicz, Marilyn. *Early Colonial Religious Drama in Mexico: From Tzompantli to Golgotha*. Washington, D.C.: Catholic University of America Press, 1970.

Rawlings, Peter, ed. *Americans on Shakespeare, 1776–1914*. Aldershot, Hants.: Ashgate, 1999.

Richards, Jeffrey H. *Theater Enough: American Culture and the Metaphor of the World Stage, 1607–1789*. Durham, N.C.: Duke University Press, 1991.

Richards, Stanley. *Great Rock Musicals*. New York: Stein and Day, 1979.

Riis, Thomas. *Just before Jazz: Black Musical Theater in New York, 1890–1915*. Washington: Smithsonian Institution Press, 1989.

Ripley, John. *Coriolanus on Stage in England and America 1609–1994*. Madison, N.J.: Fairleigh Dickinson Press, 1998.

Roach, Joseph. *Cities of the Dead: Circum-Atlantic Performance*. New York: Columbia University Press, 1996.

Rodgers, Richard. *Musical Stages: An Autobiography*. New York: Random House, 1975.

Rudy, Kathy. "Queer Theory and Feminism," *Women's Studies* 29 (2000): 195–216.

Samples, Gordon. *Lust for Fame: The Stage Career of John Wilkes Booth*. Jefferson, N.C.: McFarland, 1982.

Sandla, Robert. Liner notes to *Your Own Thing*. New York: RCA Victor, 1999.

Schiede, William H. "The Earliest First Folio in America?" *Shakespeare Quarterly* 27 (1976): 332–33.

Schlochauer, Ernst J. "Shakespeare and America's Revolutionary Leaders." *Shakespeare Quarterly* 12 (1961): 158–60.

Schoch, Richard. *"Not Shakespeare": Bardolatry and Burlesque in the Nineteenth Century*. Cambridge University Press, 2002.

Schoenbaum, Samuel. *Shakespeare's Lives*. New York: Oxford University Press, 1970.

Secrest, Meryle. *Somewhere for Me: A Biography of Richard Rodgers*. New York: Knopf, 2001.

Seilhamer, George O. *History of the American Theatre: During the Revolution and After*. Philadelphia: Globe Publishing, 1889.

Seldes, Gilbert. *The 7 Lively Arts*. New York: Harper Bros. 1924; rpt. New York; Sagamore, 1957.

Sellers, Charles Coleman. *Charles Willson Peale*. New York: Scribner's, 1969.

Shakespeare, William. *The Riverside Shakespeare*. Ed. G. Blakemore Evans, et al. Boston: Houghton Mifflin, 1974.

Shattuck, Charles. *Shakespeare on the American Stage*. 2 vols. Washington, D.C.: Folger Press, 1976, 1987.

Shields, David S. *Oracles of Empire: Poetry, Politics, and Commerce in British America 1690–1750*. University of Chicago Press, 1990.

Silverman, Kenneth. *A Cultural History of the American Revolution: 1763–1789*. New York: Crowell, 1976.

Simas, Rick. *The Musicals No One Came to See: A Guidebook to Four Decades of Musical-Comedy Casualities on Broadway, Off-Broadway, and in Out-of-Town Try-Out, 1943–1983*. New York: Garland, 1987.

Sinfield, Alan. "Making Space: Appropriation and Confrontation in Recent British Plays." In *The Shakespeare Myth*. Ed. Graham Holderness. New York: St. Martin's Press, 1993.

Smart, Jeffrey. "Lorenz Hart: This Can't Be Love." In Marra and Schanke: 167–93.

Snyder, Robert. *The Voice of the City: Vaudeville and Popular Culture in New York*. New York and Oxford: Oxford University Press, 1989.

Spewack, Bella and Sam, with lyrics by Cole Porter. *Kiss Me, Kate*. New York: Knopf, 1953.

Stein, Charles W. ed. *American Vaudeville as Seen by its Contemporaries*. New York: Knopf, 1984.

Stern, Philip Van Doren. *The Man Who Killed Lincoln: the Story of John Wilkes Booth and His Part in the Assassination*. New York: Literary Guild of America, 1939.

Steyn, Mark. *Broadway Babies Say Goodnight: Musicals Then and Now*. New York: Routledge, 1997.

Sturgess, Kim C. *Shakespeare and the American Nation*. Cambridge University Press, 2004.

Swain, Joseph P. *The Broadway Musical: A Critical and Musical Survey*. New York and Oxford: Oxford University Press, 1990.

Taylor, Gary. *Reinventing Shakespeare: A Cultural History from the Restoration to the Present*. New York: Oxford University Press, 1989.

Teachout, Terry. "Is Musical Comedy Dead?" *Commentary* 117 (June 2004): 47–50.

Teague, Frances. "Shakespeare, Beard of Avon." In Burt, *Shakespeare after Mass Media*, 221–42.

Thomson, Peter and Gamini Salgado. *The Everyman Companion to the Theatre*. London: J. M. Dent, 1985.

Tocqueville, Alexis de. *Democracy in America*. Ed. Richard D. Heffner. New York: Mentor, 1956.

Toye, William. *The Oxford Companion to Canadian Literature*. Oxford University Press, 1983.

Twain, Mark. *Following the Equator and Anti-Imperialist Essay*. Ed. Shelley Fisher Fishkin. Oxford University Press, 1996.

Usigli, Rudolfo. *Mexico in the Theater*. Trans. Wilder P. Scott. University, Miss.: Romance Monographs no. 18, 1976.

Velz, John and Frances Teague. *One Touch of Shakespeare: Letters of Joseph Crosby to Joseph Parker Norris, 1875–1878*. Washington, D.C.: Folger Press, 1986.

Villena, Guillermo Lohmann. *El Arte Dramático En Lima Durante El Virreinato*. Madrid: [Estades, artes gráficas] 1945.

Vitale, Joe. *There's a Customer Born Every Minute*. New York: AMACOM, 1998.

Wallace, Irving. *The Fabulous Showman*. New York: Knopf, 1959.

Washington, George. *The Writings of George Washington*. Ed. Worthington Chauncey Ford. 14 vols. New York and London: G. P. Putnam, 1889–93.

Wells, Stanley. *Nineteenth-Century Shakespeare Burlesques*. 5 vols. Wilmington, Del.: M. Glazier, 1978.

Wells, Stanley, and Sarah Stanton. *The Cambridge Companion to Shakespeare on Stage*. Cambridge University Press, 2002.

Westfall, Alfred Van Rensselaer. *American Shakespearean Criticism, 1607–1865*. New York: H. W. Wilson, 1939.

White, Richard Grant. "The Age of Burlesque." *Galaxy* (August 1869): 256–66.

Wilder, Alec. *American Popular Song: The Great Innovators, 1900–1950*. New York: Oxford University Press, 1972.

Williams, Elsie A. *The Humor of Jackie Moms Mabley: An African-American Comedic Tradition.* New York and London: Garland, 1995.

Willoughby, E. E. "The Reading of Shakespeare in Colonial America," *PBSA* 30 (1936): 48.

Wilmer, S. E. *Theatre, Society, and the Nation: Staging American Identity.* Cambridge University Press, 2002.

Wilson, Douglas L. ed. *Jefferson's Literary Commonplace Book.* The Papers of Thomas Jefferson, 2nd ser. Princeton University Press, 1989.

Wilson, Garff. *Three Hundred Years of American Drama and Theatre.* 2nd edn. Englewood Cliffs, N.J.: Prentice-Hall, 1982.

Wolf II, Edwin. "A Signed American Binding on the First American Edition of Shakespeare." *Shakespeare Quarterly* 12 (1961): 153–54.

Wright, Elizabeth, Louise M. Burkhart, and Barry D. Sell. "Lope de Vega in lengua mexicana (Nahuatl): don Bartolomé de Alva Ixtlilxochitl's Translation of La madre de la mejor (1640)." *Bulletin of the Comediantes* 55.2 (forthcoming).

Wright, Louis B. *The Cultural Life of the American Colonies: 1607–1763.* New York: Harper, 1962 rpt. of 1957 edn.

Culture on the Moving Frontier. Bloomington: University of Indiana Press, 1955.

"The Reading of Plays during the Puritan Revolution." *Huntington Library Bulletin* 6 (November 1934): 73–108.

Wright, Richardson. *Revels in Jamaica, 1682–1838.* New York: Dodd, Mead, 1937.

Wright, Thomas Goddard. *Literary Culture in Early New England.* New Haven: Yale University Press, 1920.

Wroth, Lawrence C. *The Colonial Printer.* Charlottesville, Va.: Dominion Press, 1964 rpt. of 2nd edn. 1938.

Zadan, Craig. *Sondheim & Co.* 2nd edn. New York: Harper and Row, 1986.

INTERNET SITES

American National Biography Online. 25 October 2005. http://www.anb.org/articles/home.html.

The American Variety Stage: Vaudeville and Popular Entertainment, 1870–1920. 27 October 2005. http://memory.loc.gov/ammem/vshtml/vshome.html.

Chicago Public Library. Iriquois Theater Fire. 25 October 2005. http://cpl.lib.uic.edu/004chicago/disasters/iroquois_fire.html.

Corrigan, Alan. "Jazz, Shakespeare, and Hybridity: a Script Excerpt from *Swingin' the Dream. Borrowers and Lenders* 1 (2005). 9 September 2005. URL http://atropos.english.uga.edu/cocoon/borrowers/index.

Disney Corporation. 29 October 2005. http://disney.go.com.

Internet Broadway Database. 29 October 2005. http://www.ibdb.com.

Internet Movie Database. 29 October 2005. http://www.imdb.com.

Jazz Standards. 29 October 2005. http://www.jazzstandards.com/index.html.

Library of Congress. 29 October 2005. http://catalog.loc.gov/.

Monaghan, Terry, "Naomi Waller, the Lindy Prima Donna." The Savoy Ballroom Website 20 August 2005. http://www.savoyballroom.com/nets/dafloor1/socdance/waller.htm.

Museum of the City of New York Website 25 October 2005. http://www.mcny.org/.

Shakespeare Birthplace Trust Website, 17 July 2002. http://www.stratford.co.uk/birthplace/barnum.html; 25 October 2005. http://www.shakespeare.org.uk.

The Shaksper-L Listserve. 29 October 2005. http://www.shaksper.net/index.html.

Tezuka's "Jungle King" and Disney's "Lion King" 18 July 2004. http://www.cs.indiana.edu/~tanaka/Tezuka_Disney/.

The Tunesmiths Database. 25 October 2005. http://www.nfo.net/cal/ts6.html.

Index